performing glam rock

performing glam rock

gender and theatricality in popular music

PHILIP AUSLANDER

THE UNIVERSITY OF MICHIGAN PRESS   *Ann Arbor*

Copyright © by the University of Michigan 2006
All rights reserved
Published in the United States of America by
The University of Michigan Press
Manufactured in the United States of America
⊚ Printed on acid-free paper

2009   2008   2007   2006   4   3   2   1

A CIP catalog record for this book is available from the British Library.

Library of Congress Cataloging-in-Publication Data

Auslander, Philip, 1956–
    Performing glam rock : gender and theatricality in popular music /
Philip Auslander.
        p.   cm.
    Includes index.
    ISBN-13: 978-0-472-09868-2 (cloth : alk. paper)
    ISBN-10: 0-472-09868-3 (pbk. : alk. paper)
    ISBN-13: 978-0-472-06868-5 (cloth : alk. paper)
    ISBN-10: 0-472-06868-7 (pbk. : alk. paper)   1. Rock music—
History and criticism.   2. Rock musicians.   3. Gender identity in
music.   I. Title.
ML3534.A9 2006
781.66—dc22   2005017928

for deanna, my own true love

acknowledgments

I would like to thank my colleagues and students in the School of Literature, Communication, and Culture of the Georgia Institute of Technology for their support and patience with my nattering about glam rock for quite a few years. I particularly want to acknowledge the students who have participated over the last three years in my Music as Performance course, the proving ground for my approach here. I would also like to thank all those, too numerous to mention, who provided me with venues at conferences and universities in which to present this material: I profited enormously from the feedback. A shout-out particularly to Vivian Patraka, whose timely invitation made it much easier for me to finish the project. And thanks to Laci Reed for canine companionship.

A number of people were kind enough to read and comment on early versions of these chapters: Susan Fast, Judith Halberstam, Jon McKenzie, Richard Pettengill, and Peter Shapiro. Thank you all. Thanks also to "anonymous" readers Will Straw and Maria Delgado for your positive reinforcement and good suggestions.

Special thanks to LeAnn Fields for her unflagging support and faith in the project.

Portions of the introduction were published originally in "Performance Analysis and Popular Music: A Manifesto," *Contemporary Theatre Review* 14.1 (2004). Portions of chapters 1 and 5 appeared in "Good Old Rock and Roll: Performing the 1950s in the 1970s," *Journal of Popular Music Studies* 15.2 (2003). An early version of chapter 6 appeared as "I Wanna Be Your Man: Suzi Quatro's Musical Androgyny," *Popular Music* 23.1 (2004). "The Inauthentic Voice: Vocal Production in Glam Rock," a schematic version of chapter 5, was published in *Kunst-Stimmen,* ed. Doris Kolesch and Jenny Schrödl (Bonn: Theater der Zeit, 2004). These materials are reprinted here by kind permission of their original publishers.

contents

illustrations

Introduction

Personal and Disciplinary Reflections

I glimpsed the first manifestations of glam rock while living in London in 1971. I was very taken with T. Rex's single "Get It On (Bang a Gong)" and bought their album *Electric Warrior* as soon as it appeared; well over thirty years later, it remains one of my favorite records. Back in the United States, I was introduced to the work of David Bowie in 1973 but did not really develop an appreciation of it until a year or two later, when I became a fan. Working in radio in the early 1970s, I had the opportunity to listen to every recording of music that was released; it was through this association that I first became aware of Slade, Gary Glitter, and Suzi Quatro, though they did not rank among my favorite performers at the time.

These fragments of musical autobiography may suggest, at first blush, that I am not necessarily the best person to write a book about glam rock. Although I was aware of it from its early stages and enthusiastic about certain of its manifestations, I was not particularly engaged by it as a genre. Then, as now, my favorite genres of rock music were psychedelic rock and blues-rock, precisely the musical precedents against which glam rockers reacted. After devoting more than five years to researching, writing, and talking about glam rock, I have come to see my status as a relative outsider as an advantage. For one thing, it meant that the research was a process of discovery: rather than remapping familiar territory, I explored terrain that was relatively unknown to me. As a nonfan with few existing prejudices or allegiances, I was able to assess the material in a fairly "objective" way. I no longer consider myself an outsider, however. Rather than writing a book about a genre of music of which I was a fan, I became a fan by writing the book.

My interest in writing about rock evolved in part from a desire to bring together my vocation as a performance studies scholar and my avocational interests as a record collector and popular music fan. I found my first opportunity to do so when working on the book *Liveness: Performance in a Mediatized Culture* (1999): the relationship of live musical performance to sound recordings and music videos became one of three paradigmatic instances of the general relationship between live and mediatized performance I discussed there (the other two were the relationship between theater and television and that between live courtroom proceedings and videotape trials). I became better acquainted through that project with writings on rock and popular music, primarily from the realm of cultural studies and media studies. I thus became aware of the centrality of concepts of authenticity to rock culture, an issue I wanted to explore further and to which I return here as a central theme.

Reading the academic discourse on rock music emerging from cultural studies, I was struck by the way that field, perhaps because of its roots in sociology and ethnography, generally emphasizes the reception of popular music much more than the performance behavior of musicians. Although scholars in communications and cultural studies often make excellent observations concerning specific genres of rock and pop music and their audiences, their remarks on performance are generally impressionistic and synoptic. Most of the work in cultural studies of popular music that focuses on production examines the sociological, institutional, and policy contexts in which popular music is made, not the immediate context of the work of the artists who make it. In contrast, my stance here is unabashedly performer-centered: I am interested primarily in finding ways of discussing what popular musicians do *as performers*—the meanings they create through their performances and the means they use to create them. Although I will not ignore the reception of these performances (particularly in the conclusion, where I discuss the social effects of glam rock), I am less concerned with the audience than with the performers themselves.

If cultural and media studies of popular music have neglected performance, performance studies has been remiss in its general neglect of musical performances. The principal journals in the field seldom publish articles about music as performance or musicians as performers, and only a small (but growing) number of papers on these topics are presented at academic conferences. At a common-sense level, the absence of music from the array of subjects considered by performance scholars seems odd—musicians are performers, after all, and it would be eminently reasonable to discuss them as such. I cannot explain fully the neglect of musical performances by performance studies, but I suspect that a partial explanation lies in the genealogy of the field. The original paradigm for performance studies resulted from a synthesis of theater studies with aspects of anthropology, sociology, and oral interpretation.[1] Theater studies generally stakes out its territory in such a way as to exclude music, and scholars in performance studies seem unfortunately to have inherited this unwillingness to deal with musical forms. Even opera, a musical form that obviously avails itself of the same means of expression as the theater, is traditionally omitted from theater historical discourse. Vera Mowry Roberts, with whom I studied theater history, argues in her introductory textbook that the history of opera and the history of theater are separate narratives because "the predominant force in opera was the music rather than the words" and "the composer . . . is the focus of attention in opera" (108). For Roberts, the fact that opera is driven by music rather than drama, by composers rather than playwrights, places it outside the realm of theater history.

The approach I have taken here in an effort to sketch what performance studies might bring to the table in discussing musical performances is to apply the concept of performance analysis to popular music. While theater scholars have long described and analyzed performances, the idea that performance analysis constitutes an identifiable—though not strictly defined—approach (as distinct from theater criticism, say) is of relatively recent vintage. Performance analysis differs from the transcription methods of ethnomusicologists and the notation methods of dance scholars in the sense that it is as much interpretive as descriptive and is not organized around a specific technical vocabulary. Whereas dance notation may be of equal value to analysts and performers, performance analysis is understood to be specifically from the spectator's point of view. Although performance analysis is a semiotic enterprise at heart, theater scholars' flirtation with the technical vocabulary of

1. For a discussion of both the evolution of performance studies and the status of concepts of performance and performativity in a variety of disciplines, see Auslander, "General Introduction."

semiotics, popular during the 1970s, has largely dissipated in favor of a less "scientific," more eclectic set of approaches drawn from reception theory, phenomenology, cultural anthropology, sociology, feminist theory, cultural and literary theory, and other theoretical orientations.[2]

Central to my understanding of performance analysis as applied to popular music is the concept of *persona,* which I have used before in discussing performance art and stand-up comedy.[3] Following Simon Frith,[4] I see the performer in popular music as defined by three layers: the real person (the performer as human being), the performance persona (the performer's self-presentation), and the character (a figure portrayed in a song text).[5] All three layers may be active simultaneously in a given musical performance. For example, when Kelly Clarkson, the winner of the 2002 *American Idol* television singing competition, sang a duet on television with country singer Reba McIntyre, they performed a

2. Patrice Pavis charts the rise and fall of theatrical semiotics as well as the current eclecticism in performance analysis (13–30). This list of contributing disciplines draws on Pavis and the authors represented in Colin Counsell and Laurie Wolf's anthology, *Performance Analysis.*

3. I find the term *persona* useful as a way of describing a performed presence that is neither a fictional character nor equivalent to the performer's "real" identity. In earlier work, I have used it as a heuristic in discussions of performance art (Auslander, *Presence* 57–81), experimental theater, and stand-up comedy (Auslander, *From Acting* 39–45, 108–25).

4. Frith proposes that we hear pop singers as "personally expressive," that is, as singing in their own persons, from their own experience. But two other layers are imposed on that one because popular musicians are "involved in a process of *double enactment:* they enact both a star personality (their image) and a song personality, the role that each lyric requires, and the pop star's art is to keep both acts in play at once" (*Performing Rites* 186, 212). Frith uses the term *persona* but only in reference to performance artists who "took themselves and their bodies as the objects or sites of narrative and feeling" (205) not in reference to popular musicians.

5. David Graver proposes that actors' presence onstage can be broken down into at least seven varieties, two of which (character and personage) overlap my categories here. Graver's "personage" is basically equivalent to my "persona"; Graver provides an eloquent definition: "personage . . . is not the real person . . . behind the character. Personage status is not a foundational reality but simply another way of representing oneself or, rather, a way of representing oneself within a particular discursive domain" (164). Using Graver's vocabulary, I am suggesting here that the musical performer's persona is the way the performer represents him- or herself within the discursive domain of musical performance.

song in which they played the roles of women competing for the affection of the same man. In addition to these characters, however, they also portrayed musical personae of the seasoned veteran singer and her young acolyte (and perhaps future competitor); these personae were delineated through the same performance as the characters in the song but were independent of those characters—the singers could have performed their personae regardless of what song they chose.[6] The presence of the performers as real people was implied through Clarkson's televised announcement that she had always idolized McIntyre and had therefore chosen her as a duet partner when she was in the position to do so by virtue of having won the competition. Whether true or not, this appeal to personal experience was layered into the performance alongside the two women's performance personae as seasoned veteran and young up-and-comer and their characters as romantic rivals; all three levels of personification contributed to the performance's meaning for the audience.

That these three signified presences admittedly are often difficult to distinguish from one another does not diminish their heuristic value. The demarcation line between real person and persona is always ambiguous in performance, for, as Richard Schechner points out, performance is always a matter of the performers not being themselves but also not not being themselves ("Performers" 88). This logic of the double negative is represented in one way by the professional names sometimes used by pop music performers, names that initially designate their personae but are later generalized to the real people. David Jones renamed himself David Bowie; David Bowie is not David Jones, yet he also is not not David Jones, as suggested by the fact that the name David Bowie belongs now to both the real person and the performance persona. The real person is the dimension of performance to which the audience has the least direct access, since the audience generally infers what performers are like as real people from their performance personae and the characters they portray. Public appearances offstage do not give

6. Graver argues that in the theater, the character's presence is dominant over the actor's presence: "We do not really see the character in a drama in addition to the actor representing that character; rather, we see the actor as a character within drama's universe of discourse" (158). I argue that this priority is reversed in the performance of popular music, that we usually perceive the performer primarily in the guise of his or her persona, with character emerging as a distinctly secondary effect.

reliable access to the performer as a real person since it is quite likely that interviews and even casual public appearances are manifestations of the performer's persona rather than the real person. Glam rockers like Bowie and Quatro consistently extended their onstage personae to public venues offstage.

I believe that this general schema can be applied to musical performers of all kinds: jazz musicians and symphony conductors present personae just as popular musicians do. I ultimately chose glam rock as a subject partly because its overt and self-conscious theatricality presents clear and dramatic cases of the creation and presentation of performance personae by popular musicians. I have focused here on both the aural and the visual means through which glam rockers asserted their personae, with particular emphasis on voice, costuming, and movement. Glam rock also cries out for discussion in terms of compelling issues in performance studies, particularly the performance of self, gender identity, and sexual identity. All of these are crucial to my analysis here and reveal important points of intersection between music and performance studies. In these discussions, I have drawn on prominent theorists of identity and gender, including Judith Butler, Judith Halberstam, and Erving Goffman. The sociocultural "gendering" of musical instruments and how instruments contribute to the gender image of a performance persona, which is a theme to which I return regularly here, is one example of an analytical trope that intersects music and performance studies.

The other main reason behind my choice of glam rock is its fascinating historical position. As someone who came of age during the Vietnam War, I have long been intrigued by the era known as "The Sixties" and its aftermath. Glam rock is a culturally significant part of that transition, part of the story of how "The Sixties" became "The Seventies." Arguably, glam rock was the first fully developed post-countercultural genre of rock music. Looking at how it was performed by contrast with the performance conventions of the psychedelic rock closely associated with the hippie counterculture can tell us a great deal about the shifts in aesthetic, political, social, and cultural priorities that unfolded at this important moment. In many ways, psychedelic rock and glam rock are polar opposites. Whereas psychedelic rock emphasized musical virtuosity and seriousness, glam rock emphasized accessibility and fun. If psychedelic rock was suspicious of spectacle and theatricality, glam rock celebrated those aspects of performance. Whereas psychedelic rock, as a countercultural form, always had an uneasy relationship to the market through which it was disseminated, glam embraced the concept of the hit single. If psychedelic rock addressed its audience as a collective whose actions could ultimately transform global politics, glam rock addressed its audience as individuals with the power to transform only themselves. All of these differences, and many others, are enacted in the respective styles of performance associated with psychedelic rock and glam rock. In chapter 1, I develop a stylistic model of the performance of psychedelic rock against which to gauge both certain maverick performers of the 1960s and the glam rockers who followed them. The relationship between psychedelic rock and glam rock is finally not one of simple opposition but dialectical; several of the most important glam rockers, including Bolan and Bowie, were active on the underground rock scene before going glam.

Although I have sought to describe the development of glam rock (largely in chapter 2) and to place it in historical, social, and artistic context, this book is intended primarily as a work of performance analysis informed by theory rather than a history or sociology of glam rock. There are two serviceable histories available: Barney Hoskyns's well-informed, journalistic *Glam! Bolan, Bowie and the Glitter Revolution,* which provides a very helpful account of the development of glam in both its American and British versions, and Van Cagle's more academic treatise *Reconstructing Pop/Subculture: Art, Rock, and Andy Warhol,* which deals primarily with the American side of the equation. Both authors provide good insights into the development of glam rock, and I have not attempted to duplicate their work. This book also should not be taken to be a comprehensive guide to glam rock as a musical genre. For a useful book of that kind, I would direct readers to Dave Thompson's *20th Century Rock and Roll: Glam Rock,* a comprehensive guide aimed at an audience of record collectors.

Although my narrative here is structured in a roughly chronological way, it is organized more as criticism than as history. Opting for depth over breadth, I discuss only a fraction of glam rockers here, focusing on the British performers and discussing the Americans primarily as context, but I have tried to treat their performances in detail. My selection of subjects was governed by their importance to glam rock (in my view, for instance, one cannot write on glam without discussing both Bolan and Bowie, without both of whom the genre probably would not have developed as it did), by the critical and interpretive issues their performances raise, and by their intrinsic interest as performers. I have also tried to include performers with differing relationships to glam rock. Whereas Bolan and Bowie were glam innovators who initiated and consolidated the style and its basic performance strategies, Bryan Ferry and Roy Wood were second-wave glam rockers who put their own particular twists on a set of existing strategies. Suzi Quatro, my subject in chapter 6, has the distinction of being the only canonical female glam rocker. The mere fact of her being a woman necessitates a different approach, including consideration of the general status of female performers in rock.

In examining performances of glam rock, I have drawn on a range of primary materials, including sound recordings, films of live performances, television performances, and interviews. Because glam rock predates MTV, most of the television performances are concert-like presentations rather than music videos, though many are lip-synched. Although lip-synched television performances may not convey much musical information, they do provide a sense of the kinds of visual performance and the performance persona the artist chose to present and are therefore of great value to the performance analyst.

I aspire with this book to make a bridge between disciplines that really ought to be in conversation with one another and to advocate an approach to talking about popular musicians as performers. However, if I succeed only in drawing renewed attention to a fascinating moment in the cultural history of rock and a body of pleasurable music that has been a significant presence in my life these past five years, I will have accomplished something eminently worthwhile.

1. glamticipations

Rock Faces the 1970s

The pause of 1970 was a strange moment. It was marked by the absence of
creative movement in rock's central core. . . . It was equally due to the
dangerous political climate that shattered the youth movement's unity and
thus drove rock away from its natural base. The breakup of bands, the
deaths, the personal crises, the restless movement of performers, the record
companies' insistent attempts to pull out solo acts from ensemble bands so
that they could be turned into superstars, all these led to a reconsideration
of what constituted the stable unit for rock.
—Philip Ennis (360)

Sociologist Philip Ennis describes the year 1970 as a "pause point"
in the development of rock music, which had enjoyed a decade of
steady ascendance up to that time (344). But the social, political,
and cultural disappointments of 1969 and 1970, including the
Rolling Stones' disastrous concert at Altamont; the shootings of
student protesters at Kent State University; the dissolution of the
Beatles as a group; the deaths of Jimi Hendrix, Janis Joplin, and
Brian Jones of the Rolling Stones; the upheaval surrounding the
1968 Democratic National Convention and the resulting trial of the
Chicago Seven all marked the point at which rock music could no
longer serve as the soundtrack of the Vietnam era hippie counterculture. After 1970, rock would have to proceed on different eco-
nomic, political, social, and cultural bases.

Ennis examines these issues in the American context, but the
same disappointment and disaffection with the counterculture was
spreading in the United Kingdom. Iain Chambers describes the
"moral retrenchment" in British politics and society at the end of
the relatively permissive 1960s: "the 1970s open, as they will close,
seated on that eternal political work horse: 'law and order'"
(106–7). Chambers indicates how this changing climate was
reflected in rock: "The full wave of the alternative politics of the

1960s had now crested. In its wake it had beached a music, now robbed of this central referent, that increasingly sounded 'loudly within . . . and hollow at the core' (Joseph Conrad)" (107). This was the backdrop against which glam rock developed as the first post-countercultural rock style to solidify as a genre practiced by a significant number of musicians.

For Ennis, the performance that epitomizes the pause point in rock was Phil Ochs's appearance at New York's Carnegie Hall in April 1970. Ochs had made a career as an unremittingly political folk protest singer and was considered one of the least compromising practitioners of that idiom. By his own testimony, Ochs was so disturbed by the political developments of the late 1960s that he "went crazy and didn't care anymore" (qtd. in Wilson 44). At Carnegie Hall, he appeared on stage wearing a gold lamé suit modeled after one of Elvis Presley's stage outfits and interspersed rock and roll and country songs from the 1950s with his usual repertoire of folk protest.

Ochs was roundly booed by much of his audience, presumably because they saw his embodiment of Elvis as a retreat from the political engagement of the 1960s back to the conformism of the 1950s against which the counterculture had rebelled. But I shall emphasize a different aspect of Ochs's performance that may also have set him at odds with the counterculture: wearing the gold lamé suit was clearly a *theatrical* gesture in conflict with a counterculture that was ambivalent, at best, about theatricality, especially in musical performances. Although it has long been conventional to describe the political protests and Yippie manifestations of the 1960s as street theater, I argue that the counterculture's deep investment in the idea of authenticity entailed a necessary antipathy to theatricality. This antipathy derived from three ideological commitments: the emphasis on spontaneity and living in the present moment, the desire for community, and the suspicion that spectacle served the interests of the social and political status quo.

In both the United States and the United Kingdom, the hippie counterculture placed a premium on personal authenticity, whether in everyday behavior, politics, or cultural expression. Stuart Hall, writing in 1969, interpreted Timothy Leary's famous hippie slogan, which he renders as "Turn on, tune in and drop out," as a call "to switch . . . to a more authentic mode of experience" (173).[1] At the

1. To Leary himself, the slogan meant that one should seek "an active, selective and graceful process of detachment from involuntary or unconscious commitments" (qtd. in David Farber 32).

level of everyday life, this meant that "what is real, is total self-expression and authenticity in the here and now. Life is a loosely-organised series of unplanned 'happenings,' with the stress on the immediacy, the spontaneous participation and the free-form expressiveness of the response" (Hall 183). Peter Braunstein also takes the happening as the central motif in his summary of the countercultural ethos:[2]

> Youth in the 1960s tended a culture of immediacy that prized such elements as spontaneity, frivolity, and amorphousness, a zeitgeist epitomized by phenomena like "Happenings" that eluded categorization. . . . By the mid-1960s, Happenings became a catch-all term to describe any type of free-form, deliberately improvised event—be it festive, commercial, or . . . romantic. . . . Happenings, along with such—in suffixed events as Be-Ins and Love-Ins, testified to the lure of the unscripted in 1960s pop culture, an aspect of its presentist, immediatist orientation. (255–56)

Theodore Roszak, writing, like Hall, during the countercultural moment, extended the themes of spontaneity and self-expression to the political realm: he describes "the prevailing spirit of New Left politics" as the idea that "at whatever cost to the cause of the doctrine, one must care for the uniqueness and the dignity of each individual and yield to what his conscience demands in the existential moment" (61).[3]

In "Spectacles and Scenarios: A Dramaturgy of Radical Activity," an essay of 1969, Lee Baxandall opposed spectacle, which is used by the reigning powers to maintain control, to scenarism, a radical strategy of subversion. Whereas subjection to "the spectacle genre . . makes you narrow and stupid," scenarism is a "a free intelligent activity" based on the construction and enactment of scenarios that are "projected and agreed beforehand in part, and in part created as opportunities and fortuities arise in performance" (259–60). The political theater associated with the counterculture, of which the San Francisco Mime Troupe was a prime exemplar, employed a dramaturgy such as Baxandall describes by emphasiz-

---

2. Although the word *happening* referred at one point to a specific genre of experimental art world performance that originated in the 1950s (see Kirby), it became a buzzword of the 1960s: any significant event or state of being was described as a happening.

3. See Doug Rossinow for further discussion of the New Left's emphasis on authenticity.

ing the spontaneous, unscripted, existential moment. Performing in parks and streets rather than theaters, the Mime Troupe created theatrical events where none were expected. The group's approach to performance was modeled on the improvisatory scenarios of the commedia dell'arte (also Baxandall's model for scenarios) that could be adapted on the spot to local conditions and audience response. This kind of theater was called guerilla theater not only because it modeled its revolutionary aspirations on those of Che Guevara but also because it was designed to occur unexpectedly and to disappear suddenly, especially if antagonistic police were to arrive on the scene (Doyle 74). In these ways, the guerilla street theater of the 1960s was theater that aspired to the condition of a happening or be-in. It was antitheatrical in the sense that it sought to undermine the ritual and institutional aspects of conventional theater as a planned event that takes place at a designated time, in a designated theater space, for an audience that is there expressly to see it. Guerilla theater was to be continuous with the life of the streets on which it occurred.

Just as the San Francisco Mime Troupe set out to create a political theater that would reflect the high value placed on spontaneity and improvisation within the counterculture, rock musicians, too, were expected to honor the countercultural ethos in their performances. In a 1974 review of a David Bowie concert that shows the persistence of this ethos after the 1960s, Chris Charlesworth makes clear how theatricality was perceived within rock culture. Charlesworth describes Bowie's show as "a piece of theatre" that "has as much to do with rock and roll as Bob Dylan has with Las Vegas." The reason for this characterization lies in the production's lack of spontaneity: the "show is a completely rehearsed and choreographed routine where every step and nuance has been perfected down to the last detail. There isn't one iota of spontaneity about the whole show." Charlesworth's overall assessment of Bowie's concert is not negative, but he is at pains to insist that what Bowie is doing is *theater,* not *rock,* a "show that belongs on Broadway" rather than before a rock audience (3).

As Paul E. Willis shows in his ethnographic study of British hippies, the hippie audience expected its cultural figures to be direct reflections of its values. As one of Willis's subjects put it, "The bands that are producing music today are coming out of this life-style, they are only projecting what we're thinking. They are coming from this life-style, they are growing from us, and they are communicating what we already know" (165). This meant, in part, that rock groups were expected to participate in be-ins and other manifestations of the counterculture and to play in parks and other unconventional venues, often for free. The idea that rock musicians were members of the community from which their audiences were drawn went hand in hand with "the prevailing aesthetic of amateurism . . . in the alternative music scene" of the 1960s that "asserted that everyone could be a star" (Lipsitz 216), the attitude celebrated by Sly and the Family Stone in their song "Everybody is a Star" (1970) and satirized by the Byrds in "So You Wanna Be a Rock and Roll Star" (1967).[4] This understanding of rock music as an arena in which participatory democracy could be enacted enshrines a paradox: the countercultural audience idolized musical virtuosity (as exemplified by the famous London graffito, "Clapton is god") but wanted simultaneously to believe that anyone had the potential to become a rock star. This attitude, however fanciful it may have been, was at the base of the counterculture's antitheatricalism.

Whereas the counterculture wanted to perceive a seamless unity between rock performers and their audiences, the theater is, as Herbert Blau puts it, premised on an "original splitting"—the differentiation of performer from audience. As a collective enterprise, the theater seems to hold out the promise of community, but always ends up asserting the basic fact that "there is no theatre without *separation*" (Blau 10). Because the hippie counterculture sought to resist this separation of performer and audience in favor of an imagined social collective, rock musicians were constrained to perform in ways that stressed their identity with their audiences. The ideology of authenticity mandated that musicians appear on stage as themselves, not as any other persona or character,[5] and discour-

---

4. The formation of rock musicians—and the idea that anyone can become a rock star—is a recurrent theme in the music. Two random examples: Chuck Berry's "Johnny B. Goode" (1958), about a guitar-playing innocent who is tapped for stardom, and Norman Greenbaum's amusing "The Tars of Inja" (1970, on his *Spirit in the Sky* album), in which he suggests that the best training for a future rock musician is to stay in his room getting stoned and practicing the guitar.

5. In a 1968 interview with Donovan, Jay Ruby suggests that for a psychedelic rock musician, any difference between onstage persona and offstage person is grounds for an existential crisis: "the conflict that the other entertainers have between their public image as an entertainer and their private image of themselves as a person is very frequently in conflict [*sic*]. That is, they have to

aged forms of overtly theatrical performance that would emphasize the differences between performers and spectators. Consequently, the counterculture evinced a general "disdain for rock theatrics . . . [that] came for some to represent inauthenticity" (Onkey 200).[6]

One of the ways that psychedelic rockers demonstrated continuity with their audiences was to present stage personae that were not dramatically different from the people one could see in the streets. Some performers, notably Grace Slick of Jefferson Airplane—who performed in a flowing white tunic at the 1967 Monterey Pop Festival—were clearly costumed; even Janis Joplin's relatively informal stage outfits were actually designed.[7] Nevertheless, the standard onstage attire for psychedelic rock musicians was basically a version of what their audiences might be expected to wear—the informal attire and casual dress wear of the time. Costuming conventions for rock musicians varied somewhat according to their musical commitments. Blues rockers, such as the members of Canned Heat and the Electric Flag, generally favored more proletarian-seeming clothing: tee shirts or work shirts with denim jeans and jackets. Male psychedelic rockers tended to wear casual dress attire onstage, ranging from turtleneck sweaters and blazers to the wide lapels and ties favored at the time, usually accompanied by dress slacks (not jeans).

Performing at Monterey, Andy Kulberg, bassist and flutist for the Blues Project, represented the less formal side of this spectrum by wearing a dark green suede jacket over a shiny, striped blue dress shirt with a dark blue turtleneck under that. Guitarist John Cipollina, of the Quicksilver Messenger Service, offered a more formal version of hippie elegance by wearing a brown fringed leather jacket, white shirt, and black tie with dark slacks. All of the styles visible onstage, including elements of cowboy fashion and the pen-

---

perform, they have to put on a face, a mask, when they appear in public. . . . you are Donovan whether you're in Carnegie Hall or whether you're sitting here in this room" (65–66).

6. One very notable exception to rock culture's distrust of theatricality is Michael Rosenbaum's 1968 essay in *Crawdaddy*, "Jimi Hendrix and Live Things." Using an interview with Hendrix as the pretext for some reflections on rock performance, Rosenbaum champions "the theater aspect of live performance," going on to say, "visual presentation . . . is as important to a live performance as is the music" (25).

7. Mablen Jones reproduces one of Linda Gravenites' costume designs for Joplin (82).

chant for big furry hats exhibited by John Phillips of the Mamas and the Papas and David Crosby of the Byrds, were also visible in the audience. Even Jimi Hendrix's flashy, Gypsy-inspired garb was only a slight exaggeration of then current Carnaby Street fashion.

Musicians' use of clothing to mark their identification with the hippie community notwithstanding, the counterculture evinced an antiocular bias. Baxandall's linking of the word *spectacle* to the evil machinations of the power structure is symptomatic of the counterculture's distrust of the visual, a distrust that stemmed from the belief that the dominant culture controlled the means of producing socially influential images (e.g., the mass media).[8] The visual manifestations of the counterculture, such as rock concert posters and underground comix, had to be readily distinguishable from their Madison Avenue counterparts and had to be perceived as unassimilable to the mainstream. As Lawrence Grossberg suggests, this antiocularity was particularly acute with respect to rock performance:

> The authenticity of rock has always been measured by its sound. . . . The eye has always been suspect in rock culture; after all, visually, rock often borders on the inauthentic. . . . It was here—in its visual presentation—that rock often most explicitly manifested its resistance to the dominant culture, but also its sympathies with the business of entertainment. (204)

Albert Goldman noted this tension in a 1968 article for *Vogue* in which he describes rock performances at the Fillmore East as "a nascent theater that is squalling already with vigor" (28). He thought that such a theater could ultimately achieve the "catharsis of the most basic instinctual appetites and fantasies" imagined by Artaud in his conception of the Theater of Cruelty (30). But Goldman also acknowledged that this theater could come into being only through collaborations between rock musicians and "the show-biz professionals whose skills they need in the theater" and

---

8. Baxandall uses the term *spectacle* in much the same way as Guy Debord does in the latter's famous work *The Society of the Spectacle* (originally published in French in 1967). One important difference between their respective understandings of the concept is that whereas Baxandall refers to spectacle as the genre of public display used by the power elite to serve their own interests, Debord characterizes spectacle in more systemic terms "as a social relation between people that is mediated by images" (12).

that such collaborations were unlikely to occur because of the musicians' ideological resistance to show business (31).

The counterculture's antiocularity clearly was not absolute: rock musicians did indeed use visual elements and effects in performance both to distinguish themselves from the dominant culture and to articulate a position toward it (Country Joe McDonald's displaying painted flowers on his face while wearing a parody of a military uniform comes to mind). Many psychedelic rock groups considered the visual aspects of performance so important that some (Pink Floyd and King Crimson among them) had members whose sole function in performance was to run the group's light show, and many psychedelic groups performed against elaborate projected images.[9] Light shows and projections, however, did not contravene the antispectacle bias of the counterculture, for three reasons. For one thing, the lighting designers and operators presented themselves as members of the counterculture (not "show-biz" professionals from the outside) who specialized in creating atmospheric effects appropriate to psychedelic music and drugs. Some lighting companies, such as Headlights and the Joshua Light Show, became sufficiently well known to merit their own billing at rock concerts. Second, the lighting operators could improvise their effects and respond spontaneously to the musicians, thus manifesting the presentism valued in the counterculture. Finally, the lighting was subordinated to the music: Pink Floyd's light artist Joe Gannon's "slides were based on the underlying rhythm of the music" (Whiteley, *The Space* 28), allowing the aural to dominate the visual. Light shows thus supported the ethos of spontaneity and preserved the primary focus on musical sound. They served chiefly to create the proper mood and ambience around a group's performance and did not involve the musicians, who generally did not interact directly with the light shows, in the creation of spectacle.

The musicians' performance styles reflected the antitheatrical and antiocular tendencies of the counterculture. Psychedelic music, often fueled by LSD and other hallucinogenic drugs, was intended primarily as an internal, individualized experience for both musicians and audience. All references to psychedelic rock as theatrical and Dionysian aside, psychedelic rock musicians usually appeared

9. For a discussion of how Pink Floyd's lightshow worked with the group's music to produce psychedelic effects, see Whiteley, *The Space* (31–33).

quite introspective on stage.[10] They generally focused their attention on each other or their instruments, especially while playing a solo, and did not play to the audience extensively. At the start of the Jefferson Airplane's morning performance at Woodstock, for instance, Slick greeted the crowd exuberantly. But when she began to sing, she closed her eyes and restricted her attention to the stage. (It was not unusual, in fact, for psychedelic rockers to turn their backs to their audiences during their performances.) Even performers whose styles involved intense physicality, such as Joplin and Joe Cocker, appeared to be directing their energies inward. In the performances documented in the film *Woodstock* (1970), both Cocker and Joplin seem to be completely wrapped up in the sound created by their backing musicians and more or less oblivious to the audience. With Joplin and Cocker, it often seemed that their physical performances resulted more from their own internal experiences of powerful emotion than a desire to communicate with their audiences.

Unlike their contemporaries in soul music and Motown, psychedelic rock musicians usually did not dance on stage. They sometimes moved or swayed rhythmically and they engaged in histrionic gestures with their instruments, but they did not dance (though members of their audiences often did). Willis points out that hippie culture generally deemphasized dance, arguing that "little of the hippy's general identity was expressed through autonomous bodily movement, so there was no demand that the music should parallel rhythmic bodily movement in a regular clear beat or encourage dancing. Beat was not a way of encouraging and reflecting physical action, but a way of demanding attention in the head" (156–57). It is also the case that the irregular, shifting rhythms of much psychedelic rock make it very difficult to dance to in any patterned way.

---

10. This and similar observations, and all of my generalizations about the performance behavior of psychedelic rock musicians, are based on close examination of documentary films, particularly Michael Wadleigh's *Woodstock* and D. A. Pennebaker's *Monterey Pop;* I have also drawn on my own experience as a concert-goer in the 1960s and 1970s. *Monterey Pop,* especially in its current incarnation as a multi-disc DVD set, is a particularly good source, in part because it includes performances by musicians in a variety of different genres—including psychedelic rock, blues rock, folk rock, pop, soul, and jazz—at the same moment in time, thus permitting comparisons of performance conventions across musical genres.

The primary impression psychedelic rockers apparently wished to create was of seriousness and concentration—in keeping with the counterculture's valorization of virtuosity, they appeared to be focused on musicianship above all, which they implied to be more important than acknowledging their audiences or creating visually interesting effects. (Blues rockers, by contrast, tended to be more ebullient—on stage, the members of both Canned Heat and the Electric Flag moved and responded to one another in ways that emphasized their pleasure in the music and one another's skills.) During the Jefferson Airplane's performance of "Somebody to Love" at Monterey, for example, lead guitarist Jorma Kaukonen looked only at his own left hand on the fretboard while playing his solo. As the song neared its end, he turned his back to the audience to conduct the band and stayed in that position until the song was over. Several psychedelic rock groups typically played a portion of their set in total darkness, as if to suggest that a visual environment conducive to meditative concentration on the sound was desirable.[11] As a member of the Paupers, a Canadian group that played at Monterey, put it, "We are trying to create a total environment with sound alone. Sound is enough. We don't use lights or any gimmicks" (qtd. in Lydon 26). The glaring, rule-proving exception to psychedelic rock's typically low-key performance style, of course, was Jimi Hendrix, who engaged his audiences directly with performances that were flamboyant, excessive, and overtly sexual, though even he often performed with his eyes closed and seemed oblivious to the presence of his audience.[12] Although many in his audiences were thrilled by his performances, other observers were put off by his theatricality, and Hendrix himself ultimately disowned the spectacular side of his performances, saying, "I never wanted it to be so much of a visual thing" and expressing the desire that "people come to listen rather than to see us" (qtd. in Waksman 205).[13]

11. These groups included the Doors, the Jefferson Airplane, and Eric Burdon and the New Animals. Scenes of the latter two groups performing in the dark appear in *Monterey Pop*.

12. I offer a brief analysis of one of Hendrix's performances in chapter 3.

13. See also Lauren Onkey's discussion of Hendrix's reception by audiences and critics in both the UK and the United States (197–200). Onkey points out that the showy performance techniques Hendrix perfected while playing on the American South's "chitlin circuit" were perceived as wild and exotic (though not specifically African-American) in the UK and by some U.S. critics as overly theatrical and as reinforcing racial stereotypes.

It is in the context of the counterculture's antitheatricalism and rock's antiocular bias that Phil Ochs's appearance in a gold lamé Elvis suit must be understood. Ennis sees Ochs's performance in 1970 as "emblematic of this moment of dissolution" of the rock culture "and the courage of some parts of the rock life to fight it" (354). In Ennis's estimation, Ochs was trying to restore vitality to rock at its moment of crisis by returning to its roots and rediscovering Elvis's originally subversive energy. But Ochs's performance can also be seen as premonitory rather than retrospective. Ochs may have received a mixed response at Carnegie Hall not only because he, the most political of folk singers, played the kind of ostensibly apolitical rock and roll that the counterculture thought it had surpassed, but also because of the overt theatricality of his performance. Unlike psychedelic rockers or the protest folkie he had been, Ochs did not present himself as an extension of his audience: the Elvis suit—obviously a *costume*—clearly set him apart as a performer. The appeal of Ochs's gesture was to the eye: to understand what he was doing, one had to *see* him dressed as Elvis; his visual performance was not secondary to his aural one. His use of the suit also brought an element of role-playing into his performance: belying the ideology of authenticity, he did not appear simply as himself. Although Ochs may have thought that his decision to appear as Elvis expressed his own emotional upheaval at the time, it is likely that at least a portion of his audience read his performance as planned and calculated (he had to obtain the suit, after all) and therefore antithetical to the countercultural ethos of spontaneity and presentism. In all these respects, Ochs anticipated aspects of rock performance after the counterculture; his performance at Carnegie Hall foreshadowed the emphasis on characterization, self-consciousness, and spectacle in the rock of the 1970s, particularly in glam.

Ochs was not the first American artist whose performances anticipated glam; there had already been intimations of the new dispensation in 1968 and 1969. I will devote the remainder of this chapter to discussing two American rock groups whose performances implied a move beyond the counterculture, Sha Na Na and Alice Cooper. (Whereas Alice Cooper is usually included among the ranks of American glam or glitter artists, Sha Na Na is not.) Each of these discussions centers on a contrast: I will contrast Sha Na Na's performance of 1950s music at Woodstock with John Lennon's performance of similar music at the Toronto Rock

Revival to show that while Lennon performed 1950s revivalism in countercultural rock terms, Sha Na Na—like Phil Ochs—looked ahead to something else. In my discussion of Alice Cooper, I will contrast the group's portrayal of a madman in "The Ballad of Dwight Fry" with a pre-glam-era song by David Bowie also on the theme of madness. This contrast reveals that whereas Bowie's treatment of the theme at that point was consistent with a countercultural perspective, Alice Cooper's recorded performance exemplified some of the crucial characteristics of glam.

Although one might assume otherwise, Sha Na Na's performance at Woodstock had much in common with John Lennon's performance with the Plastic Ono Band at the Toronto Rock Revival. Both events took place in 1969, less than a month apart—Sha Na Na performed at Woodstock on August 18, while Lennon appeared in Toronto on September 13. Both groups were quite new at the time of their respective performances. Sha Na Na was formed at Columbia University in 1969; their performance at Woodstock was only their seventh gig. For Lennon, who had not played live in three years, the Toronto concert was a first step in establishing a musical identity apart from the Beatles. The Plastic Ono Band, with whom Lennon had issued the single "Give Peace A Chance" two months earlier, had never performed in public. Both groups focused their repertoire on rock and roll songs from the 1950s: Sha Na Na were captured for posterity in the documentary film *Woodstock* performing Danny and the Juniors' "At the Hop" (1958) while the Plastic Ono Band opened their set with Carl Perkins's "Blue Suede Shoes" (1956).

Sha Na Na's and John Lennon's respective performances in 1969 reflected the surge of interest in the rock and roll of the 1950s in both the United States and the United Kingdom that lasted from about 1968 until at least 1974. (Glam rock, too, participated in this revival, and I shall have more to say about the relationship between glam and the 1950s in the next chapter.) During these years, veteran rock and roll musicians from the 1950s gained a youthful new audience, and a great many rock musicians performed and recorded their songs. This interest in the past was not a monolithic phenomenon: rock musicians performed rock and roll in different ways to convey different meanings.[14] Here, I will discuss the ways Lennon's

14. See Auslander, "Good Old Rock 'n' Roll."

performance of similar materials reflected the countercultural emphasis on authenticity and Sha Na Na's performance of 1950s music prefigured glam's celebration of artifice.

Lennon conveyed a strong sense that by playing rock and roll songs, he was digging down to the bedrock of his own artistic identity. At Toronto, Lennon introduced the Plastic Ono Band by saying, "We're only gonna play numbers we know, you know, 'cause we've never played together before." Lennon thus implied that rock and roll songs like "Blue Suede Shoes," "Money," and "Dizzy Miss Lizzie" are so basic to the vocabulary of rock that any randomly assembled group of rock musicians should be able to play them without rehearsal. (He also seemed to be evoking the amateurism prized by the counterculture by suggesting that his group of very accomplished musicians would be bashing out informal versions of well-known songs like any average garage band.)

On his album *Rock 'N' Roll,* a collection of cover versions of well-known songs from the 1950s recorded in 1973–74 and released in 1975, Lennon describes his relationship to rock and roll in explicitly autobiographical terms by associating the songs with his own youth and formation as a musician. Among the many credits listed on the album's back cover is the statement: "Relived by: JL." The front cover reproduces a photograph of Lennon in Hamburg, Germany, taken when he was twenty-two years old. Lennon is seen leaning against the side of an arched entryway, looking at passersby through hooded eyes. He's dressed in the uniform associated with the British working-class subculture of Rockers: black leather jacket, black jeans, and leather boots. This photograph evokes the historical moment in the very early 1960s when many British groups, including the Beatles, found work as cover bands, churning out versions of rock and roll songs in the disreputable clubs on Hamburg's Reeperbahn.[15]

Jon Wiener, one of Lennon's biographers, describes the significance of the song selection on *Rock 'N' Roll* in detail:

> The songs John decided to cover on *Rock 'n' Roll* were not just any old oldies. They represented his own personal musical history. John sang Buddy Holly's "Peggy Sue" on *Rock 'n' Roll*. The name "Beatles" had been inspired by Buddy Holly's Crickets and

15. It is interesting in this connection that Lennon counted the beat in German at one point during the Toronto concert, surely a holdover from those early days.

"That'll Be the Day" was the first song John learned to play on the guitar in 1957. He had sung many other Buddy Holly songs: "It's So Easy" as Johnny and the Moondogs in his first TV appearance in 1959, and "Words of Love," which the Beatles recorded in 1964. (268–69)

Wiener continues in this vein, explaining the specific associations of songs by Gene Vincent, Little Richard, Chuck Berry, and Larry Williams in terms of Lennon's history before and with the Beatles. As if to hammer home the importance of these biographical associations, Lennon himself provides a disc jockey–like spoken introduction to "Just Because," the last song on the album. He waxes nostalgic, saying, "Ah, remember this?" and tries to recall how old he was when the song was first recorded.

By performing his relationship to rock and roll as a relationship of authenticity grounded in a deep personal connection to the music of the 1950s, Lennon sought to close the gap between his performance persona and his real identity by suggesting that they were one and the same, that his audience should perceive his performances of rock and roll songs as emanating from his life experience. In strong contrast, Sha Na Na's performed relationship to the same music did not assert the same connection.[16] To the contrary: whereas Lennon presented himself as having lived and absorbed the music of the 1950s in the 1950s, the performers in Sha Na Na constructed themselves as entities without biographies. Whereas Lennon framed his performances of rock and roll as artifacts of his own history, Sha Na Na performed rock and roll as history without claiming it as their own, personal history. We are meant to take the picture of the twenty-two-year-old Rocker on the cover of the *Rock 'N' Roll* album as a point of reference for understanding the older Lennon's relationship to rock and roll music. Sha Na Na advanced no such claim about the greaser image they presented. There was no implied biographical relationship, for instance, between the preening, spitting, obnoxious Bowzer, the popular persona of Sha Na Na's bass singer, and Jon Bauman, the performer who portrayed him.[17]

Although Lennon's Rocker image and the greaser image por-

16. As of this writing, Sha Na Na still exists as a functioning group (see http://www.shanana.com). I refer to them in the past here because I am focusing on their appearance at Woodstock.

17. In fact, Bauman (who joined the group after their appearance at Woodstock) and Bowzer were originally presented as different people. In the liner

trayed by Sha Na Na are sartorially similar, there are important differences between their respective performances of these subcultural
icons. By presenting himself as a Rocker, Lennon aligned himself
with a specific, historically class-based social experience of which
rock and roll had been a part. As Stanley Cohen has shown, to be a
Rocker in early 1960s Britain was to adopt a particular social identity. Whereas the Mods, another working-class youth subculture of
the same period that I discuss further in chapter 2, were considered
exciting and newsworthy, "the rockers were left out of the race:
they were unfashionable and unglamorous just because they
appeared to be more class bound" than the seemingly more
upwardly mobile Mods (156). Insofar as Cohen suggests that the
early British pop groups also represented upward mobility through
"success stories of being discovered and making it" (152), Lennon's
assertion of his Rocker past was an act of symbolic downward
mobility, as if he were undoing the Beatles' phenomenal rise to
assert solidarity with his former working-class self.

Sha Na Na also enacted personae based on subcultural identities
with overtones of class and, in their case, race and ethnicity, but in
a spirit very different from Lennon's. Although Sha Na Na played
the music of such African-American rhythm and blues artists as the
Coasters and there was an African-American performer (Denny
Greene) in the group's original lineup, their performances revolved
primarily around two stylistic reference points: the rock and roll
purveyed by white southerners such as Elvis Presley and Jerry Lee
Lewis, and East Coast doo-wop as practiced by working-class Italian-American singers. Although several members of Sha Na Na
typically wore gold lamé suits associated with Elvis onstage (the
same outfit to which Ochs resorted), their visual image otherwise
did not correspond to those of the earlier performers they emulated. The other main costume Sha Na Na used was an outfit of
black leather jacket, jeans, and T-shirt comparable to British
Rocker attire but associated in the United States primarily with the
greaser.[18] (Sha Na Na emphasized that association by referring to
the "grease" they used to maintain 1950s-style hairdos, which they

---

notes to *Sha Na Na* (1971), the group's second album, Jon Bauman is credited
as playing piano and Bowzer is credited with production assistance. Somewhat
later, Bauman would be identified only as Bowzer: a trading card featuring
Bauman's image that accompanied the 1974 album *Hot Sox* is signed
"Bowzer."

18. Examples cited in the *Oxford English Dictionary* suggest that in the
UK, *rocker* and *greaser* can be used interchangeably to designate the same

combed continuously during their performances.) Neither the greaser outfit nor the gold lamé suit has any specific relationship to the doo-wop that makes up the largest part of Sha Na Na's repertoire since doo-wop singers, both black and white, generally wore evening wear when performing.

Unlike Lennon's Rocker image, Sha Na Na's greaser look referred neither to the performance practices associated with the music they performed nor to the typical appearance of its audiences but to a stereotypical "Italian-Americanicity."[19] Members of the group whose own names suggested a variety of ethnic heritages, including Irish and Jewish, adopted such Italianate stage-names as Tony Santini, Gino, and Ronzoni.[20] Unlike Lennon, Sha Na Na never suggested that they chose these images because they corresponded to their own social or cultural identities. If Lennon stressed the continuity between his performance persona and his real identity, Sha Na Na knowingly drove a wedge between those

---

working-class subculture. In the United States, however, the term *greaser* most often has specific ethnic, as well as class, implications. It seems to have originated around the middle of the nineteenth century in California, where it was used as a highly derogatory slang epithet to describe a person of Mexican or Spanish heritage. On the east coast of the United States, the term was applied to Italian and Puerto Rican immigrants. By the mid-1960s in California, the term lost some of its ethnic specificity when it was applied to motorcycle enthusiasts: in subcultural terms, greasers (bikers) were distinguished from surfers. A few years later, during the rock-and-roll revival period under consideration here, the term *greaser* was used in the United States to evoke an image that combined the biker reference with Italian-American identity: Henry Winkler's character on the *Happy Days* television program, Arthur (The Fonz) Fonzarelli, exemplifies this image. This is the version of the greaser image taken up by Sha Na Na, a version that evokes an ethnic stereotype in more benign terms than its exclusively derogatory application to Mexican-Americans on the West Coast. See Heather Altz for a very complete account of the etymology and usage of *greaser* and related terms in both the United States and the UK.

19. I refer here to Roland Barthes's famous 1964 essay "The Rhetoric of the Image" in which he describes a French advertisement for Italian food products as evoking "Italianicity," an identity "based on a familiarity with certain tourist stereotypes" rather than direct cultural experience (17).

20. Continuing this tradition of stage names and personae, Screamin' Scott Simon, Sha Na Na's longtime stand-in for Jerry Lee Lewis, also performs in Los Angeles as Eddie "Hong Kong" Tailor with a blues trio called Eddie "Hong Kong" Tailor and the Prom Kings. This latter group is a synthesis of two important backward-looking musical simulations of the 1970s: Sha Na Na meets the Blues Brothers. See http://www.eddiehongkongtailor.com.

two signifieds. In a 1972 interview, group member Rich Joffe defined Sha Na Na's performance style by saying, "We try to create a reality on stage but also to indicate that we're not in it really. It's definitely a theatrical thing" (qtd. in Steve Turner, "Moving History"). Fundamentally, the difference between Lennon's performance of rock and roll and Sha Na Na's is the difference between *inhabiting an identity* and *playing a role*. (It should be clear that I am not speaking ontologically here—I do not mean that Lennon really did inhabit an identity while the members of Sha Na Na merely played roles. I refer, rather, to two different modes of performing identity, neither of which is necessarily any more objectively "real" than the other but that make different truth claims.) While Lennon's performance was thus aligned with the hippie counterculture's valorization of authenticity, Sha Na Na's challenged that value by foregrounding the kind of theatricality the counterculture rejected.

Except for the presence of Yoko Ono, who busied herself with performance art interventions during an otherwise straightforward musical event, the first half of the Plastic Ono Band's performance, captured in D. A. Pennebaker's documentary *Sweet Toronto* (1988), was absolutely typical for a late-1960s rock band with countercultural affiliations. Long haired and fully bearded, Lennon wore the white suit he favored at the time. Eric Clapton dressed in denim jacket and pants; his jeans had a large appliquéd patch at the crotch of the sort favored in hippie fashion.[21] The musicians looked at each other only when necessary; Clapton, in particular, darted furtive glances at Lennon and the audience, preferring to close his eyes in concentration when playing. Since Lennon functioned as master of ceremonies, he talked directly to the audience and exhibited a little bit more showmanship than Clapton. While playing "Blue Suede Shoes," Lennon pulled his guitar up toward him and bobbed his head on the beat, but barely moved otherwise. In a telling moment at the start of "Money," Lennon suddenly "Charlestoned" his legs for a brief moment, perhaps in emulation of Chuck Berry, then immediately became more introspective, tilting his head

21. Dick Scheuring elucidates the ideology of patched jeans in the 1960s: "brightly patterned cloth remnants had to be found to decoratively patch the various holes in the trousers. Holes had to be there, as a beacon of resistance to the addictive extravagance of capitalism. The idea was to make a brand-new and fashionable pair of jeans look as if one had already been wearing them for five years without a break" (229–30).

down toward his guitar with his eyes closed, moving his head in rhythm. In an apparent act of self-censorship, Lennon reined in his rock-and-roll enthusiasm in favor of presenting the serious, musicianly image favored by psychedelic rockers.

The Plastic Ono Band came on at the end of a daylong bill that also featured such veteran 1950s rock and rollers as Bo Diddley, Chuck Berry, Jerry Lee Lewis, and Little Richard (all of whom are also included in Pennebaker's film). Although the Plastic Ono Band's repertoire included the same kinds of songs performed earlier in the day by their elders, their performance style could not have been more contrasting. Bo Diddley danced flirtatiously with his female backup singer, while his bass player played his instrument behind his head; Jerry Lee Lewis played piano with his booted foot; Chuck Berry played a guitar solo while holding his instrument down between his legs and only a few inches off the floor; and Little Richard appeared in a mirrored vest and an enormous bouffant pompadour. Despite the raucous rhythms and lyrics of the rock-and-roll songs they played, the Plastic Ono Band's performance eschewed showmanship in favor of the kind of restrained, pensive performance style favored by psychedelic rockers.

Whereas the members of the Plastic Ono Band barely moved when they played, Sha Na Na not only danced on stage at Woodstock but made dance the main focus of their performance of "At the Hop." At the start of this performance, three gold lamé-clad figures ran out on stage to a drum roll and stood with heads bowed like circus performers about to attempt a stunt. When the song began, one of the gold-suited men retired to a microphone at the back of the stage while the other two remained front and center to engage in intense, high-energy dancing. It is important that these two men *did not sing* on this occasion; they performed solely as dancers, while the others doing the singing stood to either side and behind them. The dance they performed was not at all the spontaneous, freeform style of dancing associated with psychedelic rock audiences—it was, rather, a highly choreographed set of symmetrical, unison steps. Some of the steps were adapted from well-known social dances of the 1950s and early 1960s, including the pony, the frug, and the twist. The movements of the backup singers were also clearly choreographed as they alternately leaned their mike stands forward and back.

Sha Na Na did not use an instrumental break in the song as an opportunity to show off their playing ability, as did Eric Clapton with the Plastic Ono Band and most of the acts at Woodstock. Instead, the break also featured dance, not only by the gold-clad performers but by the lead singer and guitarist as well—each exploded into exaggerated dance steps. The guitarist did not play his instrument, but held it in front of him and used it as a prop or dancing partner. At the end of the performance, the entire band ran offstage together, pumping their arms in the manner of a sports team.

Through their presentation of rock-and-roll songs, the Plastic Ono Band performed their allegiance to the counterculture just as surely as Sha Na Na issued a challenge to the counterculture through their presentation of doo-wop. The Plastic Ono Band dressed in a way that was coherent with countercultural fashion and created continuity with their audience: Clapton's patched jeans and Lennon's white suit typified different aspects of countercultural fashion. Although the music they performed provided ample opportunities for showmanship, especially in the context of a rock-and-roll revival concert, the Plastic Ono Band offered the kind of visually and physically restrained performance favored by psychedelic rockers, emphasizing seriousness and authentic musicianship over spectacle. Sha Na Na's performance, by contrast, was clearly costumed and choreographed; the group's appearance distinguished them from the spectators and marked them as performers. They did not present their performance as spontaneous and self-expressive, but as a tightly scripted, theatrical event.

The Plastic Ono Band's performance in Toronto suggested historical continuity between countercultural rock and the rock and rollers with whom they shared the bill. Lennon and the band (including Clapton) implicitly positioned themselves as heirs apparent to rock and roll, as rock musicians who remembered the past, acknowledged their debt to it, and were able to carry the tradition into the present. In a way, Yoko Ono's wailing, avant-garde, very un-rock-and-roll-like piece "Don't Worry Kyoko" (performed in the second half of the concert) was the band's strongest statement of historical continuity, for the instrumental accompaniment to Ono's unconventional keening and ululating vocal was based on the opening chord sequence from the Everly Brothers' "Wake Up Little Susie" (1957). This gesture suggested that even Ono's highly experimental approach to music making was ultimately grounded in and continuous with the rock-and-roll tradition.

Although it would be reasonable to suppose that Sha Na Na's

appearance at Woodstock also represented historical continuity by reminding the audience there of rock's precedents, their performance has been interpreted, correctly I think, not as a sign of continuity between past and present—between rock and roll and rock—but as an anticipation of historical discontinuity between countercultural rock and what came after it. Geoffrey Stokes sees Sha Na Na's appearance at Woodstock and their subsequent popularity as marking the beginning of the end for the rock counterculture of the 1960s:

> Their success was real, but . . . nonmusical. Theirs was, deliberately, a music of nonsignificance, a break from the moral and political freight that rock was bearing. Though it took nearly a decade for them to translate their live popularity to the real stardom that came when they began a syndicated TV show, they planted the seeds of rock's rejection at the site of its greatest triumph. (433)

Stokes deftly marks the historical irony of Sha Na Na's presence at Woodstock, but it is important to recognize that his comment is itself a product of the ideology of countercultural rock. As Grossberg observes, rock ideology "draws an absolute distinction between rock and mere 'entertainment'" (201); clearly, Stokes positions Sha Na Na on the wrong side of that divide. By suggesting that Sha Na Na found their true medium in television, Stokes implies that they never really belonged in rock culture.[22] (It is presumably this perception of Sha Na Na that has kept the group out of most histories of rock and rock reference books.)

French historian of rock Alain Dister also sees Sha Na Na's appearance at Woodstock as a harbinger of crucial changes in popular music culture, though he presents the moment in more positive terms by describing its relationship to subsequent developments:

> The tone [of post-countercultural rock] was established at Woodstock with the unexpected appearance of Sha Na Na. Exhausted, rock returned to its origins while making fun of itself. At first parodic, this attitude became more serious with the Flamin' Groovies, who . . . established the connection between the popular music of the 1960s and the minimalism of the 1980s for legions

22. See Auslander, *Liveness* (87–88) for a brief discussion of the uneasy relationship between television and countercultural rock.

of punk groups. The decadent New York Dolls provoked surprise in 1973. An archetypal garage band, like the later Ramones, they emphasized look and attitude without worrying too much about musical precision—a remarkable theatricalization of rock that others, such as Alice Cooper and David Bowie, exploited with much greater care and technique. (111–12; my translation)

Dister sees Sha Na Na as anticipating two distinct, though related, trends in rock in the 1970s: glam and punk.[23] Sha Na Na's artificial personae foreshadowed the theatrical aspects of punk rock exemplified by Johnny Rotten's sneering actorly presence and the Ramones' overtly synthetic group identity, uniform of leather biker jackets, and adopted Italian-Americanistic surname. Sha Na Na's emphasis on show bizzy performance techniques that were anathema to the counterculture anticipated glam rock, as did their construction of an obviously artificial (and, incidentally, somewhat homoerotic) image. Joffe, the member of Sha Na Na whom I quoted earlier, noted this similarity in 1972, citing David Bowie and Alice Cooper as other performers who were "definitely back into the show biz thing" and arguing that Sha Na Na were "just another facet of the modern rock scene" (qtd. in Steve Turner, "Moving History"). I am not suggesting that Sha Na Na directly influenced glam or punk, only that they anticipated these developments in certain respects. But the fact that Sha Na Na were well known in New York and had performed to acclaim in London in 1971 makes it possible that the early avatars of glam and punk took notice.

In 1969, the same year that Sha Na Na was formed, Alice Cooper, another American group of similar premonitory importance that had existed in one form or another since the early 1960s, began to find its niche. Like Sha Na Na, Alice Cooper[24] was intentionally anomalous in relation to the counterculture, though they cultivated an image very different from that of the cheerfully atavistic doo-wop enthusiasts. Rather than a group of refugees from the 1950s,

23. There is also a connection to disco here: the distance from Sha Na Na to the Village People is not great!

24. Originally, Alice Cooper was the name of the whole group. Vincent Furnier, the group's lead singer, eventually assumed the name for himself and retained it as his stage name when the group disbanded. Furnier supposedly discovered the name during a Ouija board session in which he learned that he is the reincarnation of a seventeenth-century witch.

Alice Cooper presented themselves as a band of trashy transvestites. The cover of the group's first mature album, *Love it to Death* (1971), shows Vincent Furnier, the lead singer who eventually took the name of Alice Cooper himself, and the other members of the group dressed in a style that combined tight-fitting leather, satin, or gold lamé pants with lacy, see-through lingerie, fringe, floor-length wraps, and copious mascara. (The now familiar, highly stylized, streaky eye makeup that Furnier still uses when he performs as Alice came later.)

If Sha Na Na's theatricalism flew in the face of countercultural values, Alice Cooper's transvestism—which explicitly anticipated glam rock's central performance strategy—prodded the counterculture at an ideologically vulnerable spot. Although it is generally conceded that the feminist and gay liberation movements were inspired by the antiwar movement, the counterculture's approach to sex and sexuality was complex and self-contradictory. Parts of the movement made a point of flouting sexual convention as a way of antagonizing the dominant culture and conceptualizing a new sexual politics (Beth Bailey, "Sexual Revolution(s)" 255–57). But the sexual politics of the hippie counterculture were basically quite conservative: "The attitude to women in the culture was far from progressive. They had a place which was certainly different from, and usually inferior to, men. . . . Generally, the hippies distrusted the women's movement, and contrasted its ideals with their notion of the *natural* female and her organic role" (Willis 128). Countercultural representations of women and sex often spilled over into misogyny, as Beth Bailey shows in her analysis of the underground comix of the 1960s ("Sex as a Weapon"). Even Roszak, otherwise a very sympathetic observer of the youth counterculture, was dismayed by what he saw as "elements of pornographic grotesquery" in the underground press (74). The relationship of women to the hippie brand of "liberation" was therefore frequently ambivalent.

Although the counterculture professed openness about sexuality and some gay people were attracted to its centers (especially San Francisco), the counterculture's actual sexual practices were generally conventional.

Hippies, due to their long hair and more "feminine" appearance, may have been conflated with gay men in the popular imagination, but this conflation did not necessarily mean that the counterculture explicitly endorsed or participated in homosexual activity. On the contrary: despite the abstract rhetoric of love and sexual freedom that dominated the movement, the privileging of masculinity through an emphasis on "groovy" heterosexual performance meant that the counterculture was often homophobic as well as sexist. (McRuer 217)

If this was true of the counterculture at large, it was particularly pronounced in the realm of psychedelic rock. During the 1960s, the number of prominent rock performers who were female or of color was observably very small, and no rock performer publicly claimed a homosexual identity.[25]

As part of its sexual politics, the hippie counterculture advocated new definitions of masculinity and femininity and embraced androgyny, especially in fashion, but androgyny of a very specific sort. In 1969, Stuart Hall took note of the "standing joke that young men and women are steadily coming to look more and more like one another," and imputes to the hippie counterculture "a greater fluidity between 'masculine' and 'feminine'" than in the dominant culture (181–82). Later in the same essay, in a chart that counterposes hippie values to mainstream ones, Hall proposes that the male/female dichotomy had been conflated into one term: youth (195). He thus suggests that the fluidity of hippie androgyny flowed in the direction of eliminating masculine and feminine in favor of a new third term thought to transcend the dichotomy. That third term, however, was to be enacted sartorially, not sexually. As George Mosse observes, the hippies' "clothes and appearance tended to blur [gender] distinctions, and yet they were not meant to question a basic heterosexuality" (263).

Although Alice Cooper's image bridged the gap between conven-

---

25. The "whiteness" of rock is one of the things that distinguish it from its precursor, rock and roll, a majority of whose performers were African-American. White rock and rollers like Jerry Lee Lewis and Elvis Presley were often said to have imitated black vocal and performance styles. The fact that a few very successful and popular psychedelic rock musicians, such as Carlos Santana, Sly Stone, and Jimi Hendrix, were not white should not be allowed to obscure the more salient fact that people of color were actively discouraged from seeking high visibility as rock musicians—see my discussion of the Chambers Brothers in *Liveness* (67) for a case in point. In chapter 6 of the present study, I discuss some of the issues surrounding the participation of women in rock. On a purely statistical basis, some number of psychedelic rock musicians must have been homosexual, yet none ever declared a gay identity publicly. Whiteley speculates that Janis Joplin never publicized her bisexuality because "the risk was too high" even within a counterculture that "outwardly embraced a freedom of sexuality" (*Women and Popular Music* 67–68).

tional notions of masculinity and femininity, hippie gender fluidity was not at all what the group's transvestism was about. The group's look constituted a discordant collision between masculine and feminine gender codes, not a quest for a third, transcendent gender identity. When asked in 1969 about Alice Cooper's sexual image, Furnier's response both echoed and challenged the counterculture. His claim that "biologically, everyone is male and female" could easily have been offered as an explication of the hippie unisex look. But Furnier went on to link this idea to the sexuality that had no comfortable place in the counterculture: "Why is everybody so up tight about sex? About faggots, queers, things like that. That's the way they *are*" (qtd. in Quigley). The next year, speaking in a more political vein, Furnier aligned himself with the identity movements that evolved, in part, out of frustration with the counterculture: "One of the things I'd like to do would be to play for Women's Liberation and Gay Liberation since so many people are trying to liberate themselves from the roles our society has imposed on them" (qtd. in Cagle 122). Furnier was also known to respond affirmatively to hecklers who would yell out "Queer!" during his performances (Senelick 445). This suggests that part of Alice Cooper's project was to question the basic heterosexuality taken for granted by the hippies even as they pursued unconventional gender roles.

It is critically important to consider the implication of Alice Cooper's undertaking this project specifically in the cultural context of rock music. There were arenas within the counterculture in which homosexuality was acknowledged and transvestism was performed before approving audiences—the San Francisco troupe the Cockettes, who performed LSD-infused drag fantasies between 1970 and 1972, was a major example. It is significant, however, that Laurence Senelick, chronicling theatrical cross-dressing in *The Changing Room: Sex, Drag and Theatre,* places the Cockettes in his chapter on alternative cabaret, not the chapter on rock music. The audience for theater or cabaret, even as subcultural a cabaret as the Cockettes, was simply not the same as the audience for rock music (which is not to say there was no overlap at all). Whereas the Cockettes' audience clearly was comfortable with the troupe's polymorphous sexuality and drag antics, the audience for a hypothetical concert of psychedelic rock across the street at the same time would not have been. And vice versa. As Senelick points out, "no distinct gay male contingent could be discerned at rock concerts. Gay youths . . . tended not to congregate conspicuously where the performers aggressively announced their heterosexual preference and the hysteria generated by the crowd was likely to be conspicuously boy-girl" (447).

Cooper was not the first rocker or rock and roller to perform a queer persona, of course. Perhaps because it has always been predicated on the spectacular display of male bodies, effeminacy and transvestism have always been present in rock performance, tendencies that first became highly visible, perhaps, with Esquerita and Little Richard in the mid-1950s. In 1973, *Creem* magazine, an American rock publication that championed Alice Cooper and many of the British glam groups, ran an article entitled "Androgyny in Rock: A Short Introduction," which both outlined the genealogy of androgynous rock performance and recognized that homosexuality and transvestism, while always present, were generally suppressed in rock culture in favor of displays of heterosexual machismo. As a consequence of rock's unwillingness to deal directly with anything other than representations of heterosexuality, cross-dressing, drag, and effeminacy functioned as markers of iconoclasm within rock culture and were usually confined to isolated gestures by mainstream figures—as when the Rolling Stones famously posed in drag for a publicity photo in 1966—or associated with such eccentrics as the Mothers of Invention, who wore dresses on the cover of their album *We're Only In It for the Money* (1967), and Captain Beefheart, the members of whose Magic Band wore dresses and lipstick on stage as early as 1968. Alice Cooper was probably the first rock band of the 1960s to build their entire image around transvestism, intentionally confronting the rock audience with a visual practice—and intimations of a sexuality—that preyed on its insecurities.

Alice Cooper also questioned some of the counterculture's most deeply held values. Whereas psychedelic rock was inner-directed and pacific, the image and music of Alice Cooper was an openly aggressive antithesis to the countercultural ethic of "peace/love."[26] Both Alice Cooper and Sha Na Na included moments in their respective performances that apparently expressed violent disdain for the counterculture. Sha Na Na were frequently introduced at concerts by an announcer declaiming: "Greased and ready to kick ass—Sha Na Na!" as if to emphasize the violence implicit in the

26. This shorthand formulation of the hippie ideology appears in David Bowie's song "Wild Eyed Boy from Freecloud" on *Space Oddity* (1972).

greaser image. Similarly, the group often taunted their audiences with such lines as "We gots just one thing to say to you fuckin' hippies and that is that rock 'n' roll is here to stay!" (*Sha Na Na*). This staged antagonism between the greasers on stage and the presumed "hippies" in the audience mimed real subcultural conflicts among such groups. The hippies in the audience knew, however, that they were not really going to get their asses kicked, in large part because Sha Na Na's theatrical performance of the greaser provided no reason to suppose that the people onstage really belonged to that subculture.

Alice Cooper enacted their aggression against the counterculture in harsher terms:

> As the band performed, Cooper [Vincent Furnier] pranced about the stage sporting greasy shoulder-length hair, his face accented by macabre black makeup that darted from his eyes and mouth. At times, Cooper donned a pink ballerina dress, topped off with a black leather jacket.[27] . . . Cooper would prowl the stage, contort his body, and spit newspaper directly onto incensed hippie onlookers. (Cagle 108)[28]

Although Alice Cooper's aggression might have seemed more genuine to the audience than Sha Na Na's, it was no less theatrical. As early as 1969, Furnier referred to Alice Cooper's stage show as "a theatrical piece" (qtd. in Quigley), as the group's use of costume and makeup clearly suggested. Furnier also attempted to establish a distance between his onstage persona and offstage life. As he later told an interviewer, he saw himself as an actor playing a role:

> It would've been a lie to have said I'm really Alice all the time, that I live in a big black house, and have boa constrictors everywhere. I thought it was much more interesting that there were two of us. Alice had a life of his own that existed only on stage, and I totally let him have the run of the stage. But then my other life was my own, and it had a lot more aspects to it than Alice's did. I did other things. I could play golf, I could act, I could write, I could be a husband. (Qtd. in Russell Hall 15)

27. It is worth noting, if only in passing, that this outfit was taken up much later by Chrissie Hynde of the Pretenders.

28. For a chapter-length discussion of Alice Cooper's theatrical tactics, see Cagle (117–27).

As Cagle observes, rock journalists were typically confused by Furnier's double identity, which they could not square with the dominant concept of rock authenticity: "most reporters had never witnessed this kind of rock and roll duality: a performer who both did and did not take responsibility for his actions on stage" (122).

In place of psychedelic rock's emphasis on love, sex, and pastoral bliss, Alice Cooper's music dealt in sonic and verbal images of violence, death, and madness. These elements were not foreign to rock culture, to be sure: "Drinks, drugs, ecstatic loss of self in illusion of every kind (especially drink and madness) . . . as a summary of sixties rock, Dionysus could not be bettered" (Padel 186). It is also true that Alice Cooper was associated in the late 1960s with a rock scene in Los Angeles (before the group moved to Detroit) that was thought to represent the darker side of the psychedelic moment (as opposed to the true hippies in San Francisco). Other groups on this scene included the Doors and the ironically named Love, who were reputed to have murdered their own roadies.[29] But Alice Cooper was different from these other groups in one crucial respect. The Dionysian mystique of the Doors and Love was underwritten by a version of the ideology of authenticity: the mystique depended on the idea that their madness was *real*—that one could see it and hear it in Jim Morrison's alcoholic ravings when on stage with the Doors and the violent rumors swirling around Love, whose lead singer, Arthur Lee, was later arrested and served prison time on gun charges. Unlike Morrison and Lee, Furnier always represented himself as an actor portraying a frenzied persona—Alice Cooper—who, in turn, portrayed a number of violent and mad characters in various songs. He did not present himself as someone spilling his own guts while in thrall to Dionysus as Morrison, in particular, so explicitly did.

The distance between Furnier and Alice Cooper is maintained even on the group's recordings. "Ballad of Dwight Fry" on *Love it to Death* provides an example. The song, whose lyric is in the first person, traces the character's descent into madness and incarceration in a mental hospital. It is probably based on Furnier's experi-

29. This is only one side of sixties rock in LA, the other side being the folk rock of groups like the Byrds and Buffalo Springfield that were much more in harmony with the counterculture. For a useful overview of the rock scene in LA, see Barney Hoskyns, *Waiting for the Sun*.

ence while being treated in an addiction rehabilitation facility. The reference to Dwight Frye (whose name is misspelled in the title) works against hearing the song purely as a recounting of personal experience, however. Frye was an actor who played secondary roles of madmen in a number of classic Hollywood horror films of the 1930s, most notably *Dracula* (1931), in which he played Renfield, the real-estate agent driven mad by vampiric blood lust after he is bitten by the count. The title thus makes it clear that the song is the ballad of someone who habitually *plays* a madman, not necessarily someone who is mad himself. The song's instrumental arrangement and style evoke the atmosphere of gothic melodrama that pervades the films in which Frye appeared. Furnier screams, "Let me out of here"; an electric guitar replicates a wolf's howl; the drummer imitates the sound of a ticking clock to indicate both the protagonist's status as a time bomb about to go insane (there is also an explosion sound effect when he does) and his whiling away the hours while incarcerated; an exaggeratedly childish female voice asks, "When's daddy coming home?"

It is instructive to contrast "Ballad of Dwight Fry" with another song also released in 1971 that conveys the first-person reflections of a mad protagonist, David Bowie's "All the Madmen," from his album *The Man Who Sold the World,* made when Bowie still exhibited some allegiance to the counterculture and before he perfected his glam rock persona and style.[30] Bowie's song, too, may be based in personal experience: not Bowie's own, but that of his half-brother, Terry Jones, who had been an important influence on the young Bowie but was permanently institutionalized in the 1960s (Cann 12). Whereas the Alice Cooper song focuses entirely on the protagonist's internal experience of going mad with no indication that his mental condition is caused by anything outside of himself, Bowie's song blames the protagonist's condition on the actions of a mysterious "they": "Day after day / They take some brain away."[31]

30. "All the Madmen" also had been released as a single in the United States in 1970.

31. Cagle's description of Alice Cooper's staging of this song is interesting in this context: "Toward the end of the number, a 'nurse' walked onto the stage and led a confused Cooper to the sidelines. Minutes later, he returned, this time wearing a straitjacket. As he darted from one side of the stage to another, he begged for the audience's mercy" (123). Cooper thus implicated the audience in his staged incarceration without implying the superiority of madness to sanity or criticizing society's treatment of the insane, as Bowie does in his song.

It becomes clear that for this singer, madness is a choice in a way that is not in the Cooper song: "I'd rather stay here / With all the madmen / than perish with the sadmen roaming free." A text spoken in the middle of the song clarifies the basis for this choice: "Where can the horizon lie / When a nation hides / Its organic minds / In a cellar . . . dark and grim." The suggestion here is that the madmen are wise but that their wisdom is not recognized by the society that keeps them incarcerated. The song's consistent verse and chorus structure and the lyrics' adherence to varied but regular rhyme schemes suggest the actual clarity and orderliness of the protagonist's mind. Here, Bowie seems to echo the ideas of the radical British psychotherapist R. D. Laing: "The madness we encounter in 'patients' is a gross travesty, a mockery, a grotesque caricature of what the natural healing of that estranged situation we call sanity might be. True sanity entails in one way or another the dissolution of the normal ego, that false self competently adjusted to our alienated social reality" (qtd. in Nuttall 124). This view of madness as a social construct used by the mainstream to repress the "organic minds" in its midst is much more in keeping with the counterculture's social perspective than is Cooper's theatrical, sensationalistic, and apolitical depiction of madness, fear, and isolation in the histrionic style of a horror movie.

Although Sha Na Na and Alice Cooper were very different groups, they can be seen, in retrospect, as having participated in a common project of redefining rock in ways that challenged the counterculture at its very height in the late 1960s. In musical terms, both Sha Na Na and Alice Cooper stressed straightforward styles—1950s rock and roll and unadorned hard rock, respectively—over psychedelic rock's emphasis on virtuoso instrumental improvisation. Alice Cooper deserves credit for anticipating glam's use of transvestism in rock performance—and thus pointing up the counterculture's actual conservatism in matters of sex and gender—but the group's introduction of self-conscious theatricality into rock music and its performance in the late 1960s, a strategy they shared with Sha Na Na, may be even more important as a harbinger of glam rock spectacle in the 1970s.

In performance, both groups stressed visual presentation as much as—perhaps even more than—the music, an emphasis that defied the counterculture's suspicion of the visual as a locus of inauthenticity. Both groups presented clearly staged spectacles and opened a gap between the figures on stage and the "real" people performing them, foregrounding constructed performance personae that denied the spontaneity, sincerity, and authenticity expected of rockers by their hippie audiences. Rich Joffe, of Sha Na Na, defined the group's desired effect by saying, "We know we've succeeded if people go around saying 'Are they for real?'" (qtd. in Steve Turner, "Moving History"). Although Alice Cooper and the glam rockers of the 1970s could easily have said the same thing, psychedelic rockers wanted their audiences to believe, without question, that they were "for real." Whereas Phil Ochs may have resorted to spectacular performance as an act of desperation that marked the end of the counterculture, Sha Na Na and Alice Cooper enthusiastically embraced theatricality and spectacle as the beginning of a new chapter in rock performance.

2. glamography

The Rise of Glam Rock

It was no longer possible to take the history of things as stage-managed by
the media and the educational system seriously. Everything we knew was
wrong. . . . Free at last or, if you like, at sea without a paddle, we
were giving permission to ourselves to reinvent culture the way we
wanted it. With great big shoes.
—David Bowie ("Foreword")

Glam cheered up the Seventies.
—Ian Penman (qtd. in Cato 125)

That the music classified as glam rock ranges from the buoyant
boogie of T. Rex, to the sophisticated, self-conscious deployment of
rock and pop styles by David Bowie and Roxy Music, to the
straightforward hard rock of Kiss, to the simplistic, minimalist pop
of Gary Glitter indicates that this rock subgenre cannot be defined
purely in terms of musical style. Glam rock is not distinctive in this
respect: no rock subgenre can ever be defined solely in musical
terms, for each one entails an ideology that is manifest not only in
music and lyrics, but also in the visual elements of performance
(costume, staging, gesture, etc.) and the visual culture surrounding
the music (album covers, posters, etc.).[1] It is never enough for rock
performers to play a certain kind of music in order to claim membership in a particular rock subgenre; they must also present the
right kind of image onstage, on screen, and in print, even when part
of the ideology is to deny the importance of the visual, as was the
case in psychedelic rock. Even more than most rock subgenres,
glam rock was defined primarily by the performers' appearances

1. For a discussion of the importance of these visual aspects of rock, see
Auslander, *Liveness* (73–81).

and personae, the poses they struck rather than the music they played.

In this chapter, I discuss the development of glam rock as a genre in both the United Kingdom, where it was a dominant rock style for several years, and the United States, where it took root only as a coterie phenomenon. In considering the music and its audiences, I point to the ways that glam destabilized conventional oppositions between rock and pop, art and commerce. As a reaction against psychedelic rock's emphasis on virtuosity, glam returned to stylistic basics and thus participated in the reevaluation of the 1950s that characterized the rock culture of the 1970s. I also examine the emergence of glam masculinity through a series of subcultural transformations from Mod to hippie to glam. Gender identity was another front on which glam challenged psychedelic rock and the hippie counterculture, not only because glam offered a new, implicitly queer, image of masculinity in rock but also because it disputed the ideology of authenticity by positing gendered identities as constructed rather than natural.

While the precise origins of many rock subgenres are difficult to pinpoint, the beginnings of glam rock are relatively easy to trace. Two British rock musicians, Marc Bolan and David Bowie, were instrumental in bringing glam rock into being at the very start of the 1970s. Both men entered the rock music scene in the mid-1960s. Bowie had been a musician, a mime, an actor, a member of various groups, and a folkie solo artist. Bolan, who had done some modeling as a teenager, began as a solo artist, then was a member of a Mod rock group called John's Children before forming his own group in 1967, an acoustic duo named Tyrannosaurus Rex that was successful on the underground music circuit and recorded four albums. By 1970, both sensed the exhaustion of the counterculture and its associated musical styles and chose to pursue a direction representing a specific repudiation of the counterculture. As rock historian Barney Hoskyns observes, "What Bowie and Bolan both saw was that 'glamour' was the antithesis of hippiedom: for long-hair puritans, glamour symbolized affluence, capitalism, 'show business'" (*Glam!* 23). In defiance of the audience with which they had previously aligned themselves, both Bowie and Bolan embraced glamour. In February 1970, Bowie experimented with a flashy new androgynous look for a London concert at which his group, the Hype, opened for sixties stalwarts and Woodstock veterans Country Joe and the Fish. The cover of his album *The Man Who Sold The World* (1971) "pictured Bowie relaxing on a day bed with the same sort of hairdo worn by Hollywood movie actresses of the forties, wearing an elegant dress, and holding the queen of diamonds playing card in his limp-wristed hand" (Charlton 257). By the end of that year, Bolan, who already wore items of women's apparel, swapped his folk guitar for an electric guitar, augmented his group to a quartet, and shortened its name to T. Rex. When Bolan appeared on the British television program *Top of the Pops* with glitter on his cheeks in 1971, the Glam rock phenomenon was fully launched in the United Kingdom.[2]

Any number of British groups and performers followed the lead established by Bowie and Bolan: Slade, Sweet, Mott The Hoople, Mud, Alvin Stardust, and Gary Glitter were but some of the more prominent to put on makeup, platform shoes, and glittering costumes. Even popular music artists not specifically identified as glam rockers, such as Rod Stewart and Elton John, took on some of the visual aspects of glam, whether in costume, makeup, hairstyle, or onstage flamboyance. While some glam rockers, notably Bolan, Bowie, and Lou Reed, professed homosexuality or bisexuality, most simply adopted glam as a provocative performance style. Sweet, for example, consciously decided to "go glam" in mid-1972, adding makeup and extravagant costumes to their act. This was probably the peak year of the glam era: "T. Rextasy" (as the British music press called the fans' rabid enthusiasm for the group) was at its most intense, and Bowie brought out Ziggy Stardust, his androgynous, polysexual space alien persona (I offer a detailed analysis of Bowie's final performance as Ziggy in chapter 4). By mid-1973, when Bowie gave his last concert as Ziggy Stardust, the most innovative phase of glam was over. Nevertheless, glam persisted as a viable rock style for a bit longer, attracting new adherents—including Suzi Quatro, Roy Wood and Wizzard, Sparks, and others—whose work constituted a second wave of glam that held sway from 1973 through 1975. Table 1 displays a partial but representative list

2. There is some debate as to whether Bolan or Bowie should be seen as the true father of glam rock. Bowie may have arrived at something like a glam style first, though Bolan probably did more to publicize and popularize glam, at least initially. Bowie has recently conceded this point—see the epigraph for chapter 3. My purposes here do not require resolution of this issue. Bowie and Bolan were both friends and rivals at this period; each seems to have influenced the other.

of canonical major and secondary glam rock artists organized by nationality and year of emergence.[3] Speaking very roughly, those listed as emerging in 1971 and 1972 can be considered first-wave glam rockers, while those listed as emerging after 1972 belong to the second wave. (By "first wave," I mean those who had a hand in creating glam; "second wave" identifies artists for whom glam was available as an established stylistic option.)

Before I am accused of promulgating a "great men" theory of glam rock's development, I hasten to add that communities, not individuals, produce musical genres; if Bowie and Bolan were the only glam rockers, this book would not exist. As Simon Frith proposes, "A new 'genre world' . . . is first constructed then articulated through a complex interplay of musicians, listeners, and mediating ideologues, and this process is much more confused than the marketing process that follows, as the wider industry begins to make sense of the new sounds and markets to exploit both genre worlds and genre discourses in the orderly routine of mass marketing" (*Performing Rites* 88).[4] (I will note in passing Frith's implication that musical genres originate with musicians and their audiences— they are not initially the cynical products of marketing departments.) The glam genre world's geographical center was London, where the musicians and record producers, music publishers, journalists, and broadcasters who created and disseminated the music were located. Bolan and Bowie were both native Londoners; glam rockers from other parts of England (Slade was from Wolverhampton, Roy Wood from Birmingham) had to spend at least some of their time in London to achieve visibility and success. Even many of the American artists associated with glam cemented that association by traveling to London: Iggy Pop and Lou Reed both appeared

3. I am referring to the year of emergence as a glam artist, not the artist's first appearance in any musical context. Many of the artists listed here had musical careers that began well before their glam phase: Bolan and Bowie had been around for over five years, Roy Wood and Lou Reed had both been in important groups of the 1960s (the Move and the Velvet Underground, respectively); Slade, Sweet, and Alice Cooper had kicked around as groups for several years before glam. I have also organized the entries in terms of a rough chronology based on the year and month when the artist first appeared on the British pop charts to give a sense of the sequence in which the artists listed surfaced.

4. Strictly speaking, rock is a musical genre of which glam rock is a subgenre. From this point on, however, I will eschew that awkward formulation and refer to glam rock simply as a genre or style.

TABLE 1.   Canonical Glam Rock Artists

UK Artists			US Artists	US/UK Artists
T. Rex (1971)	Blackfoot Sue (1972)	The Glitter Band (1974)	Alice Cooper (1971)	Suzi Quatro (1973)
Slade (1971)	Geordie (1972)	Kenny (1974)	Lou Reed (1972)	Sparks (1974)
David Bowie (1972)	Roy Wood's Wizzard (1972)	Showaddy Waddy (1974)	Iggy Pop (1973)	
Chicory Tip (1972)	David Essex (1973)	Arrows (1974)	New York Dolls (1973)	
Gary Glitter (1972)	Bryan Ferry (1973)	Steve Harley and Cockney Rebel (1974)	Jobriath (1973)	
Sweet (1972)	Alvin Stardust (1973)	Hello (1974)	Kiss (1974)	
Mott The Hoople (1972)	Mud (1973)	Sailor (1975)		
Roxy Music (1972)	Queen (1974)	Slik (1976)		

on the London scene and made albums there produced by David Bowie. Other Americans, including Suzi Quatro and Ron and Russell Mael, the founders of Sparks, achieved success after relocating to London.

The ideologues who supported glam were largely broadcasters and journalists. John Peel, perhaps the single most influential British disc jockey from the 1960s until his death in 2004, lent his direct support to both Tyrannosaurus Rex and T. Rex by playing their music on the air and insisting that they be booked where he made live appearances. Peel, who had a reputation for supporting artists he liked rather than those touted by record companies, also gave Bowie and other glam artists valuable exposure early in their careers. Similarly, the BBC television program *Top of the Pops* played a major role in presenting glam artists to the public. In print journalism, the weekly music paper *Melody Maker* devoted many column inches to glam rock in all its manifestations (more than its direct competitor, the *New Musical Express*) and covered the rising careers of Bolan and Bowie from the beginning, providing them not only with publicity but an outlet through which to express their views. In the United States, *Creem* magazine, headquartered in Detroit, played a similar role. *Creem* reported regularly on developments in the UK and provided such artists as Bolan, Bowie, Glitter, and Quatro with significant coverage (*Rolling Stone* also reported on these artists, but much less often and with noticeably less enthusiasm). In addition, *Creem* extended its support to American glam artists, including the New York Dolls and, especially, Alice Cooper, who was mentioned, if not featured, in almost every issue for several years in the early 1970s.

The confusion Frith describes as surrounding the development of a new genre was also apparent in the London glam rock world. It is visible at one level in the trial-and-error manner in which Bolan, Bowie, and the others arrived at their respective formulations of glam. Before becoming a Mod rocker with John's Children, then a psychedelic folkie with Tyrannosaurus Rex, Bolan (whose birth name was Mark Feld) had been an explicitly Dylanesque folk singer called Toby Tyler, after the hero of a Walt Disney movie. Bowie had been in a multitude of rhythm and blues and Mod rock groups, including the King Bees, Davy Jones and the Lower Third, and the Manish Boys. He, too, was a hippie folk-rocker before going glam. Gary Glitter, born Paul Gadd, had been around since the late 1950s, when he was unsuccessful rock and roller Paul Raven (he also produced records for other artists under this name). Alvin Stardust had a similar history: born Bernard Jewry, he had performed as Shane Fenton with the Fentones in the early 1960s. The group Slade had originally been called Ambrose Slade and had gone through phases as a reggae group and a skinhead outfit before settling on its version of glam. Most of the groups and performers considered to belong to the glam canon arrived there after a similar series of stylistic experiments.

The other locus of confusion in the nascent glam rock genre world was the web of shifting professional relationships that developed as the genre took shape. For example, Tony Visconti, an American musician who came to London in 1968 to work for an English production company, wrote arrangements for the Move, a highly successful British group of the 1960s, as one of his first assignments. Roy Wood, the main songwriter for the Move, would go on to found the second-wave glam group Wizzard (and was offered the opportunity to produce the New York Dolls' first album, though he was unable), while Visconti would help Tyrannosaurus Rex secure a recording deal and produced all of their albums. He continued working with the group when it became T. Rex and produced its most important recordings. Tony Secunda, the Move's manager, also became T. Rex's manager; his ex-wife, Chelita Secunda, a publicist, is often credited with having put the glitter on Bolan's face before he appeared on *Top of the Pops*. Visconti also played bass guitar in Bowie's early group the Hype and produced many of Bowie's records as well. Mike Leander, who produced and arranged some of Bolan's earliest folk recordings in 1965, would team with Paul Raven as songwriter and producer to develop the Gary Glitter persona. From a historical distance of several decades, the years from 1965 through 1970 appear as a period during which many of the principals of glam rock encountered one another professionally in what seems to have been a fairly small world, working together in various combinations and performing various roles relative to one another until successful working relationships emerged from the ferment. The process of discovering these relationships went hand in hand with the development of the genre.

Although glam was primarily British, it developed, like most forms of rock music, from cross-fertilizations of American and British popular music. I argued in the previous chapter that the impulses that led to glam were visible in the late 1960s in the work of such American mavericks as Sha Na Na and Alice Cooper. Other American artists had a direct influence on British glam. Bowie, in particular, was deeply impressed by the American groups the Stooges and the Velvet Underground and enlisted their respective frontmen, Iggy Pop and Lou Reed, for glam by producing records with them in London in 1972 and 1973. In a complicated twist, these American artists, whose work in the 1960s influenced British glam, themselves became glam artists in the 1970s through their association with Bowie. If Bowie counted some American rockers among his sources, the New York Dolls were an American group that took inspiration from early British glam. Future members of the Dolls had traveled to London in 1970, before the formation of the group, and were directly influenced by the first stirrings of the British glam music (especially T. Rex) and fashions they experienced there, as well as by Alice Cooper.[5] Arthur Kane, the New York Dolls' bass guitarist, refers to these influences as he describes the effort to con-

5. There is an interesting division of opinion with respect to the New York Dolls as a second-wave glam rock group. Hoskyns considers them "one of the only authentic American responses to British Glam Rock" (*Waiting for the Sun* 270). Cagle argues, by contrast, that the Dolls were not themselves a glam rock group but an ironic, camp response to glam, which was itself already ironic and campy in tone, thus producing layers of irony most rock fans did not understand (185–87).

struct an image for the group: "It was all a part of the glitter thing, we had the first platform shoes and boots in New York because Billy's [drummer Billy Murcia] sister was in London and she knew where to get them. Also I had seen the Alice Cooper group, when they were all wearing silver jumpsuits and I knew we had to look wilder than that" (qtd. in Antonia 22).

Whereas glam artists experienced great popularity and main-stream success in the United Kingdom, most British glam artists never found comparable audiences in the United States; even T. Rex could not replicate their phenomenal British success stateside.[6] Glam had only limited success in the United States, where it was associated largely with subcultural scenes in New York City, Detroit, and Los Angeles. New York contributed the New York Dolls and Kiss to the roster of glam artists, while Alice Cooper found its footing in Detroit (after a less successful sojourn in Los Angeles), home to a particularly raucous brand of rock that included the MC5 and the Stooges; Quatro also emerged from the Detroit rock scene. The glam scene in Los Angeles focused on fans and visiting musicians rather than local acts. LA glam was head-quartered at Rodney Bingenheimer's English Disco, a club on the Sunset Strip that opened late in 1972, where the faithful congre-gated around a jukebox that featured British glam recordings. The Bangles' song "The Glitter Years" (1988) is a bittersweet recollec-tion of the scene around the English Disco, highlighting the impor-tance of British musicians to it (the recording contains an imitation of Bowie's voice), and the home it provided to a group of disaf-fected young people. The glam set in LA marked what it considered

6. Glam rock generally is not counted as a significant phenomenon in his-tories of rock authored by American scholars. The conventional narrative is that rock lost its footing in the 1970s with the bombast and excess of stadium and progressive rock and rediscovered its original energy and impetus only with the advent of punk in 1976–77. It may be that this historical neglect of glam rock is symptomatic of the failure of most major British glam artists to penetrate the American market, though that would not account for instances in which Bowie, who did make his mark in the United States, is not granted significance. In "Periodizing the Seventies in Rock Music," an unpublished paper presented at the Fifth Annual Performance Studies Conference (1999, Aberystwyth, Wales), I argue that glam's challenge to the countercultural val-ues embraced by rock culture accounts for its frequent exclusion and devalua-tion by historians of rock music, many of whom themselves embrace the val-ues of rock culture, especially the concept of authenticity.

the death of the scene with the Hollywood Street Revival and Dance at the Palladium in October 1974, an event dubbed the "'Death of Glitter' night" (Hoskyns, *Glam!* 102).

The question of why glam took hold in the UK to a much greater extent than in the United States is open to conjecture. Michael Rosenbaum, writing in 1968, suggested that British rockers and their audiences had a more developed penchant for theatricality than the Americans, who "have put down outrageous acts as being nonmusical" (25). There is some truth to this claim: while American psychedelic rock groups purveyed the low-key, inner-directed performances I described in the last chapter, some British groups of the 1960s, such as the Who, the Move, John's Children, the Nice, and the Crazy World of Arthur Brown engaged in spectacular, often violent, action of a kind that was completely unknown to their American counterparts (it is no coincidence that two of these groups had connections with people who would later be important to glam). The Who, who habitually wore the height of Mod fashion on stage, became famous for destroying their instruments at the end of their sets. John's Children, who toured Germany with the Who in 1967, dressed in dazzling white outfits, bounced hyperactively around the stage, and not only attacked their instruments and equipment, but assaulted each other and ran through the audience. Keith Emerson, the keyboard player for the Nice, dressed in gold lamé and threw knives at his instruments; the Move were notorious for destroying television sets on stage. Arthur Brown would be lowered to the stage by a crane in long ceremonial robes, his head ablaze with a flaming helmet. The bridge between these practices in England and the American rock scene was Jimi Hendrix, who started his career in the United Kingdom and made a big impact by burning his guitar at the end of his premier performance in the United States at the Monterey Pop Festival.[7] But most psychedelic rockers in the United States never developed the taste for excessive performance exhibited by at least some of their English contemporaries. Frith places this cultural difference in perspective by suggesting that in the UK, "Rock 'n' roll never really made a decisive break from traditional English popular culture" but, rather, participated in the "show-biz tradition of *putting on the style.* It doesn't

7. For a brief discussion of these destructive tendencies in rock performance, see Auslander, "Fluxus Art-Amusement" (125–27).

have much to do with rock, it emerged from music hall and pan-
tomime, from drag acts and blue comics, from the notions of spectacle and all-round entertainment" ("Sweet Notes" 44).

It is arguably the case that glam rock's play with gender
signification also was more readily accepted in the United Kingdom
than the United States, for similar reasons. Glam transvestism was
relatively uncontroversial in Britain, perhaps because "cross-dressing has always been a part of British popular entertainment," as
Martha Bayles suggests; Frith's references to drag acts and pan-
tomime support her claim. In Bayles's estimation, the cross-dressing of Alice Cooper and the New York Dolls was "more radical"
than that of British glam artists "precisely because the practice is
less at home in the United States" (256). It is clear that the idea of a
cross-dressing rocker created a kind of anxiety in the United States
it did not create in the United Kingdom. Ron Ross identifies that
anxiety as the reason why glam rock was not widely promoted on
American radio: "programmers failed to play such hit Bowie tunes
as 'Sorrow,' because in their eyes . . . he was a glitter fag and with
so many competing singles to choose from, why let your station be
cited in the tip-sheets as promoting a queer, even a hit making
queer" ("Roxy Music"). In the United Kingdom, Bolan's and
Bowie's transvestism and their allusions to queer sexuality (sometimes veiled, sometimes overt) were certainly perceived as provocative and caused some furor, but that furor seemingly did not differ
greatly in kind from the usual generational conflicts surrounding
youth music and its attendant styles. While some parents of glam
fans characterized the performers as "evil" (qtd. in Vermorel and
Vermorel 73), most had more conventional responses. In a characteristic passage from Philip Cato's *Crash Course for the Ravers: A
Glam Odyssey,* the memoir of a British glam rock fan, Cato's
father goes into an apoplectic rage over the fact "that [the] bunch
of 'long-haired morons'" his son enjoyed watching on *Top of the
Pops* "were earning more than he was" for just playing "thump
thump thump" on a guitar—Cato Sr.'s distaste for his son's music
is archetypal and does not imply that he was in any way disturbed
specifically by the musicians' androgynous images (39–40). Another
fan reports her mother's saying matter-of-factly, again about an
image on television: "Oh . . . that's David Bowie. . . . He's gay"
(qtd. in Vermorel and Vermorel 73).

American glam artists and their supporters, apparently experi-
encing a measure of homosexual panic, were at pains to insist that

any tendency to dress lavishly and use makeup should not be taken as signs of sexual abnormality. A 1973 article on the New York Dolls and the sessions for their first album that appeared in *Creem,* for instance, carries a subtitle in the form of an editorial annotation. Underneath the title of the article, "The New York Dolls Greatest Hits Volume 1," appears the homophobic qualifier: "(They're not a fag band.—Ed.)" (Edmonds 39). In a similar vein, the group Kiss, who were inspired in part by the New York Dolls, sought to create personae in which their use of lavish costume and makeup would not be taken for effeminacy: "Glam . . . was linked with androgyny: fine for weak-wristed, lily-livered Brits, but not for the red-blooded, veins in the teeth, all-American boys. Kiss . . . helped themselves to Glam's pose and look and attitude, sidestepping its androgyny by becoming cartoons, comic-book superheroes" (Simmons 14–15). Bowie evaluates the situation in much the same terms, describing Kiss as "butch, manly glam with lots of . . . fireworks, muscle and metal. No mistaking the sexual bent of those fellas. 'Nothing ambiguous about our boys.' That's the only way Ohio could accept lipstick on males" ("Foreword"). Perhaps intimations of queer sexuality were less disturbing in the British context because the issue had recently been on the public policy agenda, leading to the decriminalization of homosexual activity in 1969.

Whatever the precise reasons, American glam remained a coterie affair; Reed was the only American glam artist aside from Alice Cooper to have a major hit with "Walk on the Wild Side" (1972). The UK charts, by contrast, were inundated with glam rock from 1971 through 1975. In Britain, glam was not just a highly successful trend in popular music—it became something like a cultural dominant. In their coffee table book *Wham Bam, Thank You Glam,* Jeremy Novick and Mick Middles argue that glam was manifest as a sensibility in all areas of British popular culture in the 1970s. Unsurprisingly, their discussion of glam rock takes up more than half of the book, followed by fashion. But fashion is actually tied for second place with football; the other categories are film, television, and even cars. For Novick and Middles, any aspect of Anglo-American popular culture and design that appeared between 1970 and 1976 and was theatrical, campy, show-offy, and outrageous qualifies as glam, including showboating footballers who had just discovered their star potential and acted accordingly, the *Charlie's Angels* television program, Stanley Kubrick's film adaptation of

Anthony Burgess's *A Clockwork Orange* (1971), and the Ford Fiesta 3.0 Ghia. The glam sensibility had to do with overt displays of sexuality, irony, a self-conscious emphasis on the artifice of show-biz "glamour," and excess: "more hair, more height, more glitter, more guitars, more drugs. . . . Moderation had ceased to exist" (Novick and Middles 140).

I have already suggested that glam rock is not so much a musicological category as a sociological one. Nevertheless, glam rock does have certain general musical characteristics worth discussing, especially by contrast with the psychedelic rock of the 1960s. Socially, glam represented a rejection of countercultural values, particularly with respect to sexual identity; musically, glam rock rejected many of the tendencies found in countercultural rock music. As I have noted, psychedelic rock emphasized instrumental virtuosity, especially the prowess of electric guitarists like Eric Clapton and Jimi Hendrix. The music featured extended instrumental improvisations, often borrowing harmonic and rhythmic concepts from jazz (indeed, the highest praise one could accord to psychedelic rock was that it approached the sophistication of jazz). Jerry Nolan, a drummer who eventually joined the New York Dolls, sums up this music in colorfully negative terms: "These were the days of the ten-minute drum solo, the twenty-minute guitar solo. A song might take up a whole side of an album. I was fed up with that shit. Who could outplay who? It was really boring. It had nothing to do with rock & roll" (qtd. in McNeil and McCain 117). As Nolan implies, glam rock sought in various ways to bring rock back to a more primordial state. For T. Rex, Bolan developed a sound that emphasized the shuffle and boogie rhythms and blues progressions of the early rock and roll of the 1950s, an approach that influenced many other glam rockers. The New York Dolls themselves played a straightforward, energetic rhythm-and-blues-based style of rock reminiscent of the early Rolling Stones. They also played such blues and rhythm and blues classics as "Don't Start Me Talkin'" and "Stranded in the Jungle" alongside their own songs.

Although the work of glam pioneers Bolan and Bowie is distinctive and individual, and glam groups like Roxy Music, Queen, and Sparks wrote songs that sometimes bordered on the jazzy or classicizing pretensions of progressive rock, a formulaic, commercial glam rock sound emerged as the style became more popular in the UK. Producers and songwriters, among whom Nicky Chinn and

Mike Chapman (known collectively as Chinnichap) were the most successful, developed numerous hits for performers and groups including Alvin Stardust, Gary Glitter, Sweet, Mud, David Essex, the Arrows, Suzi Quatro, and many others.[8] In place of psychedelic rock's emphasis on the virtuoso electric guitar, formulaic glam rock emphasizes drums and voices as its primary instruments. It typically features a mid- to fast-tempo foot-stomping rhythm that remains constant throughout the song; frequently, the songs open just with drums. Glam rock songs are usually based on three standard chords; the organization of verses and choruses is highly conventional. Glam melodies, which often support shouted lyrics, tend to be monotonous (in the sense of not involving much movement up and down the scale), and are highly repetitive. Often, a repeated riff substitutes for a developed melodic line. As opposed to the sometimes lengthy improvisatory excursions undertaken in psychedelic rock, glam rock songs tend to be short; Nolan's remark that the New York Dolls were "bringing back the three-minute song" (qtd. in McNeil and McCain 117) pertains to glam rock in general. Most glam rock groups employed standard rock instrumentation (two guitars, bass guitar, drums). The keyboard instruments crucial to the progressive rock that emerged at the same time as glam appear occasionally but—with some exceptions, especially in Bowie's work—are not the dominant sound. Guitar solos, the staple of psychedelic rock, are infrequent in glam, and usually brief when they do appear. (Important exceptions are the space Bowie gave to Mick Ronson to play some lengthy solos during concerts and Bolan's desire to be seen as a guitar hero.) Although psychedelic rock produced its share of love songs, there was also an emphasis within countercultural music on socially and politically conscious lyrics. Most glam rock, especially British glam beginning with T. Rex, reacted against the obligation to be socially conscious by returning to rock and roll's favorite themes: girls, cars, dancing, and sex (Bowie added to that list self-conscious reflections on rock stardom). In many respects, Gary Glitter's "Rock and Roll (Part 2)" (1972) epitomizes formulaic glam rock. The song has no lyrics aside from "hey" and, in some performances, the words "rock and roll," but consists only of an insistent beat played on drums and bass guitar, male vocals that are often just sounds (some sexual in nature), and an isolated electric guitar riff that appears at regular intervals.

8. For a detailed discussion of Chinnichap, see Hoskyns, *Glam!* (40–48).

The fact that Chinnichap and other producers were able to develop a commercially successful, formulaic version of glam rock has led some commentators to want to distinguish the music they made from the ostensibly more serious work of artists like Bowie, Reed, and Roxy Music. Dick Hebdige, for example, divides the glam rock audience into "two distinct factions. . . . One was composed almost entirely of teeny-boppers who followed the mainstream glitter bands (Marc Bolan, Gary Glitter, Alvin Stardust). The other, consisting of older, more self-conscious teenagers, remained fastidiously devoted to the more esoteric artists (Bowie, Lou Reed, Roxy Music)" (62). Although Hebdige is not arguing here for the superiority of the esoteric artists (whom he accuses of "morbid pretensions to art and intellect") over the mainstream ones, his categories still suggest a desire to inscribe glam rock within familiar binary oppositions: mainstream versus avant-garde; commerce versus art; childish versus mature, and so on. While I would not argue that all glam artists are of equal artistic merit, I wish to avoid the trap of stratifying the genre into "high glam" and "low glam." For one thing, it makes little sense to discuss a mass cultural form such as rock music in terms of a dichotomy between art and commerce since rock, no matter how much some artists and fans may rail against "the machine," is produced as a cultural commodity. All of the artists Hebdige lists, and many others, whether mainstream or esoteric, sought to sell records and concert tickets in the same marketplace, vied for spots on the same television programs, competed for coverage in the same papers and magazines, and so on. As Frith puts it, glossing Lester Bangs, "There's no distinction between puppets and artists (that's just a comfy critical fantasy)—all rock stars are strung up one way or another" ("Sweet Notes" 44).

An examination of the British pop charts raises some doubts about the empirical grounding of Hebdige's position. I looked at three artists—Bowie, Glitter, and T. Rex—and their performance on the charts over roughly a two-year period during their respective glam rock heydays: June 1972 through June 1974 for Bowie and Glitter, and February 1971 through March 1973 for Bolan with T. Rex. During that time, Bowie placed eleven songs on the charts— eight reached the top ten, though none reached number one. His records were on the charts for a total of 104 weeks. Glitter placed eight records on the charts during the same period; all eight went to the top ten and three achieved number one status. Glitter's time on the charts added up to 94 weeks. Marc Bolan and T. Rex made it to the chart with nine songs, all of which hit the top ten, four reaching number one. His music was on the chart for a total of 111 weeks. Although it is observable that T. Rex and Glitter, the more "mainstream" artists, reached number one while Bowie did not, this hardly makes a compelling case for labeling him "esoteric," especially when all three artists placed roughly the same number of songs in the top ten during the periods examined. Neither does the fact that Bolan's songs stayed on the charts seven weeks longer than Bowie's contribute much to that case. That Bowie reached the charts more frequently than either Glitter or Bolan and was on them for ten more weeks than Glitter could be taken to mean that he was actually the most mainstream artist of the three! I would go so far as to argue that glam rock transcended the kinds of distinctions on which judgments of what is mainstream or esoteric are typically based. More than one critic observed that Roxy Music, for instance, succeeded in creating "an across-the-board teen and intelligentsia appeal" (Nicholl 50) and a figure like Roy Wood, whose approach to composition involves stark juxtapositions of radically different musical styles yet had hit singles, is impossible to classify in those terms.

Hebdige's claims about the bifurcation of the glam rock audience according to age are also open to question. In the absence of a full-scale ethnographic survey of glam rock audiences, anecdotal evidence will have to suffice. It is clear from documentary films of Bowie and Bolan in live performance that large portions of both audiences behaved in a manner befitting the teeny-bopper (i.e., they dressed up to resemble their musical idols, sang along, greeted familiar songs with elation, swooned ecstatically when appropriate, etc.). Both audiences also seemed to have contained a full complement of avid teenaged girl fans. While the older, more fastidious fans Hebdige describes undoubtedly existed, it seems unlikely that they constituted the greater part of Bowie's audience or that they were completely absent from Bolan's. Ian Taylor and David Wall, sociologists who published some ethnographic work on glam rock audiences in 1976, offer an analysis that partly supports Hebdige's contentions while also pointing toward a somewhat different conclusion:

> In the interviews we carried out in Sheffield with schoolchildren aged 12–18, we confirmed that Bowie was definitely the most pop-

ular figure among the older age groups, but we also discovered that his name was mentioned as important by all the other groups. The older children who identified with Bowie tended to interpret his music as . . . a music to be listened to for its intellectual content, but amongst the younger groups, Bowie's name as mentioned alongside those of Glamrock artists like Gary Glitter, the Sweet, Slade and others; and he was described in terms of his visual impact and only very loosely in terms of his material. (117)

Taylor and Wall's findings do bolster Hebdige's assertion of an older audience for Bowie,[9] to be sure, but they also imply that the more accurate perception may be that all glam rock audiences included young people of various ages. The question of which artists attracted older or younger fans may not be as important as the disparities in how differently aged members of the same audience perceived and understood the artist. Cato's testimony as a glam rock fan in *Crash Course for the Ravers* supports this view: it is clear from his book that the teenaged Cato listened to the music produced by all of the participants in the genre, regardless of their ostensible appeal to different groups defined by age or otherwise. He did not like them all equally, of course, but his evaluations were not necessarily based on the dichotomy of esoteric versus mainstream—danceability, a factor that cuts across those categories, was a significant consideration, for instance.

In challenging what they perceived as the musical self-indulgence of psychedelic rockers, glam rockers sought to move rock forward by looking backward to the more basic rock and roll of the 1950s. As Jim Farber puts it, "A sound with a retro appeal, glam gave rock & roll its balls back. While the previous psychedelic trend encouraged decadent solos and haughty musicianship, glam revived the hard, mean chords of Chuck Berry and the Rolling Stones in the Fifties to mid-Sixties" (144). We have seen that glam rockers were not the only rock musicians looking back at the time: Paul Du Noyer observes, "Whether guided by nostalgia for their own

9. In the context of the dichotomy between the "intellectual" and the "visual" set up by Taylor and Wall, a dichotomy that clearly reflects the values and prejudices of the hippie counterculture that also colors the authors' ultimately negative assessment of the glam rock's social impact, I resist the implication that Bowie's older fans were more "sophisticated" than his younger ones. Mapped onto Taylor and Wall's dichotomy, an endorsement of "sophistication" would be tantamount to valuing "material" over "visual impact," or text over performance.

teenage years in the Fifties, or by the fashion for 'rootsy' forms like country, blues and Southern funk, figures like Bob Dylan and Eric Clapton embraced the 'authenticity' of acts such as The Band and Credence Clearwater Revival" (13–14). In the spirit of a counter-cultural quest for authenticity, the Band and Credence Clearwater Revival embraced fifties blues and rock and roll as folk music (the names of these groups alone betoken a yearning for directness and simplicity [the Band] or hearken back to earlier, regionally defined forms of popular entertainment [the tent show or revival meeting]). In 1969, Albert Goldman characterized Credence Clearwater's interest in rock and roll as a quest for musical purity that involved "turning their backs on theatricalism" and "holding themselves down to the hard dense core at the heart of rock" (129). By contrast, glam rockers' version of the 1950s, like Sha Na Na's, was distinctly theatrical.

On the commentary track of the DVD release of the concert film *Ziggy Stardust and the Spiders from Mars: The Motion Picture,* director D. A. Pennebaker makes a comparison between Bowie's onstage persona and that of the 1950s rock and roller Jerry Lee Lewis, of whom he says, "he takes on a character that you suspect isn't really there." This comment, somewhat surprising on its face, makes an important aspect of glam's revivalism clear: glam rockers not only looked to rock and roll as an antidote to what they heard as the musical pretensions of psychedelic rock but also because rock and rollers had embraced showmanship and performed obviously constructed onstage personae. Glam's treatment of rock and roll was much closer in spirit to Sha Na Na's depthless simulation than to John Lennon's autobiographical excavation. Glam rockers embraced the fifties as a matter of style, of surface, not depth. In this respect, glam should be seen in relation to the widespread commercialized nostalgia for the 1950s that permeated both the United States and the UK in the 1970s. The glam version of the fifties was not the authentic fifties valorized by musicians in search of roots, but the artificial, stylized fifties celebrated, for instance, by *Happy Days* on television (in which glam rocker Suzi Quatro appeared as Leather Tuscadero), *Grease* on the stage, and *American Graffiti* and *That'll Be the Day* at the movie theater.[10]

Many British glam rockers referred very self-consciously to the

10. Strictly speaking, *American Graffiti* is set in 1962, but its atmosphere is redolent of the 1950s.

1950s. Words like *teenager, jive,* and *jukebox* appear with startling regularity in the lyrics to British glam rock songs, as do fifties-style doo-wop backing vocals on the recordings. Glam rockers sometimes performed songs from the 1950s or early 1960s: Bolan, for example, recorded Eddie Cochran's "Summertime Blues" early on and "Do You Wanna Dance" and "To Know Him is to Love Him" somewhat later in his career. Hello covered the Exciters' "Tell Him" in 1974; Glitter recorded any number of well-known songs from the 1950s; and Slade had one of the first glam hits with Little Richard's "Get Down and Get with It," which they recorded in 1971. Quatro exhibited a penchant for recording vintage songs with her name in them: the Everly Brothers' "Wake Up, Little Susie" and, of course, Dale Hawkins's "Suzi Q." Glam artists also lovingly, but irreverently, plundered the music of the 1950s, taking from it at will in their own compositions. I shall mention only a few scattered examples of a very widespread phenomenon: Bolan's rewriting "Duke of Earl" as "Monolith" (from *Electric Warrior*);[11] Bowie's sampling of the line "Look at those cavemen go" from "Alley Oop" in his "Life on Mars"; and Roy Wood's reconfiguring Del Shannon's "Runaway" into "Everyday I Wonder." Just as important as the plundering of specific songs is the use of recognizable styles and conventions of earlier music. Wood, in particular, did this repeatedly with Wizzard, mining styles ranging from rockabilly to Brill Building to Phil Spector's "Wall of Sound" (I discuss his work in detail in chapter 5). Les Gray, the lead singer for Mud, frequently sang like Elvis, particularly on "The Cat Crept In" (1974); Chinnichap, Mud's producers, wrote songs specifically to exploit this ability of Gray's. And Roxy Music appropriated the idea of the dance introduction song, a type of song very popular in the 1950s and early 1960s, for "Do The Strand" (1973). Glam rockers' general take on the music of the 1950s was neither nostalgic nor satirical.[12] Rather, they treated rock and roll as a pleasurable source

11. In some studio conversation recorded during the sessions for *Electric Warrior,* Bolan refers to the song as "Duke of Monolith."

12. There were a few exceptions. Glitter's "Rock and Roll, Part 1" (1972), the Rubettes' "I Can Do It" (1975), and David Essex's relentlessly name-checking "Rock On" (1973) could all fairly be described as nostalgic, as could the group Showaddy Waddy. As their name suggests, they were more or less the British equivalent of Sha Na Na. Mott The Hoople took a distinctive approach: songs such as "Golden Age of Rock 'N' Roll" (1974) and "Saturday Gigs," which include a number of stylistic flourishes that evoke the 1950s and early 1960s, do not look back to that era but actually recount the group's own history.

of found musical objects that could be revamped or incorporated into new compositions.

As important as these musical appropriations were glam rockers' borrowings from the fashions and performance conventions of the1950s. Hair was swept up and greased back; sideburns grew long. In emulation of Elvis and Gene Vincent (and their models, James Dean and Marlon Brando) Alvin Stardust and Suzi Quatro swathed themselves in leather. Drape coats associated with the 1950s British Teddy Boy subculture reappeared as well. The Glitter Band (Gary Glitter's backup group, who also recorded and performed without him) and Wizzard, among others, revived the practice of including a horn section; their saxophonists would bob back and forth while playing or lift their instruments above their heads in emulation of 1950s showmanship. Andy Mackay, the woodwind and keyboard player for Roxy Music, emulated the great rhythm and blues saxophonists such as Big Jay McNeeley by indulging in all manner of byplay with his instrument, including playing it upside down.

It is noteworthy in this connection that a number of glam groups danced on stage. In a televised performance of "Devil Gate Drive," for example, Quatro and her group executed a clearly choreographed routine that began and ended with Quatro, flanked by her guitarist and pianist, sauntering in a manner reminiscent of Dorothy's strolling down the Yellow Brick Road with her male cohorts in the film *The Wizard of Oz* (Quatro, "Devil Gate"). In between, they performed unison line dance steps during the choruses that included foot stomping, kicking, sliding movements, and "hand jive" gestures derived from social dances of the 1950s. Mud had even more elaborate choreography for a television performance of "Tiger Feet." Here, the group itself was bordered on each side by a pair of what can only be called go-go boys, clad in closely fitted T-shirts, who performed energetic dance routines that borrowed from the frug and other familiar social dances. Near the end of the song, the group and dancers joined together in a chorus line, kicking and gesturing from left to right and back again (Mud, "Tiger Feet").

Having mapped the genre world and musical terrain of glam rock, I shall focus now on the variety of masculinity that developed there. (I am focusing on masculine gender performance because glam rock was almost completely male dominated. I discuss Quatro, the one female canonical glam rocker, in chapter 6; I will have more to say about the gender politics of glam there.) In their groundbreaking 1978 essay "Rock and Sexuality," Simon Frith and Angela McRobbie state boldly that "any analysis of the sexuality of rock must begin with the brute social fact that . . . rock is a male form" (373). To their credit, Frith and McRobbie qualify this statement by asserting that this male form does not subtend a monolithic definition of masculinity: "masculinity in rock is not determined by one all-embracing definition. Rather, rock offers a framework within which male sexuality can find a range of acceptable heterosexual expressions" (375). Frith and McRobbie go on to suggest that rock and pop music, as cultural discourses, generally work to define and reinforce normative gender and sexual identities. In this essay, Frith and McRobbie were able only to raise questions about glam rock—"Why did youth music suddenly become a means for the expression of sexual ambiguity?" (384)—not to answer them, because their framing of the issue did not allow for the possibility that rock can express counternormative versions of masculinity. Clearly, glam's performance of masculinity at least alluded to queer identities.

An important precedent for glam's version of masculinity was the comportment of the male Mod. The Mods, short for *modernists,* were a youth subculture that emerged in postwar Britain, after the Teddy Boys and alongside the Rockers.[13] George Melly, who traces several stages in the evolution of the Mods as well as their relations with the Teds and the Rockers, defines the original Mods as "a very small group of young working-class boys who . . . formed a small, totally committed little mutual admiration society devoted totally to clothes." Whereas the Teds had used style as a sign of aggression, Melly states that the Mods were not interested in using fashion as anything other than an end in itself: "They were true dandies, interested in creating works of art—themselves" (168). The Mods' primary fashion influence was, in Melly's view, "the East End Jewish tradition of good tailoring, as exclusive in its way as Savile Row, if based on a different premise: the necessity to reveal conspicuous expenditure rather than to conceal it" (169).[14] The other ingredient in the Mods' blend of dandyism, fashion sense, narcissism, and conspicuous consumption was "a strong

13. For a useful discussion of the development of the Mods and Rockers, see Cohen (150–61).

14. For more on Mod style, see Hebdige (104–5).

homosexual element" (Melly 167). Jeff Nuttall memorably describes the confluence of Mods and art students that took place in the early 1960s:

> Purple hearts [amphetamines] appeared in strange profusion. Bell-bottoms blossomed into wild colors. Shoes were painted with Woolworth's lacquer. Both sexes wore makeup and dyed their hair. The art students brought their acid color combinations, their lilacs, tangerines and lime greens, from abstract painting. . . . Everywhere there were zippers, leathers, boots, PVC, see-through plastics, male makeup, a thousand overtones of sexual deviation. (30–31)

Both Bolan and Bowie identified with the Mod subculture as teenagers. From 1964 through 1966, Bowie played with a number of Mod groups, including the King Bees, the Manish Boys, and the Lower Third. He hung out, and sometimes played, at the Marquee Club in London, an important Mod haunt (where he would return in 1973 to film his final appearance as Ziggy Stardust, *The 1980 Floor Show* television special). Typically, Bowie remained at a distance from the subculture even as he participated in it; his song "The London Boys" (1967) emphasizes the drug abuse associated with the Mod lifestyle and suggests that the benefits of belonging to the subculture were outweighed by the harm done to the individual (in chapter 4, I show that Bowie had much the same kind of relationship to the hippie counterculture a few years later). Bolan's identification with the Mod lifestyle was, by contrast, uncritical. As early as 1962, when he was fifteen and still Mark Feld, Bolan was interviewed for an article in *Town* magazine entitled "Faces Without Shadows" (the word *Face* was used to signify a prominent Mod) where he was quoted extensively on the Mod lifestyle, saying, "I've got 10 suits, eight sports jackets, 15 pairs of slacks, 30 to 35 good shirts, about 20 jumpers, three leather jackets, two suede jackets, five or six pairs of shoes and 30 exceptionally good ties" (qtd. in Paytress, *Bolan* 17). It took until 1976 for Bolan to respond explicitly to Bowie's caustic evaluation of Mod life, but he eventually did with his own nostalgically celebratory song "London Boys," which he recorded with T. Rex.

The Mods were what Hebdige calls a "spectacular subculture," and Bolan, Bowie, and others clearly carried the "overtones of sexual deviation" and the emphasis on creating spectacle, and on making a spectacle of oneself, from Mod into glam. The Mods' focus on fashion, on the expression of identity through clothing and makeup, became central to glam, as was the idea of self-creation. A person was not born a Mod but became one, and became one by creating a signature look, perhaps even creating one's own clothes. Mark Paytress, Bolan's biographer, describes the Mods' emphasis on custom clothing: "Rejecting the idea of the sartorial readymade, these bricoleurs continually adapted and evolved their style. Any combination was possible for the early Modernist: functional garments for the country gentleman juxtaposed with sportswear, ladies' fashions complementing city slickers' suits" (*Bolan* 18–19). This notion of creating, rather than following, fashion is at the heart of glam style as well, reflected in Bolan's combinations of women's jackets and shoes with T-shirts and slacks; the custom-made jumpsuits Bowie wore while developing the Ziggy Stardust persona; Gary Glitter's exaggerated silver lamé space suits; Slade's Noddy Holder's mirrored top hat, often accompanied by a plaid shirt and striped pants; Quatro's leather cat suit, and so on. Whereas psychedelic rock musicians tried to look like their audiences, many glam rock fans tried to duplicate the looks of their favorite performers. Glam musicians' participation in fashion bricolage implicitly invited their fans to do the same. Jeremy Novick recounts his Friday night ritual as a glam fan: "Home from school, straight upstairs to my room to sort out what I was going to wear. . . . Getting ready. I loved getting ready. Trying on this, seeing what that looked like. What do you think? That top with those trousers?" (Novick and Middles 101).

After youthful stints as Mods, Bolan and Bowie each passed through a hippie phase during which he identified with the counterculture; again, Bolan's identification seems to have been more wholehearted than Bowie's. I shall save discussion of these two artists' countercultural periods for later chapters; here, I focus more generally on the relationship of glam to the gender norms of the 1960s counterculture. Countercultural masculinity and glam masculinity were both androgynous and feminized, but in very different ways and to different ends. The gentle, introspective, passive male image portrayed in the hippie subculture of the 1960s was a feminized male image posited in specific opposition to a brand of aggressive masculinity thought to have underwritten the war in Vietnam (Kimmel 269–70). However, as I suggested in the previous chapter, this soft masculinity was presumed to be heterosexual in nature; by contrast, glam masculinity, like Mod masculinity before it, alluded to the possibility of homosexuality or bisexuality. Countercultural androgyny, derived perhaps from the view that every individual has "both masculine and feminine desire[s],"[15] was seen as natural and, therefore, as a reaction against a dominant culture that sought to suppress innate androgyny in favor of supposedly stable masculine and feminine identities. As we saw from my discussion of Alice Cooper in the previous chapter, the gender-bending of glam challenged both the dominant culture's standards of masculinity and the androgyny favored by the hippie counterculture, for glam did not posit androgyny as a "natural" state. To the contrary: glam rockers specifically foregrounded the constructedness of their effeminate or androgynous performing personae. Even though most glam rockers made no claim to being anything other than heterosexual men, glam rock departed from both normative masculinity and countercultural gender identities in favor of "a new and radically fluid model for sexual identity: no longer defined by its permanence, but the multi-coloured result of constant change and reinvention" (Haynes, "Foreword" xi). The title of Reed's Bowie-produced glam rock album, *Transformer* (1972), and the pictures of Reed in makeup on the front cover and in exaggerated male and female drag on the back encapsulate this commitment to an idea of sexual identity as something not rooted in "nature," but flexible and open to question.

The use of makeup in glam rock illustrates clearly how glam posited sexual identity as constructed. The centrality of makeup to glam is indicated by Lou Reed's having devoted an entire song to the subject, the appropriately titled "Make Up," on his *Transformer* album. The song is partly a list of cosmetics, including brand names. The consumer of these items is referred to as a "slick little girl," but the chorus, which represents a rare moment of explicit political engagement for glam rock, implies strongly that the "girl" in question is not female: "We're coming out / Out of our closets / Out on the street." That the title of the song is not hyphenated suggests that "make up" can be taken here as a verb as well as a noun: to make oneself up, to invent or transform oneself. In this context, the list of products and beauty rituals in the song underlines the procedures used to construct a feminized male image. Sim-

---

15. Anthony Easthope, *What a Man's Gotta Do: The Masculine Myth in Popular Culture* (Boston: Unwin Hyman, 1986), as quoted in Whiteley, "Little Red Rooster" (97). I have taken this brief quotation somewhat out of context.

ilarly, both *Ziggy Stardust and the Spiders from Mars: The Motion Picture,* the documentary film of a Bowie concert in 1973, and a U.S. television appearance by the New York Dolls on *Don Kirschner's Rock Concert* in 1974 begin with the application of makeup. Bowie is seen having makeup applied by a makeup artist; the New York Dolls are seen circulating a lipstick among themselves as if they were sharing a joint, each man applying it to his lips before passing it on to the next. In these performances and Reed's song, wearing feminine cosmetics is presented as an act of transgression against dominant concepts of masculinity and a fundamental aspect of glam rock performance. But the emphasis on the application of makeup in the transformation of male images into feminine or androgynous ones demystifies the glam image itself and emphasizes the constructed nature of glam masculinity.

It is also important that most glam rockers used cosmetics to create neither the illusion of female identity nor that of a seamless, androgynous blending of masculine and feminine. Unlike countercultural unisex fashion, the combination of masculine and feminine codes in glam costuming and makeup did not blur distinctions between men and women: glam rockers were clearly *men* who had adopted feminine decoration. For his Ziggy Stardust makeup, David Bowie employed feminine cosmetics, but created an image so exaggerated as to appear more alien than feminine.[16] Sweet is another case in point: although their use of eye makeup and glitter did give the members of the group a feminine look, it was so overstated, patterned, and stylized that it could not be mistaken for the normal use of cosmetics by women other than Las Vegas showgirls. In conjunction with the tribal-looking jewelry sometimes affected by Sweet, their makeup took on something of the aura of such traditional male uses of makeup as war paint.[17] Sweet's androgyny

16. In an article entitled "David Bowie's Makeup Do's and Don'ts," Bowie reveals what cosmetics he uses to achieve the Ziggy Stardust look. The article is a parody of a beauty tips feature one might find in a women's magazine, perhaps with a female star as its subject. The original source of this article is unknown to me; it circulated as an insert in a Bowie bootleg LP, *Dollars in Drag.*

17. For a photograph of Sweet, see Novick and Middles (41). It is possible that Sweet was parodying the counterculture's enthusiasm for American Indians, with whom the hippies identified as fellow outsiders. Sweet's tribal warrior look may also shed some light on one of the ironies of glam rock: the use of glam songs as rousing anthems by professional sports teams. Gary Glitter's "Rock and Roll (Part 2)" and Queen's "We Will Rock You" and "We Are the

was thus more a collision of male and female gender codes than a true subsumption of both to a third possibility.

In light of the overtly fabricated, patched together, and made-up nature of glam performance personae, it is intriguing to find a cluster of references to gothic horror in glam rock, particularly to *Frankenstein*. These include Alice Cooper's "The Ballad of Dwight Fry" (discussed in the previous chapter), the New York Dolls' "Frankenstein," and Edgar Winter's instrumental "Frankenstein."[18] (Although Winter is not primarily a glam rock artist, he had a glam phase. The title of the album on which "Frankenstein" appears, *They Only Come Out at Night* [1973], is suggestive of such gothic horrors as werewolves and vampires. Winter appears in full glam drag on the cover.) Within glam rock itself, Alice Cooper has exploited the gothic connection the most, building first his stage shows, then his entire career around it. The British stage musical *The Rocky Horror Show* (and its filmed counterpart, *The Rocky Horror Picture Show* [1974]), while not direct products of the glam genre world, also underlined the association of glam rock with gothic, as did Brian DePalma's film *Phantom of the Paradise* (1974), in which glam rock figures as part of a plot derived from *The Phantom of the Opera* with a helping of *The Picture of Dorian Gray* mixed in. At one level, the association of glam with gothic horror, particularly the Hollywood films of the 1930s satirized by *The Rocky Horror [Picture] Show* that popularized the nineteenth-century novels on which they were based, makes perfect sense. As Harry M. Benshoff has shown in *Monsters in the Closet*, those films, many of them directed by the avowedly gay James Whale, contain multiple, coded references to homosexuality and reflect a covert queer sensibility based on an identification of the queer and the monster as the Other. References to gothic horror occur frequently enough in glam rock to justify a brief discussion of the parallels between glam rock and the gothic.[19]

Champions" (both 1978) are commonly used in this context. The ironies of using songs produced by musicians who affected a homoerotic style in the context of professional team sports abound. But as a look at Sweet and most other glam rockers makes clear, glam was hardly devoid of machismo.

18. Photographer Mick Rock uses a quote from *Frankenstein* ("I saw the dull yellow eye of the creature open; it breathed hard, and a convulsive motion agitated its limbs") as one of the epigraphs for *Blood and Glitter,* his book of glam-era images.

19. There is another rock genre called goth rock, a somewhat later development that grew out of punk in the late 1970s and whose focus on monstros-

Commenting on contemporary reviews of *Dr. Jekyll and Mr. Hyde,* Judith Halberstam describes the gothic novel as a "cross-dressing performance" whose stylistic excesses are understood as feminine dressing up and whose pages are filled with instances of "grotesque transvestism" (*Skin Shows* 61). The transvestism of glam rock is similarly grotesque, and glam rock personae often border on the monstrous (it should be clear that I am not using these terms pejoratively: the excessiveness of both gothic and glam are central to the pleasures each provides). Gary Glitter, seven feet tall on high platform shoes, wrapped in silver and covered with glitter, hair a bouffant nightmare, shoulders unnaturally wide, lurches across the stage like Frankenstein's monster. (Actually, his own description of seeing himself on film refers to a more contemporary icon of gothic horror: "I've never seen such a freak in all my life. I was really shocked, y'know—I looked like something out of *The Exorcist*" [qtd. in Kent 29].) For a television performance of "Blockbuster," Sweet's bass player, Steve Priest, the member of the group given to the campiest looks and performances, appeared wearing a World War I piked German military helmet; a Nazi military jacket complete with swastika arm band; a Hitler mustache on his otherwise femininely made-up face surrounded by shoulder-length, femininely coiffed hair; tight black pants; and high silver platform boots. This outfit combines any number of loaded signifiers in a whole that is simultaneously excessive, transgressive, and incoherent. As Halberstam says of the novel *Frankenstein,* "the sum of [its] parts exceeds the whole" (*Skin Shows* 31).

Halberstam describes the gothic novel as "cannibalistic" with respect to its sources, arguing that *Frankenstein* and *Dracula* "exemplify models of production and consumption which suggest that Gothic, as a genre, is itself a hybrid form, a stitched body of distorted textuality" (33). As I showed in my discussion of glam rock's relationship to the rock and roll of the 1950s, glam rockers consumed existing music in the making of their own, thus generating songs that often are monstrous effigies made up of parts of

ity and morbidity relate it to nineteenth-century gothic fiction. Goth has something of a genealogical relationship to glam: for instance, the Damned, a punk group that would later turn goth, were the opening act on T. Rex's last tour in 1977 and recorded Sweet's "Ballroom Blitz"; other connections of this kind could be discovered. Here, I am using the presence of references to gothic fiction in glam rock to outline some conceptual similarities between the two genres without suggesting that glam is a version of the gothic.

other textual bodies. Bolan's early piece "Sally Was an Angel" (ca. 1967), for instance, grafts Bolan's own lyrics onto the melody of "Heartbreak Hotel" (Bolan, *The Best*). His "Woodland Rock" (1971) combines parts of Little Richard's "Long Tall Sally" (1956) with Chuck Berry's "Too Much Monkey Business" (1958), Beach Boys backing vocals, psychedelic backward-masked guitar, and animist lyrics. Rock music is intrinsically intertextual, of course, and many songs contain elements (e.g., lyrics, chord changes, bass lines, riffs) that recall other songs. But glam rock characteristically makes free with existing songs, styles, and even voices to such a degree that it challenges "rock's mythology of original expression" (Toynbee 47), leading one commentator to note, "The idea of individual creativity that had been current in the sixties was replaced by a delight in plagiarism—everyone was free to steal" (Street 172).

A case in point is Slik's late glam opus "Forever and Ever" (1976), which opens with an explicit reference to gothic horror, the first bars of Bach's "Toccata and Fugue in D Minor," widely known as the music the Phantom of the Opera plays on the organ. The first section refers to the end of a love relationship against a background of what sounds like monks chanting: the male singer refers ominously to burning candles and a promise he intends to keep. The tempo is deliberate, punctuated by a throbbing, heartbeat-like pulse on the bass guitar (the atmosphere created is close to that of Blue Oyster Cult's "Don't Fear the Reaper"). As the section nears its end, the pace picks up and the song transforms into a medium-tempo, early-sixties-style pop-rock ditty about eternal love featuring a piano-dominated arrangement with horns and a slightly nasal vocal reminiscent of Bobby Vee. At the end of this section, the organ and creepy vocal return, only to yield again to the happier sound. Although the song's schizoid structure may effectively convey the idea that loving devotion and psychotic fixation are two sides of the same coin, its heterodox combination of conflicting stylistic elements, many of them clearly borrowed, is what stands out. In addition to Bach and Bobby Vee, the song probably cannibalized glam rock itself, since another of its likely points of reference is Roy Wood's "Forever," a recording that alternates between two different styles in a similar manner (and possesses a similar title) that appeared three years earlier.

I am not arguing that a sustained critical comparison of gothic and glam is worthwhile or even possible, only that there are certain striking parallels between two genres considered to transgress and question the norms of their respective art forms. They partake, intriguingly, of shared means, including self-conscious stylistic excess and overstatement, the violation of boundaries, transvestism, and the assertion of the constructedness of identities and texts. Here, finally, is Halberstam's description of the relationship of the gothic novel to literary realism: "the Gothic, the 'amplitude of costume' and the feminine guise which is worn by an author, plays homosexual to the healthy and appropriately garbed heterosexuality of realism. Gothic is the debased and degenerate cousin who calls too much attention to himself by an outrageous and almost campy performance of all the tricks of the literary trade" (*Skin Shows* 61–62). If I were to substitute glam for gothic and make other cannibalistic adjustments to this text to suture it into the context of rock music, I could produce a very accurate and pithy description of the relationship between glam rock and psychedelic rock that would go to both the textual and performance practices of the two genres. Glam indeed "played homosexual" to its assertively hetero predecessor, and Glam Rock would certainly be the campy cousin who could be relied upon to behave inappropriately at any Rock family reunion.

Whereas psychedelic rockers downplayed the visual aspects of their performances, glam rockers went in precisely the opposite direction and emphasized costume, makeup, hairstyle, and movement. Producer Mike Chapman's comment on Sweet's music could be generalized to all of glam rock: "those records were styled to be watched as well as listened to" (qtd. in Cato 45); consequently, television became one of the genre's primary media. Glam's valorization of style and pose over authenticity may be its most profound challenge to the 1960s counterculture. The ideology of sixties rock insisted that the musician's performing persona and real self be presented and perceived as identical—it had to be possible to see the musician's songs and performances as authentic manifestations of his or her individuality. Glam rockers specifically refused this equation. By insisting that the figure performing the music was fabricated from makeup, costume, and pose, all of which were subject to change at any moment, glam rockers insisted on the constructedness of their performing identities and implicitly denied their authenticity.[20]

20. Hoskyns's treatment of the authenticity issue in his history of glam is uneven. On the one hand, he decries rock's ideology of authenticity because it

Glam returned to cultural and social images that the hippie counterculture thought it had displaced and rendered obsolete, such as the Mod, the Teddy Boy, and the rock and roll of the 1950s. By cobbling together songs out of existing and outmoded styles, thus making the creation of music an act of consumption as well as production, glam defied the emphasis on individual creativity, originality, and expression so central to the countercultural ethos. Glam rock also mounted an assault on the whole idea of the "natural" so dear to the counterculture; even Bolan's and Bowie's respective moves from hippie to glam personae suggested that all social identifications are temporary, self-selected constructs rather than expressions of an essential, natural identity. Certainly, there was nothing "natural" about glam rockers' androgynous personae, which were clearly and overtly constructed as bricolages of bits of masculine and feminine gender coding in clothing, makeup, and behavior used in playful and self-conscious ways. That the images they drew on to create glam masculinity were overtly queer in emphasis challenged the counterculture's tacit assumption that heterosexuality is "basic," to quote Mosse. The choice of adopting that pose in the public arena of popular culture was an important act signifying a freedom of choice in constructing one's own identity that flew in the face of both normative and countercultural mores.[21]

In discussing two songs and their respective value as glam rock anthems (or glamthems, if you will), Van Cagle opts for Lou Reed's

---

masks the fact that all rock performers are in show business and construct their images very carefully, and implies that glam rock at least acknowledged its status as entertainment and made no claim that its performers were authentic. On the other hand, a concept of glam authenticity that is very close to garden variety rock authenticity starts to creep in when Hoskyns argues that performers like Bowie and Reed, who could make some claim to a perversity in their private lives that corresponded with their stage images, were more authentically glam than Alice Cooper, who made a very clear distinction between his stage persona and his private persona (*Glam!* 14, 49–50, 72).

21. The attentive reader will probably have realized that most of the musicians referred to here did not perform under the names they were given at birth. Essentially all glam rock artists, with the perhaps ironic exception of Suzi Quatro, performed under fabricated names. Even the more "natural" seeming names, like Marc Bolan, David Bowie, and Lou Reed, were invented by the artists. Other glam artists like Alvin Stardust, Gary Glitter, and Johnny Thunders of the New York Dolls had obviously fabricated names. The artificiality of these names is another gesture in the direction of indicating the constructed nature of glam personae, as well as a tribute to the idea of self-invention.

"Walk on the Wild Side" over Mott The Hoople's "All the Young Dudes" (1972). Although Cagle finds "All the Young Dudes" to "suggest rather progressive notions concerning gay sexuality," he feels that it pulls its punches in order to appeal as broad an audience as possible (149). "Walk on the Wild side," by contrast, "presents a more candid approach to the themes that were by this point steadily defining the genre" (152). I am sympathetic with Cagle's approach: the identification of certain songs as anthemic is a common practice in rock fandom and criticism. Identifying a song that may be considered anthemic within a certain genre has the virtue of forcing the chooser to be clear about what he or she sees as defining the genre in question.

I have reservations, however, about Cagle's analysis. For one thing, he does not acknowledge the many other possible glamthem contenders. Both "All the Young Dudes" and "Walk on the Wild Side" are to some extent Bowie products: he wrote "All the Young Dudes" and produced Mott The Hoople's recording of it and also produced "Walk on the Wild Side" for Reed, who wrote it. The Bowie oeuvre alone offers several other songs that deserve consideration: "Changes," with its exhortation to "Turn and face the strange" would surely be one, as would "Oh You Pretty Things" and even "Rebel Rebel." Approaching the concept of a rock anthem more in the spirit of a manifesto or statement of purpose than a declaration of allegiance, early glam hits like T. Rex's "Hot Love" and Slade's "Get Down and Get with It" would qualify. Paytress makes an argument for T. Rex's "Metal Guru" (1972) as glam's "defining anthem" because "it epitomized Glam Rock's pop disposability" (*Bolan* 209–10); Glitter's "Rock and Roll (Part 2)" could equally well qualify as the definitive statement of glam rock's retrospective and reductivist tendencies. This leads to my second reservation about Cagle's approach: as crucial as creating spaces for the performance of gay sexuality and queer masculinity unquestionably was to glam rock, it was not the whole story. Glam was also about revisiting the rock and roll of the 1950s in search of more direct and straightforward musical models than psychedelic rock offered; returning spectacle and theatricality to rock performance and spectatorship through movement, makeup, and outrageous fashions; reveling in the constructed nature of performance personae; and treating existing music, musical styles, and even specific voices, as source material to be plundered at will. In fact, rock-and-roll revisionism became such a dominant aspect of glam—particularly the second wave—that critical commentary leaned toward defining a new genre, labeled *nouveau rock,* as a subset of glam.[22] These other tendencies were not at odds with glam's performances of a queer masculinity: all were means by which glam performed itself as the queer member of the Rock family, and the pool of potential anthems is correspondingly deep.

The final comment I wish to make concerning Cagle's approach to the anthem question has to do with the fact that he bases his assessment almost exclusively on the songs' lyrics; he has little to say about them musically or in terms of performance. This is a serious omission, since he is actually discussing specific recorded performances, not just compositions. Consideration of the recordings as performances rather than texts opens up other avenues of interpretation, even with respect to the performance of sexuality. If one were to read the lyrics of T. Rex's "Hot Love," for instance, it would appear to be a heterosexual love song of a kind fairly common in rock. At moments, the protagonist is surprisingly gallant and deferential toward the female love object ("may I hold your hand?"); ultimately, however, he celebrates her youth, sexuality, and availability. But consider Hoskyns's description of the recording:

> In essence the song was nothing more than a twelve-bar blues, but it had little to do with the crude grit of Chicago's South Side, or even with the earnest twiddling of the British blues boom. It was a pop blues delivered with mincing swishiness, in a cheek-suckingly camp voice flanked on its fruity "la la la" fade-out by a pair of wailing falsetto clowns called Flo and Eddie. (*Glam!* 4)

All of the features of "Hot Love" that made the recording a distinctive experience for Hoskyns and align it with glam's performance of queer masculinity are contained in the *performance,* in the voices and how they were deployed, not in the song itself—neither its twelve-bar blues structure nor its lyrics themselves gave rise to the swishiness, campiness, and fruitiness that Hoskyns heard on the record. I raise this issue to suggest that perhaps the category of rock anthems needs to be expanded to include anthemic perfor-

22. The term *nouveau rock* started to appear around 1974, in reference to glam artists whose work and personae clearly reflected a fifties influence including (according to Gambaccini 14) Suzi Quatro, Gary Glitter, Sweet, Mud, Alvin Stardust, Wizzard, and Barry Blue.

mances, not just songs. Certainly, Bolan's legendary performance of "Hot Love" on *Top of the Pops* with his face flecked with glitter was such a moment, its importance contained at least as much in his visual performance as in the song. By proposing the concept of the anthemic performance, I am foregrounding the importance of performance, in all of its aspects, to the creation of musical meaning. In the next four chapters, I will turn to the work of specific performers and examine in detail not just the music they made but the way they performed that music.

3. king of the highway, queen of the hop

Marc Bolan and the Evolution of Glam Style

> We couldn't have pounced without Marc Bolan. The little imp opened the
> door. What was so great, however, was that we knew he hadn't got it quite
> right. Sort of Glam 1.0. We were straining in the wings with versions 1.01
> and 1.02, while Marc was still struggling with satin. But boy,
> he really rocked. He did, y'know?
> —**David Bowie, 2001 ("Foreword")**

> What they tried to do with David Bowie was create another Marc Bolan.
> —**Marc Bolan, 1973 (qtd. in Crowe 38)**

In the first epigraph above, David Bowie uses the language of technological innovation to acknowledge Marc Bolan's status as the
first artist to put glam rock on the map, with the caveat that
whereas Bolan created the glam prototype, he, Bowie, developed it
further. This claim is obviously somewhat self-serving on Bowie's
part, but it is also an instance of turnabout as fair play, as the second epigraph shows. In any case, Bowie's comment contains a
grain of truth. Bolan bridged the gap between psychedelic rock and
glam rock but was a transitional figure who neither let go completely of the values inherent in the former style nor pushed the latter style to its limits. Bolan undertook the transition intentionally
and knowingly. He marked it self-consciously in various ways,
most conspicuously by renaming his group late in 1970. Tyrannosaurus Rex, founded in 1967 after Bolan ended his association
with John's Children, was an acoustic duo beloved of a coterie,
underground audience; T. Rex, the augmented, electrified glam
rock version, was for several years a streamlined, hit-making
machine whose British audiences responded with a fervor not seen
since the mid-1960s. T. Rextasy was the new Beatlemania.

71

I begin this chapter with a discussion of Tyrannosaurus Rex, the group with which Bolan became a fixture on London's underground music scene in the late 1960s. I focus primarily on the group's musical style and its relationship to psychedelic rock to show that Tyrannosaurus Rex developed a kind of music that responded to the interests of the hippie counterculture but that was not entirely within the conventions of psychedelic rock. In the second section, I examine the musical transition Bolan undertook as he moved from psychedelic music to glam rock and from Tyrannosaurus Rex to T. Rex, a transition that unfolded gradually through a series of incremental stylistic changes that led to a significantly different sound. In the final part of the chapter, I look at the same transition in terms of Bolan's physical performance style with the two groups and suggest that Bolan established the basic elements of glam rock performance style through the implicit queerness of his persona and the self-conscious, highly theatrical manner in which he presented himself on stage.

Although there is some dispute as to whether Bolan truly embraced the countercultural ethos or simply latched onto it as a means of advancing his musical career, the music he made with Tyrannosaurus Rex exemplifies many of the characteristics of psychedelic rock and reflects hippie values. Not entirely of their own volition, the group met one of the primary criteria for acceptance by the hippies, who "liked 'progressive' or 'underground' music which was not disseminated widely, and not represented in the current 'top 20s'" (Willis 107). Although Tyrannosaurus Rex released five singles from 1968 to 1970, not one even came close to the top twenty and they did not receive extensive radio or television exposure. That the four albums they released during the same period fared much better (the first reached number fifteen, the third number twelve) is consistent with the inclinations of the countercultural audience, which favored the album over the single as the more serious, less commercial type of musical commodity.[1]

Tyrannosaurus Rex traveled the circuit of underground music venues, appearing regularly at Middle Earth in London and com-

---

1. As Sheila Whiteley points out, the antipathy toward singles and the music industry commercialism they represent was shared by psychedelic rock musicians and their audiences, all of whom preferred the LP as a format that allowed for fuller musical statements (*The Space* 37–38).

parable clubs in other English cities, as well as at colleges, sharing bills with the likes of Donovan, the Nice, Fairport Convention, the Jimi Hendrix Experience, and many other prominent rock and folk-rock musicians of the time. (On a tour of the United States in 1969, Tyrannosaurus Rex played at many of the most important medium-sized psychedelic rock venues in the country, including the Family Dog in San Francisco, the Grande Ballroom in Detroit, the Café Au Go Go in New York City, and the Boston Tea Party.) The group played the first free concert in London's Hyde Park in June 1968, along with Pink Floyd, with whom they appeared fairly often and also shared management.[2]

Bolan's music with Tyrannosaurus Rex partook of the "implicit pastoral-arcadian spirit of Hippie culture" identified by Stuart Hall, who describes "the fondness for Tolkien's Hobbits" as one symptom of that spirit (179), a fondness evident from the fact that the club Middle Earth was named after one of the realms in Tolkien's *Lord of the Rings* trilogy. Bolan did indeed admire Tolkien's books; the second member of Tyrannosaurus Rex, percussionist and vocalist Steve Porter, became Steve Peregrine Took in honor of one of Tolkien's characters (the hobbit Peregrin Took) "probably at Bolan's command" (Paytress, *Bolan* 93). Bolan's own diminutive stature (he stood about five feet four inches) and energetic music earned him the critical sobriquet "the Bopping Elf."[3] The titles of Tyrannosaurus Rex's albums also reflected a commitment to Tolkienesque fantasy, mythology, and chivalry: their first album is called *My People Were Fair And Had Sky In Their Hair But Now They're Content To Wear Stars On Their Brows* (1968); their second *Prophets, Seers and Sages, the Angels of the Ages* (1968); their third simply *Unicorn* (1969). In some cases, the Arcadian flavor of Bolan's songs is evident from the titles alone: "Woodland Bop," "Lofty Skies," "Find a Little Wood," " 'Pon a Hill." In

2. The best source for primary information about Marc Bolan's musical career is Cliff McLenehan's exhaustive *Marc Bolan 1947–1977: A Chronology*, which proceeds almost day by day. Bolan has also been well served by Mark Paytress's fine, full-scale biography, *Bolan: The Rise and Fall of a 20th Century Superstar*. A good source of discographic information is John and Shan Bramley, *Marc Bolan: The Legendary Years*.

3. As if to preempt Randy Newman's later parodic declaration in song that "Short people got no reason / To live" ("Short People," 1977), Bolan sang in "Spaceball Ricochet" (from *The Slider*, 1972), "I know I'm small / But I enjoy living / Anyway."

others, it is present in the description of characters: the titular figure in "Stacey Grove," from the first Tyrannosaurus Rex album, for example, "drinks acorn juice [while] roasting his feet by the furnace of peat" *(The Definitive)*. His early songs contain too many references to elves, witches, warriors, princesses, kings, druids, and poetesses to inventory; and many of the love songs of this period are addressed chivalrously to the singer's "lady love."

Bolan often represented himself in interviews as having been exposed to magic at an early age when he lived with a wizard in France.[4] Some of his songs themselves refer to spells, such as the cheery injunction to "Catch a bright star and place it on your forehead / Say a few spells and baby there you go" of "Ride a White Swan" (1970) or the more ominous "Iscariot" from *Unicorn,* a song that itself seems to be an incantation of some kind: "A mare of wood / Elder, elm and oak . . . / Will keep you fair / If you jest me no joke" (Tyrannosaurus Rex, *The Definitive*). Bolan aspired to produce his own epic fantasy tale, "The Children of Rarn," as a book or concept album. "It's about prehistoric earth," he explained to an interviewer, "before the dinosaurs were heavy creatures. There were two races of people then, the Peacelings and the Dworns" and a third group of beings called Lithons, all locked in complex, antagonistic relationships (qtd. in Hodenfield 25). Although the project never came to fruition, bits and pieces of it showed up in some of his songs.

Besides these fantasy-laden compositions, Bolan also wrote songs for Tyrannosaurus Rex that reported on the counterculture by chronicling aspects of the underground scene or portraying particular hippies, although more as types than as individuals. "Charlie" (1966), a piece that never made it past the demo stage, describes a character with a "Biblical beard and long black flowing hair" who is ubiquitous on the scene but whose precise identity is unknown. His behavior typifies that of the hippie toward the "straights": he "smiles and politely says 'how do you do' / As you walk away, he makes faces after you" (Bolan, *The Best*). Although the song seems benevolent toward Charlie as the kind of idiosyncratic character and scene-maker prized within the counterculture, Bolan's representation of him is not wholly positive; he comes off as somewhat annoying and interfering.

The counterbalance to "Charlie" is "Scenescof," from the first Tyrannosaurus Rex album, the main character of which is a nega-

---

4. The "wizard" was Riggs O'Hara, an American actor with whom Bolan lived in London and traveled to Paris (Paytress, *Bolan* 45–46).

tive "straight" who scoffs at the underground scene (hence his name) and has stolen the singer's girlfriend. "Child Star," also from the first album, probably a fanciful self-portrait, depicts a young musical genius possessed of "elvish fingers" and "Beethoven hair" who composes in bed while sipping tea. "Chateau in Virginia Waters," from the same album, "romanticized a middle-class Surrey hippie idyll" (Paytress, liner notes) in its portrayal of an aspiring poetess (Tyrannosaurus Rex, *The Definitive*). These songs, and many others like them, are thematically close to a number of pieces recorded by Donovan in 1966, including "The Trip" and "Sunny South Kensington," which describe his countercultural adventures and the people he encountered on them in Los Angeles and London, respectively. (One difference is that whereas Donovan namechecks such well-known figures as Bob Dylan, Allen Ginsberg, Jean-Paul Belmondo, and Mary Quant, Bolan's characters constitute less rarified company.)

Bolan's use of language in the lyrics for these early songs is very much in keeping with countercultural modes of expression. While the majority of Tyrannosaurus Rex's songs are narratives, the precise actions being described are often obscured beneath layers of ornate, anachronistic linguistic flourishes and references to mythology and lore, both known and invented. Such verbal stylistics made many of the songs seem obscure, as if their meanings were available only to initiates possessed of the arcane knowledge required to parse them. As Willis points out, the underground audience "wanted conventional meaning to be undercut," preferring "a rich ambiguity" to straightforward " 'meaning.' " All of this served to create "a sense of esotericism and of élitism. They had a music which only they could appreciate" (159–60). Bolan's songwriting catered to these countercultural preferences, as did his diction when singing. He often slurred his words, rendering them virtually unintelligible and therefore more appreciable for their abstract sonic qualities than their discursive meanings (though he generally included printed lyrics with the albums to allow for close study).

Although Bolan probably did not make extensive use of psychedelic drugs in the 1960s, his partner Took did, and the music they made together reflects the psychedelic influence.[5] In its very first

---

5. The evidence assembled by Paytress suggests that Bolan was not a drug user in the 1960s and did not write Tyrannosaurus Rex's songs under the influence (*Bolan* 162), though he did go through a period of substance abuse later on. Took's enthusiasm for drugs was one of the factors that led to his leaving the group in 1969. He died in 1980 as a result of substance abuse.

incarnation, Tyrannosaurus Rex was a five-man, electrified rock group, but that version sank on its maiden voyage. Precisely how the group quickly became a duo consisting of Bolan on acoustic guitar and lead vocals and Took on hand percussion and backing vocals is not entirely clear,[6] but the result was a kind of psychedelic folk music rather than rock—one critic described it as "jug-band psychedelia" (qtd. in McLenehan 35).[7] (This is another parallel with Donovan, who, like Bolan, began as a Dylanesque folkie then gravitated toward a more psychedelically inflected, yet still largely acoustic, style.) Regardless of the extent to which Bolan and Took themselves used drugs, their music was perceived as expressive of the hallucinogenic experience. One of the subjects of Willis's ethnography of British hippies singled out Tyrannosaurus Rex, along with Pink Floyd, as producing music that spoke specifically to the drug culture: "A good example is Tyrannosaurus Rex, if you listened to them and you'd never tripped you wouldn't have a clue

6. Took was the drummer in this earliest incarnation of Tyrannosaurus Rex that apparently performed only once, in the summer of 1967. Following this woefully unsuccessful debut, Bolan's record company repossessed his electric guitar and equipment, and Took sold his full drum kit for money to live on, settling for a set of bongos. The two persevered nevertheless, as an acoustic duo (Paytress, *Bolan* 88, 92–93).

7. Although most psychedelic rock bands were heavily influenced by the electric Chicago blues, there was a folkier side to psychedelic music. In the United States, this aspect was represented particularly by the Byrds in Los Angeles and several less well known groups associated with the San Francisco scene, such as Kaleidoscope, which performed on a variety of Eastern instruments as well as rock and folk instrumentation; It's A Beautiful Day; the Peanut Butter Conspiracy; and H. P. Lovecraft. (A different version of psychedelic folk flourished in New York City's Greenwich Village, with groups like Jake and the Family Jewels and Cat Mother and the All-Night Newsboys, whose first album was produced by Jimi Hendrix.) A number of the psychedelic rock groups in San Francisco, including Jefferson Airplane, Quicksilver Messenger Service, and the Grateful Dead, had originated in that city's burgeoning folk music scene in the early 1960s, an influence that is quite apparent in their music. In the United Kingdom, the roster of psychedelic folk artists included Fairport Convention, Donovan, and especially the Incredible String Band, a duo from Scotland who played a plethora of acoustic instruments and wrote LSD-inspired songs in a folk vein. Tyrannosaurus Rex was often compared with the Incredible String Band, presumably because both were acoustic duos performing on the circuit of psychedelic music clubs, but the comparison is not substantial. As Bolan himself said, "The difference is that they're folk musicians. I come from rock and roll" (qtd. in Marsh, "Marc Bolan" 38). For a good account of folk rock and psychedelic folk, see DeRogatis (47–62).

Tyrannosaurus Rex, ca. 1968. *From left:* Steve Peregrine Took, Marc Bolan. © MichaelOchsArchives.com.

about what they're singing about, but after you'd tripped and listened to them, you'd actually understand some of what they're singing about" (146).

Sheila Whiteley argues that psychedelic rock contains specific aural codes that "convey a musical equivalent of hallucinogenic experience" (*The Space* 3), and Tyrannosaurus Rex's music has characteristics that can be interpreted that way. One such characteristic, "the manipulation of timbres (blurred, bright, overlapping)" (Whiteley, *The Space* 4), is a central aspect of the Tyrannosaurus Rex sound: Bolan's vigorously strummed acoustic guitar was set off by the much duller timbres of Took's usually rapid tapping on bongos and African talking drums, which were juxtaposed in turn with the brighter timbres of finger cymbals, toy xylophones, bells, wooden flutes, and whistles. In many instances, these latter sounds, and others that border on pure noise, appear on the recordings unexpectedly and do not necessarily reappear at rhythmically

predictable intervals. By using such atypical instruments, Tyrannosaurus Rex provided "unusual, bizarre and exotic sounds" that
reflected "the 'head'-centered nature of the hippy culture, and the
general emphasis on expanded awareness" (Willis 159).

Unlike their occasional bill-mates Pink Floyd and a great many
other psychedelic rock groups, Tyrannosaurus Rex did not engage
in lengthy instrumental improvisations; instrumental solos of any
duration were extremely rare in their work, in fact. The music was
about creating textures through the layering of voices and a somewhat limited, if unconventional, palette of instrumental sounds, not
about demonstrating individual instrumental virtuosity in the manner of, say, Cream. But Bolan and Took used their voices as their
central improvising instruments in a fashion that paralleled the
instrumental jamming of psychedelic rock groups.

Bolan sang in a high-pitched, somewhat nasal, heavily vibrato-
laden tenor voice that was completely idiosyncratic and unmistak-
able. Describing Bolan's peculiar way of singing at this time presented a challenge to journalistic music critics, some of whom rose
to the occasion. Allen Evans, of the *New Musical Express*,
described the duo's manner of singing as "quivering and tremulous"; another critic warned the listener: "Do not adjust your
record players, this is how Marc Bolan and Steve Peregrine sing—
as if they're about to break out crying" (qtd. in McLenehan 40, 35).
Chris Welch vividly described the duo in his review of the song
"Pewter Suitor" (1969) for *Melody Maker*: "Their rattling pots and
tiny voices get quite heated at the end, rather like a couple of rough
gnomes, bashing each other with toadstools" (qtd. in McLenehan
43). Even less generous was Dave Marsh, who commented that
with Tyrannosaurus Rex, "Bolan often came on like a demented
vacuum cleaner or a chimney sweep gargling charcoal" ("Marc
Bolan" 38). Steve Turner simply threw in the towel by saying that
Bolan had "a voice which sounded like . . . (well what *did* it sound
like?)" ("Marc Bolan").

"Weilder [*sic*] of Words," a three-part composition from Tyrannosaurus Rex's first album, provides abundant examples of their
approach to singing. The recording begins with wordless, indeed
nonsyllabic, falsetto vocalizations in two-part harmony over a
strummed acoustic guitar. A conventional verse/chorus structure
ensues for three verses describing a bohemian artist (it may be
another self-portrait), with Bolan's voice backed by Took, who

alternately hums, sighs, and sings harmony on the last lines of each verse. The choruses have no words, consisting only of harmonized "la la la"s. The second section, introduced by a fingerpicked acoustic guitar figure, consists of the name Robard de Font Le Roy, with the first name repeated ("Robard, Robard de Font Le Roy"), sung to the fingerpicked melody over and over again by both voices. This section has an experimental feeling not only because of its radical use of repetition and its consequent challenge to discursive meaning, but also because the singers continuously try out different voices and vocal relationships to one another *(The Definitive)*.

On the first two repetitions of the name, Took's backing vocal is lower than Bolan's lead, but then Took goes up to falsetto on the third repetition, and back down on the fourth. For several repetitions, Took alternates between high and low backing vocals and Bolan, too, varies the pitch of his singing. At the end of this section, Took stops singing the name and switches to scat-sung syllables behind Bolan's final iterations of Robard de Font Le Roy. The third section consists of Bolan and Took vocalizing nonsense syllables (punctuated by the occasional "yeah"), often in falsetto, over a rapidly strummed guitar. This last section is energetic, almost vehement at moments (it conveys something of the "rough gnome" effect Welch described) before the tempo slows at the very end. It is essentially a vocal jam, a full minute in duration, that gives the singers ample opportunity to engage in improvisational vocal play that can be heard as consonant with the hippies' emphasis on spontaneity and being in the moment.

"Weilder of Words" is a good example of how Tyrannosaurus Rex developed a version of psychedelic music that foregrounded singing and acoustic musicianship rather than the electric guitar. Like many others of the group's songs, it describes a character, presumably a poet, that a countercultural audience would find appealing in language that signifies more on the level of sound and surreal (or perhaps hallucinatory) imagery than as straightforward exposition: "His opera is torn thru' the haste / of operatic oyster eating evenings of waste." But instead of yielding to instrumental passages and solos, the verses lead to scat singing and ever more abstract vocal jamming that constitutes a vocal equivalent for the progressive dissolution of established structures to be found, for instance, in Pink Floyd's early instrumental pieces. In "Astronomy Dominé" and "Interstellar Overdrive," both from the group's first album *The Piper at the Gates of Dawn* (1967), riffs established at the start of the piece and conventional instrumental sounds give way to looser, more improvisational structures and unconventional noises.[8]

There were, however, some important ways in which Bolan's music for Tyrannosaurus Rex differed from psychedelic rock and folk; in retrospect, these differences are suggestive of subsequent developments. For one thing, the songs are mostly very brief: few are over three minutes in duration and many are under two minutes. As Willis notes, psychedelic rock "had a commitment to larger forms, oppositions and variations, which rock 'n' roll did not" (168); in this respect, Bolan's music, which consisted largely of brief, unitary statements in a basic verse/chorus form, was more in the spirit of rock and roll than that of psychedelic rock. This spirit also manifests itself in his penchant, curious in an underground context, for writing lyrics about cars. The automobile was hardly an object of veneration to the antitechnocratic, antimaterialist, anti-big-business hippie counterculture, yet Bolan offered songs like "Hot Rod Mama" (whose lyric actually refers to motorcycles, a vehicle with some countercultural cachet)[9] and, particularly, "Mustang Ford," which, like "Hot Rod Mama" appears on the group's first album and comes across like a mock car commercial ("It's all put together with alligator leather"). The opening of "Mustang Ford" is a call-and-response sequence initiated by one voice chanting "Boogedie" to elicit a response of "car-bu-re-tor." The song evokes the spirit, if not precisely the sound, of the Beach

8. Paytress notes that Bolan was very impressed with Pink Floyd's first album and with the group's original guitarist and songwriter, Syd Barrett, whom he described as "one of the few people I'd actually call a genius . . . he inspired me beyond belief" (qtd. in *Bolan* 100).

9. Although certain automobiles, such as the Volkswagen Microbus, became iconic within the American hippie counterculture, greater symbolism was attached to the motorcycle, as evidenced by the movie *Easy Rider* (1969) and songs like Arlo Guthrie's "Motorcycle Song" (1967) and, especially, Steppenwolf's "Born to be Wild" (1968). The hippies' enthusiasm for the motorcycle may have stemmed in part from a perceived affinity with the bikers, an older subculture with which they shared some values, particularly a sense of existing permanently outside of and at odds with the dominant culture. This perceived affinity led the hippies to romanticize the likes of the Hell's Angels, with disastrous results at Altamont when the biker "security guards" hired by the Rolling Stones killed a spectator.

Boys, Jan and Dean, and all the other groups of the early 1960s to record songs about hot rods (Tyrannosaurus Rex, *The Definitive*).[10]

The other important thing that set Tyrannosaurus Rex apart from other psychedelic groups was Bolan's voice and his and Took's manner of singing, particularly in the use of falsetto and heavy vibrato. On the one hand, this completely individual vocal sound fit in with the counterculture's emphasis on "extremity and flamboyance of style . . . as the expression of the particular of the special [*sic*]" (Willis 101); Bolan's unique vocal style could certainly be heard as exemplifying the ethic of doing your own thing in defiance of convention. But it is also the case that such highly mannered voices were extremely rare in psychedelic rock. The genre's normative male voice was a baritone tenor, and while some male singers were certainly capable of vocal extremes (Marty Balin of the Jefferson Airplane comes to mind, as does the less well known David Michaels of H. P. Lovecraft, a classically trained singer with a four-octave range), the overwhelming majority of singers in psychedelic rock adopted straightforward, unadorned vocal styles and did not employ such overtly artificial vocal techniques as tremolo, vibrato, and falsetto.[11] Such vocal techniques (the falsetto in particular) were used commonly in such earlier genres as rock and roll, doo-wop, and surf music, and also had a place in the soul music that was contemporaneous with psychedelic rock, but psychedelic rockers shied away from them. Some of the very rare exceptions are instances in which the singer specifically seeks to evoke one of those other genres, as when Pigpen breaks into falsetto during the Grateful Dead's version of "Turn On Your Love Light" (*Live/Dead*). The song was originally recorded by Bobby "Blue" Bland in 1959; the

10. Although Bolan's fixation on automobiles appears repeatedly in his songs, he never acquired a driver's license. He is seen driving in the film *Born to Boogie* (1972) but was able to do so only because the sequence was shot on private property. In one of the many heavy-handed ironies of rock history, Bolan was killed in 1977 at the age of twenty-nine when a car in which he was a passenger went out of control.

11. It is worth noting here that unconventional voices were more welcome on the folkier end of the psychedelic musical continuum. Donovan frequently used a very mannered, breathy, vibrato-laden voice, and Robin Williamson of the Incredible String Band slid around pitches rather than hitting them squarely.

Dead's version incorporates elements of blues, rhythm and blues, and gospel.

The lack of interest in stylized vocal techniques in psychedelic rock undoubtedly resulted in part from the emphasis on instrumental rather than vocal virtuosity: it was much more important to be a great guitarist than a great singer, with the result that many groups, including the Grateful Dead and the Quicksilver Messenger Service, were very strong as instrumentalists but relatively weak vocally. I would also link the mostly straightforward vocal styles of psychedelic rock to the countercultural ethos of authenticity: a highly mannered voice, after all, seems theatrical, artificial, and perhaps unmasculine—one commentator described Bolan's voice at this time as possessing a "soft but sinister androgynous vibrato" (Thomas 34). In opting for a highly mannered vocal presentation, Tyrannosaurus Rex set themselves apart stylistically from psychedelic rock in ways that anticipated glam in its use of sexually ambiguous and artificial-seeming voices.

Bolan's move away from his brand of psychedelic folk music and toward glam rock unfolded over a period of about a year and a half beginning in October 1969, a time that saw the production of two transitional albums and major personnel changes in the group. Bolan's desire to move the group's sound more toward rock was first evidenced by somewhat hesitant changes in Tyrannosaurus Rex's instrumentation. At a London concert in April 1969, Bolan played electric guitar for one song, and Took "moved from percussion to bass guitar" for a few numbers (McLenehan 48). In McLenehan's estimation, Bolan clearly "wanted to go electric" at this point, but Bolan's own assessment of the April concert was that it had been a disaster, and "it seems that he wasn't quite sure how to achieve his aims" within the structure of the group as it then was (McLenehan 42). In July 1969, Tyrannosaurus Rex issued an uncharacteristically "heavy" single, "The King of the Rumbling Spires," that effectively melded the group's continued interest in Tolkienesque mythology with an electric, rock-oriented sound *(The Definitive)*. The single was not a success with audiences, however, probably because it neither gave the group's core hippie following what they expected nor made sufficient appeal to a broader audience.

The most significant change to take place during the transitional period was Steve Peregrine Took's departure from the group. Bolan and Took parted company in October 1969, immediately after a tour of the United States. Took was replaced by Mickey Finn, who, as Bolan cheerfully admitted in interviews, was not a musician but a visual artist, a fairly successful muralist who had done psychedelic exterior decor for businesses that included the Beatles' Apple boutique. Tyrannosaurus Rex had always been dominated by Bolan (the group performed only his songs), but Took had been able to contribute musical ideas and was a significant presence as percussionist and vocalist. Although Finn learned to play the congas and bongos and became a passable percussionist, there was no sense in which he was Bolan's musical partner.

The changes in the group's sound discernable on *A Beard of Stars,* the last Tyrannosaurus Rex album, and *T. Rex,* the first T. Rex album, both of which came out in 1970, reflected relatively gentle shifts in musical priorities rather than any kind of sudden overhaul. The songs on both albums remained largely within Tyrannosaurus Rex's pastoral-Arcadian mode and still referred to the worlds of legend and lore, wizards and witches. The rapidly strummed acoustic guitars and hand percussion are still present on *A Beard of Stars,* as are some of the musical eccentricities ("Organ Blues," for instance, is a glacially paced twelve-bar blues accompanied by a minimalist pattern of slowly changing chords played on a dime store organ, punctuated by a slow pulse on the tablas and sung in an odd, chanting, double-tracked voice). But a short instrumental called "A Beard of Stars," the opening track on that album, suggests difference within continuity. The only instrumental sounds are of electric guitar and finger cymbals: the cymbals represent the kinds of unusual sounds on which Tyrannosaurus Rex's earlier style had been built, while the presence of the electric guitar marks a significant deviation from that style.

Syllabic scat singing and some of the vocal playfulness that distinguished the earlier Tyrannosaurus Rex from the run of psychedelic music were still present on *A Beard of Stars,* as on "The Woodland Bop," though the scat singing there is no longer experimental but is confined to repeating the melody. Bolan's lead vocals are as mannered as ever, perhaps even more so. The earlier vocal jamming has disappeared, to be replaced by more conventional background vocals, albeit often in falsetto, that echo the lyrics of the lead vocal and harmonize with it. In many cases, electric guitar lines and solos appear at moments that previously would have been given over to vocal jamming. Rather than a dialogue between two singers, much of the music on *A Beard of Stars* seems more like a dialogue between Bolan the vocalist and Bolan the electric guitarist. Structurally, these songs proceed conventionally from verse to chorus to guitar solo, with none of the surprising shifts found in earlier compositions. In sum, the new Tyrannosaurus Rex sounded a lot like the old one, but the sound was formalized and shorn of some of its previous eccentricities. The final track on the album, "Elemental Child," pointed toward the future in its focus on Hendrix-influenced rock guitar playing.

The album *T. Rex* continued the formula of combining gestures toward a rock sound with Tyrannosaurus Rex's typical themes and musical concessions to the counterculture, including some vocal raving, use of the toy xylophone, and other somewhat idiosyncratic choices. "The Time of Love is Now," for instance, which features the recorder, could have appeared on virtually any Tyrannosaurus Rex record. A pattern of alternating songs that emphasize the electric guitar with songs that are more acoustically based emerges on this album and sets the pace for the next two T. Rex albums, *Electric Warrior* (1971) and *The Slider* (1972), the recordings that defined the high point of T. Rextasy.[12] If the arrival of the electric guitar was the most significant sonic change introduced on *A Beard of Stars,* the more extensive presence of the electric bass guitar has the same status for *T. Rex.* Producer Tony Visconti had played that instrument with T. Rex in concert on a few occasions; the group's commitment to the instrument became official with the hiring of bassist Steve Currie in November 1970 (though he did not play on the album). The bass guitar gave the T. Rex sound more depth and punch; the presence of a bass player also brought the group one step closer to standard rock instrumentation—the hiring of drummer Bill Fifield (renamed Bill Legend) early in 1971 completed that part of the transition. The other highly significant instrumental change was the addition of a string section, arranged by Visconti. From this point on, the combination of electric rock instrumentation with orchestral strings would be part of the T. Rex sound.[13]

12. In many cases, Bolan's songs did not have rigidly fixed identities as either acoustic or electric numbers. Bolan often tried them out both ways before settling on which instrumentation to use for the recording. Even after choosing electric instrumentation for a particular song, he might perform that song on the acoustic guitar on some occasions.

13. Visconti notes that after he added strings to two Bolan hits, "Ride a White Swan" (1970) and "Hot Love" (1971), he was able to persuade Bolan to use strings on "Get It On (Bang a Gong)" (1971) and all subsequent single releases (liner notes).

One noteworthy feature of *T. Rex* is the presence of two songs Bolan had recorded before: "One Inch Rock," which appeared on the first Tyrannosaurus Rex album, and "The Wizard," which had been Bolan's first single, dating back to 1965. In retrospect, one can interpret the presence of these earlier songs, both of which deal with the supernatural, on the last album to reflect the themes that typified Tyrannosaurus Rex and its link to the hippie counterculture as Bolan's final gesture to the underground. These two recordings also include the last instances of what I have been calling vocal jamming before the solidification of T. Rex's glam rock sound. Both recordings place a great deal of emphasis on this practice. The 1968 recording of "One Inch Rock" features a scat refrain that is repeated four times at the very start before it recedes behind the lead vocal to become the backing vocal pattern. The 1970 version starts off in the same way, but instead of giving way to the lead vocal, the scat pattern leads to a loose, improvised-sounding exchange between two voices (Bolan's and possibly Finn's). The section ends with a repetition of the scat figure, which then becomes background for the lead vocal. All told, there is about a minute of scat singing before the verse starts. This constitutes almost half of the recording and contrasts sharply with the ten seconds of scat that precede the verse in the earlier recording. It may also be significant that Bolan's diction is radically different here than on the earlier recording. On the earlier one, he slurs the words beyond recognition, perhaps in keeping with the hippie counterculture's preference for ambiguity. That the diction on the later recording is very clear and every word is understandable may be symptomatic of Bolan's wanting to reach a more conventionally minded audience.

If "One Inch Rock" is a brief ditty, "The Wizard," at almost nine minutes, is an epic. It begins portentously with the sounding of gongs and multiple cymbals as the melody fades in. In most respects, the song is typical Tyrannosaurus Rex: the rapidly strummed acoustic guitar is there, accompanied by conga drumming and a "dye dye dye" chorus. The electric guitar is used only to provide accents. The second part consists of an extended vocal jam in which Bolan scats, makes mouth percussion noises, screams, moans, caterwauls, eventually repeating the phrase "he was a wizard and he was my friend he was" over and over in multiple voices. His vocal jamming is highlighted by recording production techniques—his voice is double tracked, with an echo effect added in some places. It is also provided with extravagant, shifting musical settings, sometimes involving a string section in addition to strummed acoustic guitar and congas, sometimes an electric guitar, sometimes a solo violin, sometimes combinations of all three. This excessive vocal jam goes on for nearly six minutes and seems cathartic, as if Bolan had to go over the top before he could move on from his pastoral-Arcadian themes and psychedelic vocal play, neither of which appear to any significant extent on the very next T. Rex album.

That album, *Electric Warrior,* and its follow-up, *The Slider,* represent the mature T. Rex style. As a group with full rock instrumentation, T. Rex now had a fuller, deeper sound. Whereas Tyrannosaurus Rex's sound, made up of high-pitched voices and acoustic guitars, was brittle and almost shrill at times, T. Rex's sound was characterized by the contrast between Bolan's high, breathy voice, the even higher falsettos of backing singers Howard Kaylan and Mark Volman,[14] and the depth provided by two percussionists, an electric bassist, and Visconti's string arrangements, which often emphasized cellos and basses that reinforced the bottom end. Bolan typically contributed several guitar tracks: on "Rabbit Fighter" (from *The Slider*) for example, there are multiple acoustic rhythm guitars and two electric lead guitars all playing at once. The result on *Electric Warrior* is a sound that is full and bottom heavy but also crystalline: each instrument and voice has its own presence. On this album, Bolan generally plays his guitar solos at the lower end of the instrument's range, adding further heft to the overall sound. Several tracks on *The Slider,* particularly the hit "Metal Guru," tend more toward a Phil Spectorish "Wall of Sound" production: all the same elements are present, but the sound is more homoge-

14. Howard Kaylan and Mark Volman, whom Bolan met during Tyrannosaurus Rex's 1969 tour of the United States, are American singers whose joint career has taken them from the mid-1960s pop group the Turtles, to Frank Zappa's Mothers of Invention, to their own group as Flo and Eddie. Their extraordinary falsetto background vocals were an integral part of the T. Rex sound on record, though they were never members of the group. In live concerts during the years of T. Rextasy, Currie and Finn would try to reproduce their contributions to the recordings. In later incarnations of the group, Bolan would sometimes be accompanied on stage by other background singers.

nized. The lead vocals are further back in the mix, and it is harder to identify individual instruments.

The relationship between lead and background vocals on T. Rex's recordings is entirely conventional: the background singers either repeat phrases already sung by the lead, sing the same line as the lead, or provide wordless background. Entirely unconventional, however, are the falsetto backing vocals provided by Kaylan and Volman. These are just as extreme in their way as Bolan and Took's vocal jamming had been in an entirely different way. Rather than suggesting the loose, improvisational atmosphere valued by the hippie counterculture, Kaylan and Volman's singing suggests an excessive, camp version of doo-wop. On the recordings, their voices were often electronically distorted to sound otherworldly.

Other aspects of the songs on these two albums evoked the 1950s. Many are composed around conventional blues progressions and shuffle rhythms. One song on each album ("Monolith" on *Electric Warrior* and "Baby Boomerang" on *The Slider*) is explicitly in the doo-wop tradition. As if twitting the underground for its emphasis on musical originality and uniqueness, Bolan plagiarized himself by using exactly the same shuffle (which was not original to him) as the basis for "Telegram Sam" on the later album as he had for "Get It On (Bang a Gong)" on the earlier one. The gambit paid off, as both songs were big hits ("Get It On" reached number one in the British charts in July 1971, while "Telegram Sam" got there barely six months later in January 1972).

There are faint echoes of earlier pastoral-Arcadian themes in the songs on these albums, but they are extremely muted by comparison with Tyrannosaurus Rex. They do not appear in contexts that suggest an underlying mythos, but rather as heightened expressions of sentiments conventional to popular songs. "Mystic Lady," from *The Slider*, for example, calls the titular character a "Sorceress" and refers to the night and the moon. But a description of the sorceress as wearing dungarees and a chorus of "Baby baby baby" make it clear that the singer's imputation of a supernatural identity to a woman should be taken figuratively, rather than literally as in his earlier songs. To a certain extent, references to legend and lore are replaced by references to space travel and technology that create an atmosphere of science fiction rather than Celtic mythology. "The Planet Queen" from *Electric Warrior* is clearly a cousin of the "Liquid Poetess" of "One-Inch Rock." But whereas the Liquid

Poetess casts a spell and shrinks the protagonist to a height of one inch, the Planet Queen uses his "head like an exploder." And while the Liquid Poetess lives in a shack, the chorus of "The Planet Queen" mentions a flying saucer.[15]

In keeping with these references to a popular cultural take on technology, Bolan's automobile fixation came into its own in T. Rex. Five out of the thirteen songs on *The Slider* contain clear and significant car-related images, including "Buick McKane," in which the singer's love object is named after an automobile. Two songs released on singles in 1972, "Cadillac" and "Thunderwing" (whose subject is a car), continued the trend, as did "Jeepster" from *Electric Warrior*. In the songs on *The Slider*, in particular, Bolan engages with the world around him by making references to contemporary popular culture rather than arcana: in the course of the album, he mentions Bob Dylan, John Lennon, legendary disc jockey Alan Freed, the eccentric homeless composer Moondog, Italian film director Pier Paolo Pasolini, and Max's Kansas City, a bar in New York City.

Since "Metal Guru," the opening song of *The Slider*, is often nominated as a quintessential example of glam rock, it is worthwhile to try to identify what makes it so. At two and a half minutes long, the song has the brevity of classic rock and roll. It is in 4/4 time played at a steady, moderate tempo that remains constant from start to finish. This rhythm is the overwhelming feature of the recording: the drums are accentuated in the mix, each downbeat a crash. The lyrics are highly repetitious and have no obvious meaning (it is not at all clear just what a "metal guru" is) but are catchy and easy to sing along with, in part because of a relentless AABB rhyme scheme reinforced by internal rhymes. The lyrics, too, closely reiterate the rhythm: the scansion is such that each syllable or pause accentuates a beat.

The recording starts off energetically, with pounding drums, strummed acoustic rhythm guitar, and electric guitar all accentuating the bar lines. In the middle of the second bar, all three vocalists (Bolan, Kaylan, and Volman) enter with an exuberant, almost shouted "Wah ah ah yeah" that rises then falls in pitch; it yields to

15. At one point, Bolan said that he saw himself as a "science fiction writer who sings" (qtd. in Steve Turner, "Marc Bolan") and claimed to American radio interviewer Michael Cuscuna that he had three science fiction novels on the verge of publication in Great Britain. This claim is an example of Bolan's notorious propensity in interviews to exaggerate his achievements.

nonsyllabic vocals until Bolan begins singing the lyrics. The verses feature a melodic pattern that rises similarly through each verse, then falls back down at the start of the next. Kaylan and Volman's backing vocals also emphasize this rising and falling motion. The instrumental sound becomes denser as the song proceeds: the rock instrumentation is joined first by strings that reiterate the rising and falling melody yet again, then by a horn section. The song's bridge consists solely of the rising and falling melody sung by the backing vocalists and reiterated by the strings, followed by a very brief two-bar electric guitar solo that is not prominent in the mix. The coda is exuberant: voices, saxophones, and strings all play the same two-bar phrase (also the first line of the song) through ten repetitions.

The thumping rhythm around which all else is organized, the short melodic line with a clear rising and falling action, and the repetition of simple lyrics all suggest that "Metal Guru" is not particularly "'head'-centered." It is not music to accompany spiritual exploration, self-examination, or hallucinatory images: it is extroverted, rooted in the here and now, and demands an immediate physical response. It is music for dancing, as ably demonstrated by the teenaged participants on *Top of the Pops* and other television programs. Unlike psychedelic rock, it is not concerned with the demonstration of virtuosity, but with the production of readily accessible, pleasurable music.

Bolan's singing voice was as important a component of T. Rex as it had been of Tyrannosaurus Rex. I indicated earlier that Bolan sang in a voice higher than the normative male rock singer's voice of his time. Although this remained true after the transition to T. Rex, Bolan's vocal delivery changed in important ways. These were incremental changes, more quantitative than qualitative, but they created an effect that was different from that of Tyrannosaurus Rex. Bolan's voice remained quavery and light, but his singing on *Electric Warrior* and *The Slider* is much more obviously controlled than with Tyrannosaurus Rex. His diction is crisp; his *s*'s sibilant to varying degrees (sometimes slightly, sometimes extremely). He continued to use vibrato, but more selectively, generally saving it to accentuate the ends of lines. Whereas the vocal extremes and experimentalism of Tyrannosaurus Rex created the impression of spontaneity and improvisation, Bolan's recorded performances with T. Rex create almost the opposite impression of a singer marshaling his vocal resources in carefully calibrated and entirely premeditated performances. Listening to the multiple takes of the songs on these two albums that are now available,[16] it becomes clear that Bolan's vocal performances were carefully planned: his vocals are almost the same on every take, down to each placement of vibrato, each seemingly spontaneous yelp, hiccup, or exclamation, even when the lyrics vary from take to take. Bolan's vocal performances, always mannered, now seemed calculated as well, belying the spontaneity valued by the hippie counterculture.

Bolan's voice also hints at a queer sexual identity. His high pitch, prissy diction, and hissing "s" sounds seem precious and effeminate, as do Flo and Eddie's falsetto backing vocals. In both musical and medical discourses, the high-breaking male voice and falsetto, along with trill, vibrato, and tremolo, all devices Bolan and his backup singers used, are considered "unnatural" and indications of "deviant" sexual inclinations (Elizabeth Wood 31–32). Bolan's voice was sometimes heard as unnatural—Nancy Erlich, reviewing a 1971 T. Rex performance at the Fillmore East in New York City for *Billboard,* referred to Bolan's "expressive stylized unreal vocals" (qtd. in McLenehan 85)—and was often described as "fey." Barney Hoskyns's reaction to Bolan's voice on "Hot Love," which I quoted at the end of the previous chapter, suggests that he heard Bolan's voice as a queer voice.

Bolan frequently created cognitive dissonance by performing hard-rocking songs or heterosexual love songs in a queer voice normally considered to be at odds with both. This combination implied a bisexual persona, a suggestion reinforced by Bolan's self-description in the song "Ripoff" (from *Electric Warrior*) as both "the king of the highway" and "the queen of the hop." The two sides of Bolan's ambivalently gendered persona are illustrated on the covers of *Electric Warrior* and *The Slider:* the silhouetted electric guitarist edged in gold against a black background standing in front of his huge amplifier on the cover of *Electric Warrior* depicts Bolan in the iconic image of macho guitar hero (his pose is somewhat reminiscent of Led Zeppelin guitarist Jimmy Page's stance), while the cover of *The Slider,* which Paytress describes accurately as a "monochrome image of Bolan playing Twenties vamp Theda Bara playing the Mad Hatter" (*Bolan* 213), presents him as an elusive, feminine seductress.

16. Studio outtakes from the recording sessions for *Electric Warrior* are readily available on the 30th Anniversary CD edition issued in 2001 and the earlier *Electric Warrior Sessions* CD (1996).

Although Bolan's voice and T. Rex's group sound would never cease to be distinctive, the transition from Tyrannosaurus Rex to T. Rex was largely a transition from a group that was idiosyncratic in ways that endeared it to the underground to a musically more conventional group that could attract a broader audience. One of the central means by which Bolan effected the transition was to transform himself from a folky acoustic guitar strummer into an electric rock guitarist. It may seem a bit paradoxical that taking up the electric guitar and remaking himself into a guitar hero was a means by which Bolan distanced himself from the hippie counterculture and psychedelic rock, given the emphasis on electric guitar virtuosity within those contexts. As I have shown, however, the initial appeal of Tyrannosaurus Rex to the counterculture was not based on their identity as rockers, but rather as purveyors of a different kind of psychedelic music that was more folk in orientation, both musically and in its thematic emphasis on pastoral-Arcadian subjects. The electric guitar was not a part of that vision.

Bolan's adopting the electric guitar as his primary instrument went hand in hand with his turning away from the fantasy themes that had endeared him to his countercultural audience. In the end, however, it seems that Bolan's decisive break with the underground came about not because of his having electrified his music or specifically because he stopped producing Tolkienesque fables. It was, rather, because he sought to have hit singles and a bigger audience. "Reaching a wider public is what we want," Bolan said early in 1971. "If 'underground' means being on a show screened at midnight and watched by fifteen people—then we're out of it" (qtd. in Steve Turner, "Marc Bolan"). Bolan's eagerness to move beyond the confines of a small but enthusiastic hippie audience that prized his music in part for its obscurity and difficulty by embracing commercialism earned him the enmity of the waning underground scene.

In strictly musical terms, the transition from Tyrannosaurus Rex to T. Rex was gradual, and there were many continuities between Bolan's music for both groups. The change in physical performance style entailed in this transition, which also unfolded over a period of time, was far more dramatic, though it began simply enough: Bolan stood up while playing. The significance of this posture is clear in the context of Tyrannosaurus Rex's relationship to the counterculture. A crucial influence on Tyrannosaurus Rex's performance style was a concert Bolan attended in 1967. His producer at the time, Simon Napier-Bell, has described its impact:

> It was a Ravi Shankar performance of Indian music. . . . It was an incredible contrast to what we'd just experienced on the John's Children tour. This man played to a hushed, reverential audience in the simplest possible way imaginable—seated on a carpet and surrounded by joss sticks which filled the air with a pungent smell. That really tripped Marc's mind. I think that was the moment he realized what he should be doing. (Qtd. in Paytress, *Bolan* 89)[17]

Tyrannosaurus Rex fully adopted Shankar's performance style, including the carpet, the incense, the seated posture, and even the reverential audience. The group's original underground audience was uninterested in dancing or singing along; they valued music "for *listening to*" (Willis 156) and acted accordingly. Visconti described the audience at Middle Earth by saying, "the circle of fans around [Tyrannosaurus Rex] were silent and waving like a wheat field to the music" (qtd. in Chapman, "Marc Bolan"). (This was another reason for the hippies' later dissatisfaction with T. Rex: the group began to attract a younger and more vigorously responsive audience whose behavior alienated the remnants of the hippie audience.)

A publicity photograph from 1969, reproduced in Paytress's biography, shows Bolan and Took in their personae as countercultural musicians. Both are seated cross-legged on the floor, which is how they performed. Each is wearing his characteristic version of hippie fashion: Took is dressed in the long cloak in which he appeared frequently; his hair falls onto his shoulders and he has a wispy mus-

---

17. Although Tyrannosaurus Rex took up an Indian performer's style and there were references to the East in their work ranging from the song "Eastern Spell" *(The Definitive),* which reflects the counterculture's enthusiasm for all things associated with the East, to miscellaneous references to jasmine tea and other exotica, to some of the instruments Took used and some of the vocal styles Bolan and Took employed, they were never as seriously interested in Eastern music, culture, religion, or philosophy as George Harrison, the members of the Incredible String Band, or even Donovan. For a brief discussion of the influence of Eastern mysticism on the hippie counterculture, see Stuart Hall (178). Roszak traces this influence back to the Beat generation's interest in Zen Buddhism (124–54). Whiteley notes the influence of Eastern music on psychedelic rock at various points in *The Space Between the Notes.*

Marc Bolan, guitar hero, performing with T. Rex in 1972.
© MichaelOchsArchives.com.

tache and goatee. Bolan wears an ornately brocaded, high-collared white shirt, bell-bottomed dark pants, and pointy suede boots; his curly, studiously unkempt hair drapes over his collar. Took's appearance refers to his hobbit affiliation, while Bolan comes across somewhat as the troubadour he sometimes called himself. Each is playing an exotic-seeming musical instrument: Took taps on an African drum, while Bolan plays an acoustic guitar with a pear-shaped body that makes it seem more like a lute or bouzouki. Both appear to be lost in musical concentration: Took looks down, his eyes unfocused, while Bolan's half-closed eyes seem to be gazing upon an internal space.

This photograph provides a good sense of the image Tyrannosaurus Rex presented in concert, an image of meditative young hippie musicians who were serious about their music, esoteric in their interests, and concerned to provide their audiences with a thoughtful experience. Once it solidified, T. Rex's image was in stark contrast to that of the two gentle hippies: Bolan stood up and was in almost constant motion while playing his electric guitar; he wore vividly colored, extravagant outfits, makeup, and glitter; and he addressed himself directly to his audience. The former bopping elf became "a sinister little angel out of the densest and most exotic prison visions of Jean Genet. With glitter around his eyes and stars in his hair and dressed in satin and sequins and girl's shoes from Anello and Davide's, Marc is the Queen of the Hop, right in the middle of the Mick Jagger gap" (Thomas 32).

Looking back in 1973 on his own recent achievements, Bolan commented that "ninety-five per cent of my success is because of the way I *look*. You have to accept that. . . . The Beatles were *mop tops*. The Stones were dirty, never-washed bad boys. That's what people pick up on. The music is secondary" (qtd. in Crowe 40). This statement, which clearly defies the underground's emphasis on "the sound" and distrust of the visual aspects of performance, also demonstrates Bolan's understanding of how performance personae function and are constructed in the context of popular music. His first step in constructing the T. Rex image was his selection of Finn to replace Took. Bolan did not choose Finn for his musical prowess but for how he looked and, more particularly, how they looked together. Bolan and Finn made an attractive male couple, a fact that Bolan exploited. The gatefold cover for the final Tyrannosaurus Rex album, *A Beard of Stars,* consists of two sepia-toned close-up photographic portrait heads, with Bolan's face on the front and Finn's on the back. Opening the gatefold and looking at the whole image, one sees the dark-haired Finn (whose resemblance to Took was striking) looking straight out at the viewer, while Bolan, wearing a frilly collar, looks fondly toward Finn, his eyes gazing off into the middle distance. The cover for *T. Rex* shows the two of them standing side by side in a field, Finn a little bit behind Bolan (a pose they would repeat in publicity photographs); both are looking out at the viewer. These images seem calculated to suggest a (fictional) musical partnership with strong homosocial overtones.[18]

18. Although Finn was presented on the covers of these two albums as Bolan's equal partner, that was never the case. It is significant that he was

Bolan's physical performance with T. Rex underwent a stepwise transformation similar to that of the group's music. If a performance of "Jewel" filmed for German television[19] (probably in February 1971) is any indication, the trio version of T. Rex performed much in the manner of a psychedelic rock group. "Jewel," from the first T. Rex album, was one of the songs Bolan used in the early days of the new group to demonstrate his prowess on the electric guitar: live performances of the song generally ended with an extended guitar solo. The television performance is in this vein, and the performance is physically subdued in a manner suitable to a display of musical seriousness. Bolan, dressed in a tie-dyed T-shirt, played standing up, but was mostly still when singing at the microphone; both he and bassist Steve Currie looked down at their instruments and their own hands when playing and soloing, glancing at each other only occasionally to coordinate their efforts. During Currie's bass solo, Bolan played a tambourine, his face lowered as if he was entirely focused on his colleague's work.

When playing his extended solo, Bolan employed a variety of gestures rock guitarists commonly use as physical representations of the music they are playing: lifting the guitar while playing higher notes is an example. Bolan not only lifted the guitar but also lifted his shoulders and raised himself up on his heels as he played higher notes, letting both the guitar and himself fall back down as he moved to lower pitches. Enacting the well-worn analogy between rock music and sexual arousal, Bolan opened his mouth and sighed at climactic moments in the solo. Bolan also frequently used physical gestures to mark structural transitions in the music. At the start of his guitar solo, he leaned back from the instrument while simultaneously drawing his right hand away from the strings and back to them in a sweeping gesture. At the end of that gesture, he placed the guitar in a position almost perpendicular to his body. This gesture, too, is sexual in nature, evoking the cliché of the phallic guitar. But

---

always positioned *behind* Bolan in these images. *T. Rex* was the last album on whose cover Finn appeared at all. Although he continued to be represented as the second most important member of the group in album credits and some publicity shots, the covers to *Electric Warrior, The Slider*, and *Tanx* (1973) feature photographs of Bolan alone. Whereas the cover for *A Beard of Stars* showed Finn as the other side of Tyrannosaurus Rex, the front cover of *The Slider* shows Bolan's face in a photograph by Ringo Starr and the verso shows Bolan in the same pose, shot from the rear.

19. All of the German television performances discussed here are available on *The Best of Musik Laden* DVD.

it also had a musical meaning: it served to mark the end of the verse/chorus section of the piece and the beginning of extended instrumental solos. By moving his torso and arm away from the guitar and repositioning it, Bolan suggested that he needed to get into the correct physical relationship to his gear in order to do the hard work of soloing that lay ahead.

A performance of "Jeepster" (from *Electric Warrior*) also made for German television (but in the fall of 1971 when the group had become a quartet) proceeded similarly. Bolan wore a soft button-down blue shirt and jeans. His movements were again keyed primarily to the music: he moved his head to the beat and also shook it to emphasize points in the lyrics. He lowered his eyebrows in an expression of concentration and earnestness; at some points, he closed his eyes. He moved his lower body more than in the performance of "Jewel," primarily in rhythmic response to the music. When he played his guitar solo, he held his mouth in a pout or moue, an expression that here seemed to reflect the concentrated effort required to perform the solo. When performing a shorter solo at the end of the song, Bolan became more animated, his facial expression one of high drama. This transition is reflective of the music: the solo he was playing was more aggressive and dissonant than the earlier one and the performance itself was building toward its conclusion. Bolan's switch to a more overtly theatrical style of physical performance marked those musical developments.

By the time of a second television performance of "Jeepster" for British television that dates from early in 1972, roughly three months after the one just discussed, Bolan's physical performance is radically different even though the musical one is not (T. Rex, "Jeepster"). He wears a garish, glittering leopard print tailcoat and makeup. He is animated and moves constantly throughout the performance, which is mimed and lip-synched. Bolan uses the guitar much more as a dancing partner than as a musical instrument. Even when the recording to which he is miming indicates that he should be feigning playing the guitar, he often employs it as a prop with which to react to the music much more than the putative source of the music. Similarly, his movements, gestures, and facial expressions, which are far more exaggerated than in the earlier performances I have discussed, are not musically motivated to anything like the same extent. Rather, Bolan took a vocabulary of movement and gesture that is associated in musical performance with the physical expression of musical sound, structure, and the emotions attendant on playing, and used it essentially as an autonomous choreographic language from which to build physical routines.

It would be easy enough to dismiss this divorce of physical performance from the musical sound it is conventionally supposed to express on the grounds that this was a mimed performance. I argue, however, that what Bolan did when freed from the obligation to play and sing gives us an idea of the visual conception he had of his performance persona at this point. This supposition is borne out by looking at a third performance of "Jeepster," filmed live by former Beatle turned filmmaker Ringo Starr at the Empire Pool, Wembley in March 1972 for use in the film *Born to Boogie,* released in December of the same year. Bolan appeared in a white satin jacket with broad lapels, shiny green satin bell-bottoms, and a T-shirt with his own face on it peeking out from under the jacket (there was also a life-size cutout figure of him on stage). Bolan used many of the same gestures and physical routines in this performance as in the televised one. While singing, he stood at the microphone, rocking side to side to the beat. On the second line of each chorus, however, he moved away from the microphone to indulge in a bit of physical business. Near the end of the song, he turned his profile to the audience, put his hand on his hip and squealed girlishly, then crouched into a Chuck Berry–like duck walk, stood back up part way and Charlestoned with his knees bent, then stood up fully. None of these movements had any specific formal or thematic association with the music being played or the effort and pleasure of producing it. It seemed, rather, that Bolan performed them for their own sake. During "Baby Strange" at Wembley, Bolan sucked in his cheeks and made his moue again. But this time, it did not denote concentration and the effort of playing guitar: it was purely a part of his feminine male persona. Bolan was showing off and playing to the crowd at these moments, without question, but in a way that abstracted musicianly gestures from their usual functions and meanings, transforming them into pure spectacle and subordinating musical expressivity to the presentation of his persona.

In a 1968 essay for *Crawdaddy* addressing the question of physical performance and theatricality in rock music, Michael Rosenbaum draws a distinction between what he calls internal and external styles. "Briefly, the Internal is spontaneous emotional movement by a performer or group. Theater springs from the motion that comes from intensity of musicianship." The External, by contrast, "can be defined as theater set apart from the music"

(25). As Rosenbaum indicates, the hippie counterculture valued the internal and regarded with suspicion any action that smacked of externality. As Rosenbaum also points out, however, there is no clear-cut distinction between the two categories: actions perceived initially as internal gestures can become externalized through repetition. When Jimi Hendrix immolated his guitar at the Monterey Pop Festival, for example, his action was perceived as an internal gesture to which he was moved on the spot (regardless of whether or not he planned it in advance). If he had burned a guitar at any subsequent performance, it would have been perceived as external since repetition seems to be at odds with the spontaneity of the internal gesture. There is a paradox here, of course. After Monterey, Hendrix's audiences all wanted to see him destroy a guitar and may even have felt disappointed if he did not.[20] Had he burned a guitar at every performance, however, his doing so would have been perceived as calculated and insincere. By taking gestures, movements, and facial expressions associated with musical expressivity, and therefore with internality, and converting them to self-consciously executed, clearly external routines, Bolan dramatized this issue, mocked the counterculture's emphasis on the value of spontaneity, and laid the foundations for a new kind of rock performance that courted overt theatricality.

The self-consciousness and externality (in Rosenbaum's sense) of Bolan's physical performances were evident in part from his use of movements associated with other performers (though not necessarily created by them), including Eddie Cochran's twists and turns and any number of movements appropriated from Hendrix. He employed a variety of such movements, notably Mick Jagger's strut, in which the head faces the audience while the body is in profile, and Pete Townshend's famous "windmill" guitar gesture. Bolan was direct and unabashed about these appropriations and their purpose: "We're the best visual band in the world. I've watched Pete [Townshend] and I've seen Hendrix. I've seen 'em all for years. I've copped everything they did" (qtd. in Marsh, "Marc Bolan" 40). It is clear that Bolan's emphasis on the visual aspects of musical performance flew in the face of psychedelic rock's belief

---

20. Michael Lydon relays this exchange between fans at a Hendrix concert: "'Will he burn it tonight?' a neat blonde asked of her boyfriend, squashed in beside her on the packed floor of the Fillmore auditorium. 'He did at Monterey,' the boyfriend said" (67).

that "the sound is enough." But Bolan goes further here by suggesting that the characteristic physical gestures employed by particular musicians do not belong to them. Rather than seeing such gestures as authentic (internal) expressions of particular subjectivities, Bolan treated them as bits of spectacle to be gathered up and used as he saw fit to create an impressive performance. His selection and arrangement of other people's routines inevitably appeared external, planned, and self-conscious. Bolan's physical performances with T. Rex seemed to result from deliberation rather than choices made on the fly and were as mannered and stylized as his vocal performances.

Another aspect of Bolan's performance style that made it seem self-conscious was the way he set specific gestures or routines apart from the overall flow of his performance. For instance, both Hendrix and Bolan simulated masturbation on the guitar as a substitute penis (Hendrix likely learned this routine while a journeyman on the southern chitlin circuit, while Bolan likely acquired it from observing Hendrix). But whereas Hendrix incorporated this particular act seamlessly into his physical performance, Bolan framed it in ways that set it apart from the rest of what he was doing. The difference can be seen by contrasting Hendrix's performance of "Foxy Lady" at Monterey with Bolan's of "Get It On" at Wembley.

After singing the last verse before his guitar solo, Hendrix stepped away from the microphone, leaned back, and lifted his left arm high above his head as he played high notes with just his right hand all the way down on the fretboard (Hendrix was left-handed). Then he started to move, boogying across the stage to his left, swinging his left arm up and away from the guitar after playing, so that his arm movements punctuated the rhythm. Arriving at his destination, Hendrix bent over the guitar toward the audience, humped his pelvis against it in time to the solo he was playing, then straddled the guitar, slowly bringing it up between his legs as he simultaneously pivoted his body to his right toward another section of the audience. After pivoting, he carefully lifted his left leg over the guitar, "dismounting" from it, then turned back a bit to his left toward the center section of the audience. He moved the guitar to his left side, perpendicular to his body and stroked the neck in a masturbatory gesture. After this climactic gesture, he stepped back up to the microphone and resumed singing. In the course of this complex set of movements, Hendrix clearly treated the guitar alternately as instrument, dancing partner, sex partner, and phallus. He moved like a dancer, fluidly and seamlessly, from one position or tableau to the next, always in relation to the music he was simultaneously playing. His movements thus seemed to be internal, motivated directly by his immediate experience of playing the music, an effect reinforced by the fact that Hendrix's eyes were closed throughout the performance and the way he often lowered his head as if he were completely caught up in the act of playing. He seemed confined to his own experience and indifferent to an audience whose response he appeared not to notice.

Bolan's performance of guitar masturbation occurred at a similar point in the song: he had finished the verses and was playing a guitar solo. But whereas Hendrix used his movements as a physical expression of what he was playing, Bolan used them to define a separate moment in his overall performance. He stopped playing and marched in place at the microphone, clapping his hands above his head to incite the audience. He paraded around the stage hitting two tambourines against each other and, at one point, joined Finn at the congas and played them briefly. It seemed at this point as if Bolan had been cut loose from any specific musical responsibilities and was mischievously looking for onstage opportunities. He strutted back center stage with one tambourine, crouched down facing the audience with the neck of his guitar jutting up from his crotch (an image that was repeated endlessly in the group's publicity) and began rubbing the tambourine against the strings on the body of the guitar. He slid the tambourine up and down the neck and strings, rising to more of a standing position. When he reached "climax," he flung the tambourine up the neck of the guitar into the audience. He then moved back to the microphone and resumed clapping his hands over his head and inciting the audience before returning to his guitar solo.

Rather than containing the masturbation routine within his playing of a guitar solo, Bolan clearly demarcated it as a separate, almost autonomous, part of the performance. He framed the event by standing at the microphone, not playing but addressing the audience, both before and after it. The sheer length of the bit also made it feel autonomous; whereas Hendrix incorporated all of the physical action I described into a forty-second solo, Bolan devoted well over a minute to the masturbation scene alone; several minutes elapsed from the time he ceased his guitar solo to the point at which he resumed it. This hiatus in the solo also marked the sounds he produced by rubbing the tambourine against the guitar as not belonging to the solo. Whereas the sounds Hendrix produced by stroking the neck of his guitar fit the compositional logic of his solo, the sounds Bolan produced came across more as by-products of his physical action. And while Hendrix at least appeared to be wrapped up in his own experience of the music and indifferent to the audience, Bolan addressed the audience directly, served as its cheerleader, and played his entire performance to it.

Performance theorist Richard Schechner includes in a list of fundamental modes of performance the categories "doing" and "showing doing." To do is simply to carry out an action; " 'showing doing' is performing: pointing to, underlining, and displaying doing" (*Performance Studies* 22). Using these terms, one could describe Hendrix as simply "doing" the actions he performed: they seemed to flow out of him naturally. Bolan, on the other hand, did not just carry out certain actions but also pointed to and underlined the fact that he was carrying them out.[21] His style therefore falls under the heading of "showing doing" rather than simply doing. Rosenbaum's terms align roughly with Schechner's: in the context of rock performance, gestures that appear internal would be perceived as "doing," while external, more overtly theatrical gestures would be a form of "showing doing." It should be clear that I am not making a statement about the performers' intentions or methods here: it is perfectly possible that Hendrix's seemingly spontaneous, internal "doing" was in fact carefully planned and choreographed, just as it is perfectly possible that Bolan was behaving spontaneously at Wembley. The distinctions among internal and external, doing and showing doing, are primarily differences in the *impression* created by certain performed actions on the audience and not necessarily differences of intent or procedure on the part of the performers.

At some point in all of T. Rex's concerts prior to mid-1973, drummer Legend and bassist Currie would leave the stage to Bolan, who would perform on acoustic guitar. In the Wembley footage,

21. Critical reaction to Bolan's self-conscious performance style was not always positive. Don Heckman, writing in the *New York Times* of a 1972 T. Rex performance at Carnegie Hall, for instance, chided Bolan by saying, "One is constantly aware of the mannerism rather than the music, of the self-consciousness rather than the total energetic performance" (qtd. in McLenehan 117). A critical stance such as Heckman's, which sees mannerism and self-consciousness as necessarily in conflict with "the music," clearly reflects the countercultural values Bolan was challenging.

Bolan sits down cross-legged on the stage and plays by himself before he is joined by Finn on bongos. The practice of performing an acoustic set was fairly common among rock groups in the early 1970s: Led Zeppelin usually included such a set in their concerts, as did the Rolling Stones, the Grateful Dead, and such lesser-knowns as Wild Turkey (whose acoustic set I witnessed at the Roundhouse in London in 1971). Susan Fast characterizes this moment in Led Zeppelin's concerts by saying that "the acoustic set in performance involved band members . . . losing the readiness of 'action' that comes with standing and, especially, moving—of commanding, dominating, owning the performance space by using all of it. By sitting down, band members became passive, vulnerable, much less powerful" (82). Fast goes on to suggest that fans perceived the acoustic set as a moment of greater intimacy between musicians and audience and also a demonstration of true musicianship. In the case of T. Rex, it had another meaning as well, since it represented a step back in time for the group, a momentary reversion from T. Rex to Tyrannosaurus Rex, especially when Finn joined Bolan (indeed, this sequence in *Born to Boogie* probably provides some sense of what the later Tyrannosaurus Rex looked like in performance).

The language Fast uses in her description of Led Zeppelin's acoustic set suggests that this performance practice has a gendered dimension. As Fast implies through her description of a transition from activity to passivity, the binary opposition that Hélène Cixous identifies as the dominant characterization of masculinity and femininity in Western societies (68), it is a moment at which male rock musicians surrender their machismo to occupy a more feminine position. The passivity and vulnerability of the seated position is underscored by the substitution of the acoustic guitar for the electric guitar. Mavis Bayton points out that in the 1960s, the acoustic guitar became a feminized instrument, associated with such folky female performers as Joni Mitchell, Joan Baez, and Judy Collins. By contrast, "playing electric guitar is 'masculine'" (Bayton 38–39). By moving back and forth between his presence as standing electric guitar hero and seated acoustic strummer, Bolan implicitly moved among a number of gender identifications, especially since his version of the guitar hero figure was an effeminate one.

This multiplicity of performed gender identities was dramatized in a 1973 appearance by T. Rex on *The Cilla Black Show* on BBC Television. First, the whole group mimed a performance of "Mad

Donna," with Bolan "playing" electric guitar and vamping in a feather boa (another idea he probably borrowed from Hendrix, who wore one at Monterey, though it could also have been a response to Bowie, who also used a feather boa as an accessory in his Ziggy Stardust concerts). At the end of that performance, Bolan conspicuously swapped his electric guitar for an acoustic instrument, sat down on a stool next to a seated Cilla Black, draping her with his boa. The two singers then performed a version of Bolan's "Life's a Gas" as a romantic duet, with Bolan playing a conventionally masculine role and Black a conventionally feminine one (*Marc Bolan*).[22]

This performance illustrates what Judith Butler calls the "proliferation" of gender identities that has the effect of destabilizing gender norms (31). Bolan first occupies the masculine position of electric guitarist, but does so queerly by wearing a feminizing feather boa. His switch to acoustic guitar and his taking up a seated posture are signs that he is moving to the feminine realm represented by Black; he surrenders the boa—initially a sign of queerness—to her, thus converting it from a sign of perverse gender identity to a normative sign. Although Bolan is feminized by playing acoustic guitar while sitting down, he is masculine within that feminine posture by virtue of the fact that he plays the masculine role in the romantic duet with Black. Of course, he sings that role in his typically queer voice. This seemingly simple television performance unpacks into a dizzying array of malleable, overlapping gender identifications; as Butler suggests, this proliferation of gendered identities indicates the intrinsic instability of all such identities.

Even though the musical and performance styles that led to the T. Rextasy of 1971 and 1972 were in many ways direct challenges to the values and aesthetics of the hippie counterculture, there were other ways in which Bolan never fully divorced himself from that connection. The persistence of the acoustic set suggests that T. Rex did not so much replace Tyrannosaurus Rex as swallow it whole. Producer Visconti observes, "Even when we were making the pop albums and the flower children were no more he said we had to

---

22. McLenehan describes this performance uncharitably as "firmly in the realms of kitsch" (145). I disagree—I find the duet with Cilla Black to be rather affecting. The fact that a song Bolan wrote for himself works well as a romantic duet is a tribute to his songwriting skill.

include some special effects like flanging and phasing for 'the heads'" (qtd. in Chapman, "Marc Bolan"). Several of the recordings on both *Electric Warrior* and *The Slider* also contain a few seconds of studio chat, and several songs do not have clean endings but just dissolve as various musicians stop playing. The inclusion of these informal moments gives even very tightly constructed pop songs a little bit of the spontaneity so prized by the underground.

Bolan's continued desire to be perceived as authentic in hippie terms is nowhere more evident than in the film *Born to Boogie*, directed by Ringo Starr. The parts of the film shot live at Wembley show T. Rextasy in full force: Bolan performs the preening glam star to a throng of youngsters who love every minute of it. Interspersed with this footage, however, is ponderous material shot on John Lennon's estate that features an unfortunate staging by T. Rex and entourage of the Mad Tea Party from *Alice in Wonderland*, a countercultural favorite for its hallucinatory imagery and elements that can be interpreted as drug references, all commemorated in Jefferson Airplane's "White Rabbit" (1967). The scene is little more than embarrassing (though it does contain an interesting miniconcert by Bolan on acoustic guitar accompanied by a string ensemble under Visconti's direction), and the other nonconcert footage betrays the listlessness and directionlessness of many underground productions. Much as Bolan may have relished his association with the iconic Starr, the film is not so much T. Rex's version of the Beatles' seminal rock film *A Hard Day's Night* (1964) as it is T. Rex's version of the Beatles' own self-produced debacle, the television film *Magical Mystery Tour* (1967).

The other important limitation to Bolan's Glam 1.0 was the fact that the rest of T. Rex comported themselves entirely as a conventional rock band. Whereas most later glam rockers would find ways of allowing whole groups to function as glam ensembles, at least sartorially, T. Rex always appeared to consist of an extraordinary glam front man backed by a regular rock group with which he did not interact significantly.

These constraints notwithstanding, Bolan more than deserves credit for having pioneered glam rock. He demonstrated definitively that a performance persona is not an organic outgrowth's of a musician's individuality and relationship to a community but a performative construct. I have shown in this chapter that he developed through both his vocal and physical performances a queer persona whose implied gender and sexuality were polymorphous and malleable, a persona that would serve as the basic template for glam rockers' self-presentations. Inseparable from the development of such a persona, Bolan introduced a heightened, self-consciously theatrical style of performing rock that flew directly in the face of psychedelic rock's emphasis on inner-directed, serious-seeming musicianship. John Street has summarized the transition from psychedelia to glam by noting that the countercultural "injunction to 'feed your head' was superseded by 'the exhortation to paint your face'" (172). No single figure embodied the spirit of that cultural transformation or urged it on more energetically than Marc Bolan.

4. who can i be now?

David Bowie and the
Theatricalization of Rock

What I'm doing is theatre and only theatre.
—David Bowie, 1976 (qtd. in Rook 134)

If Marc Bolan brought an implicitly theatrical sensibility to bear on the performance of rock music, David Bowie sought explicitly to perform rock *as theater*. Bowie achieved the synthesis of rock and theater toward which he had worked since the mid-1960s with his creation of glam icon Ziggy Stardust, the bisexual space alien, in 1972. Bowie not only envisioned the rock concert as a staged, costumed, and choreographed theatrical performance, he understood his own performing and his relationship to his audience in actorly terms rather than the communitarian terms that defined performance for psychedelic rockers. Rather than developing a consistent persona, Bowie sang in many voices and from many subject positions without identifying clearly with any of them. By asserting the performativity of gender and sexuality through the queer Ziggy Stardust persona, Bowie challenged both the conventional sexuality of rock culture and the concept of a foundational sexual identity more fully and directly than Bolan.

In the first two sections of this chapter, I discuss aspects of Bowie's career prior to the Ziggy years that contributed to his development of the glam rock persona: his interest in theater and his equivocal relationship to the counterculture and rock culture of

"Who Can I Be Now?" is the title of a song David Bowie wrote and recorded in 1974 during the sessions for his *Young American* album. It was not released until 1991 when it appeared as a bonus track on the CD version.

the 1960s. I suggest that his basic assumptions concerning rock performance were analogous to those of a stage actor in that he saw
himself moving from role to role rather than developing a single
persona even as he positioned himself within the countercultural
arena. In discussing Bowie's development of the Ziggy Stardust persona in the third section, I show how Bowie borrowed a set of
tropes associated with outer space from psychedelic rock only to
put them to very different ideological use. In the penultimate section, I discuss the ways Bowie posited gender and sexuality as performative through his articulation of his public image both onstage
and off. The chapter ends with an analysis of how the various
themes Bowie explored in the early 1970s—gender performance,
theatricality, challenges to the ideology of authenticity—came
together in his concert performances as Ziggy Stardust.

In light of the countercultural antitheatricalism I discussed in chapter 1, it is highly significant that one of Bowie's primary models for
his own artistic practice in the mid-1960s was the theater. Not the
radical experimental and political theater that burgeoned during
the war in Vietnam, but the musical theater. As early as 1966, Bowie
had been involved in a project for a musical entitled *Kids on the
Roof* that never came to fruition (Cann 25). Bowie reiterated the
desire to produce a stage musical numerous times during the early
part of his career, though none of these ventures was ever realized.
Three of his first eight albums began as concepts for stage musicals.
Bowie's first, eponymous album, issued in 1967, contained material
left over from *Kids on the Roof*. The album that made Bowie a star,
The Rise and Fall of Ziggy Stardust and the Spiders from Mars
(1972), was originally imagined as a show for London's West End.
And *Diamond Dogs* (1974) contained songs Bowie wrote for a
planned stage or television version of George Orwell's *1984* in
which he was to star—this production was announced at the same
time as a plan to bring *Ziggy Stardust* to Broadway (Harvey).
    From the perspective of popular music culture, the musical the-
ater is a highly problematic form. Although the musical theater and
popular music enjoyed a symbiotic relationship until the advent of
rock and roll in the mid-1950s, their relationship became one of
mutual antagonism thereafter (Bering 110–11).[1] This schism only

---

1. Prior to the rock era, songs from musicals often became pop hits, further
enhancing the popularity of the plays from which they came. Although this

widened in the 1960s, due partly to the increased political and cultural radicalism of rock and the perceived conservatism of the musical stage. *Hair* (1967) and other so-called rock musicals notwithstanding, rock musicians and composers have not been welcomed on that stage anymore than musical theater performers are thought to belong in rock (Wollman). By aligning himself with a cultural form regarded as inauthentic by rock standards, Bowie placed himself somewhat at odds with the rock culture he also wanted to join.[2]

Bowie pursued his theatrical ambitions in part by gaining what he considered the necessary skills. In 1967, he studied dance at the Dance Centre in London and mime and movement under Lindsay Kemp.[3] He performed with Kemp's troupe in a piece called *Pierrot in Turquoise,* and later developed his own mime play on "an anti-communist theme," *Yet-San and the Eagle,* which he performed in 1968 at the Royal Festival Hall on a bill that included Tyrannosaurus Rex and on a tour during which he opened for Marc Bolan's group (Cann 46). In interviews, Bowie often distanced him-

---

phenomenon persisted into the rock era (the score for *Hair* generated at least three chart hits in 1969: Oliver's "Good Morning Starshine," "Hair" by the Cowsills, and the Fifth Dimension's version of "Aquarius/Let the Sun Shine In"), the relationship on which it was based became obsolete as the cultural realms of musical theater and popular music became ever more discrete. Recent years, however, have seen an inversion of the original relationship: now, the musical theater frequently borrows songs that originated as pop hits. Typically, each play is built around the work of a single artist or group, the songs inserted into a (usually) fictional plot. The first such play was *Mama Mia!* (1999), developed from songs by Abba. Other examples include *Movin' Out* (2002), from Billy Joel's music, *We Will Rock You* (2002), based on material by Queen, and *Tonight's the Night* (2003) from Rod Stewart's hits. Broadway promises a plethora of such plays in 2005, including *Good Vibrations,* from the Beach Boys' music, *All Shook Up,* based on Elvis Presley's hits, and *Lennon,* developed from John Lennon's music. The remarkable global success of this genre demands critical analysis.

2. The Bonzo Dog Doo Dah Band (later known as the Bonzo Dog Band), a British rock group with a penchant for satire to whom I shall also refer in future notes, were well known on the underground scene. On their first album, *Gorilla* (1967), they satirized the earnestness of *The Sound of Music* through a mocking performance of the title song in which a solemn testimonial to the emotional experience of seeing the film version of the play is followed by a cacophony as the hills come alive with multiple styles of music simultaneously. (Of course, the Bonzo Dog Band, like The Mothers of Invention, also satirized the counterculture and rock music as well.)

3. For more on Lindsay Kemp, see Senelick (409–13).

self from his identity as a musician in favor of describing himself as a theater artist. In 1972, for example, he told Charles Shaar Murray of the *New Musical Express*, "I don't profess to have music as my big wheel and there are a number of other things as important to me apart from music. Theatre and mime, for instance" (48).[4] That same year, he was quoted in *Rolling Stone* as saying, "I feel like an actor when I'm on stage, rather than a rock artist" (Ferris 94). At the height of his success as Ziggy Stardust, Bowie emphasized to Murray the importance of mastering conventional theatrical skills: "There are going to be a lot of tragedies and a lot of clangers dropped over the next few years when a lot of bands try to become theatrical without knowing their craft" (48).

Bowie's first album, *David Bowie* (1967), clearly reflects his theatrical ambitions. Perhaps because he wrote many of the songs with a stage musical in mind, it is not a rock album but a pop album with overtones of theater music, cabaret, and music hall. Bowie's chief idol at this time was not a rocker but the British theater composer, actor, and singer Anthony Newley, and Bowie's singing on the album is very much in emulation of Newley's all-out, histrionic delivery and intermittent Cockney accent.[5] Looking back on this period, Bolan remarked of his friend that "all his songs were story songs. . . . They had a flavour, a very theatrical flavour" ("Music Hall" 14).

Simon Frith observes,

> In the British . . . tradition popular music has always featured the character song. . . . The lyrical and narrative convention here is to use the song to portray a character while simultaneously drawing

---

4. One can get a sense of Bowie as a mime from a routine he performs during the song "Width of a Circle" in D. A. Pennebaker's 1982 documentary *Ziggy Stardust and the Spiders from Mars: The Motion Picture*. Accompanied by music, Bowie mimes walking along the stage's invisible fourth wall behind which he seems imprisoned. Finding a crack in it, he pushes the two sides apart. Inserting himself into the opening, he becomes a bird flying to freedom.

5. Newley is not the only singer Bowie has imitated. On "Black Country Rock" (on *The Man Who Sold the World*, 1971), Bowie reproduced his friend Bolan's distinctive vocal warble (his voice was even modified technically to sound as much like Bolan's as possible). "Queen Bitch," a song on *Hunky Dory* (1971), features a replication of Lou Reed's songwriting and singing styles. The device of singing in other people's voices is not ancillary to glam rock—I discuss it in detail in chapter 5 in relation to Roy Wood, for whom it is a central strategy.

attention to the art of the portrayal. The singer is playing a part, and what is involved is neither self-expression . . . nor critical commentary. . . . The art of this sort of singing becomes a matter of acting, and there is always a question concerning the singer's relationship to his own words. (*Performing Rites* 171)

Bowie's first album is very much in this tradition. Most of the songs represent specific characters and contain enough information about those characters to constitute complete dramatic narratives. Several are portraits of distinctly English character types: "Uncle Arthur," who discovers he would rather continue to live with his mother, work at "the family shoppe" and be "well-fed" than have a life of his own with a wife; the protagonist of "Maids of Bond Street," a successful businesswoman whose slick, attractive exterior masks inner loneliness and frustration; and the World War I veteran whose lover left him while he was away fighting for his country ("Rubber Band"). Stylistically, these songs are in a music hall or cabaret vein ("Maids of Bond Street," a waltz, even features a Paris café accordion), though they also strongly resemble the portraits of social types recorded by the Kinks in 1965 and 1966, including "Dedicated Follower of Fashion," "Sunny Afternoon," and others. These songs, written by Ray Davies, anticipated Bowie's use of music hall style to point up the quiet desperation of everyday English lives.[6]

The singing on this album is indeed "a matter of acting": Bowie changes his delivery and vocal tone according to the character he is describing. The most actorly song on the album, "Please Mr. Gravedigger," is something of a tour de force. Bowie does not exactly sing—he uses a sort of pop *Sprechstimme* without musical accompaniment but against a background of sound effects (tolling bells, pouring rain). He portrays a man who stands day after day by the grave of a young girl he murdered and who is now planning to dispatch the graveyard functionary. Bowie's depiction of an oddly sentimental but very straightforward psychopath, down to such character details as the cold from which he suffers as he digs a grave in the rain, is highly effective.

6. Davies was also very interested in bringing together theatricality and rock, but his conception of theatricality involved constructing rock albums and concerts with clear, often overtly didactic, plots and characters—*Preservation* (1973–74) was the first of several rock operas the Kinks recorded and performed on stage. See David Dalton for an overview of the Kinks' career and an account of this aspect of their work.

The question of Bowie's relationship to his characters is broached in part because he neither presents a consistent persona on the album nor sings in a single voice. Self-expression and critical commentary both require a defined and stable position from which to speak: Bowie provides no such position. Some of his lyrics are in the first person, some in the third. His voice and accent change according to the character he portrays: the jaunty narrator of "She's Got Medals," who chuckles as he comments on the character he describes, a woman who dresses as a man to join the army; the snuffling killer of "Please Mr. Gravedigger"; the protagonist of "Rubber Band," characterized by a posh accent and high-strung vocal tone. One can hear this album as anticipating in miniature Bowie's basic performance strategy. If Bolan showed, contra rock's ideology of authenticity, that it was possible for a rock musician to shift personae at will, Bowie went a step further by demonstrating that a rock performer could take on multiple personae in the manner of a music hall singer or an actor.

Frith analogizes popular musicians with film actors: "a pop star is like a film star, taking on many parts but retaining an essential 'personality' that is common to all of them and is the basis of their popular appeal" (*Performing Rites* 199). Bowie often described himself as an actor but in terms that suggested stage acting rather than film acting. In the summer of 1971, he announced his plans for the near future by saying, "I'm going to play a character called Ziggy Stardust. We're going to do it as a stage show. We may even do it in the West End. When I'm tired of playing Ziggy I can step out and someone else can take over for me" (qtd. in Harvey). In an interview published in July 1972, a year before Bowie announced the "death" of Ziggy Stardust from the stage of the Hammersmith Odeon in London, he told Murray that he planned to spend "another few months getting [Ziggy] entirely out of my system, and then we'll don another mask" (50). Although Bowie eventually became a successful film actor, he imagined himself early on as a stage actor who would take on a series of roles without necessarily articulating a single, consistent persona through them.[7]

Although the conceit that Ziggy would be one of Bowie's many roles, a role that someone else could take over, makes perfect sense

---

7. Since 1976, Bowie has enjoyed a substantial career as a film actor, although that facet of his work lies outside the range of this study. For a discussion of Bowie's performances of gender and sexuality on film, see Anne Rice.

from a stage actor's point of view, it points to a way of thinking about performance that is foreign to rock. The whole notion of self-consciously *acting* the role of rock star rather than presenting oneself as one is antithetical to the ideology of authenticity. (This is related to the concept of "showing doing" I discussed in the previous chapter: neither Bolan nor Bowie was content simply to perform the role of rock star—both also pointed self-consciously to the conventionality of that role.) Bowie's performance practices also differed from those of other performers who presented obviously constructed personae, such as Alice Cooper and Gary Glitter. Cooper, Glitter, and, for that matter, Bolan after he made the transition to T. Rex, each performed one persona with which they were so closely identified that no one could imagine anyone other than Vincent Furnier portraying Alice Cooper or Paul Gadd playing Gary Glitter. When a musician, like a film actor, is closely identified with a single persona, it becomes easier to imagine that persona, however artificial, as an authentic expression of the performer's self. Bowie's distinctive refusal of this kind of continuity in favor of the stage actor's continual transformation from role to role set him apart from rock culture.

Bowie's eagerness to present his work as theater raised the suspicions of those invested in rock's ideology of authenticity. Ben Edmonds summarized this reaction from the perspective of 1976: "What critics have always found lacking in Bowie's music was *commitment*. It's hard to imagine a young David Jones [Bowie's real name] hearing Elvis or Little Richard on the radio late at night and dedicating himself forever to rock & roll. Like any actor, his commitment was not to the form but to his ability to manipulate that form to inspire commitment in his audiences" ("Bowie"). Without questioning Bowie's abilities as a musician and performer, the "official" rock culture of the 1970s (represented especially by critics) often found it hard to embrace Bowie because his actorly stance made it impossible to equate his performances with the real person.

The redoubtable American rock writer Lester Bangs exhibited both this qualm with respect to Bowie and rock's more general distrust of theatricality. In his 1974 review of *Diamond Dogs* for Creem magazine, Bangs excoriated Bowie's "same old theatrical delivery" as "sterilely distasteful artifice" and accused Bowie of failing to convey "real commitment [that word again!], a certain last-ditch desperation" that Bangs considered a sign of authenticity

("Swan Dive" 118–19). Here, Bangs clearly upholds the ideology of rock by associating commitment and personal expression with authenticity, and theatricality and artifice with its opposite. By contrast, Bangs wrote favorably about Bowie's 1975 "plastic soul" disco album, *Young Americans,* also for *Creem,* precisely because this time he felt Bowie's singing to be genuinely emotive. "[H]e's found his own voice at last," declared Bangs, "Bowie has dropped his pretensions . . . and in doing that I believe he's finally become an artist instead of a poseur . . ." ("Chicken Head" 132–33). Although the "soul boy" persona Bowie constructed for this material, his first full change of persona after Ziggy Stardust, was just as carefully authored a role as Ziggy had been, Bangs nevertheless granted Bowie his seal of approval because he heard Bowie as performing himself rather than a character.[8]

It is worth noting in passing that rock critics have also been troubled by Bowie's early admiration for Anthony Newley. In praising *Young Americans,* Bangs took the position that Bowie's having found his own voice meant that he no longer had to "cop . . . licks from Anthony Newley" ("Chicken Head" 132). In an overview article from 1984, Mick Farren criticized Bowie for having wanted to be "the next Anthony Newley. *Anthony Newley?* What lurked in the psyche of young David that wanted to be Anthony Newley?" (193). Farren goes on to express his revulsion at Newley's theatrical performance style and the echoes of it in Bowie's singing. From Bowie's own point of view in the mid-1960s, Newley might have seemed a good choice of model. He was, after all, a very successful, distinctly British theater composer, singer, and actor who had had hit productions in the West End and on Broadway and had also placed a dozen records on the British pop charts between 1959 and 1962. It is probably fair to say that this combination of theatrical success and pop success was attractive to Bowie, given his own aspirations. But to rock critics, Newley represented a cultural realm that is the ideological antithesis of rock.

Bowie's commitment to a theatrical conception of rock performance was initially problematic from his public's perspective as well as that of rock critics. When Bowie announced from the stage of the Hammersmith Odeon in London on July 3, 1973, that the

---

8. Susan Fast suggested to me that Bangs's ability to hear Bowie as authentic when he embraced an African-American musical style may reflect the frequent association of blackness with authenticity in the discourse of rock.

performance he and his band had just completed was "the last one we'll ever do," the music papers proclaimed Bowie a "Rock 'n' Roll Suicide" who had "Kill[ed his] Concert Career."[9] What Bowie had announced, in fact, was the relatively unremarkable actuality that he intended to disband that particular group and retire the Ziggy Stardust character, an intention he had also announced a year earlier. But because the discourse of authenticity is paradigmatic in rock, neither his fans nor the reporters could hear Bowie repeating his actor's intention to play other characters: because they perceived Ziggy Stardust as equivalent to Bowie, what they heard was his announcing an intention never to perform again. Ron Ross identified this tension between Bowie's theatrical conception of his work and the rock audience's expectations nearly a year earlier in an article for *Phonograph Record* describing Bowie as "assum[ing] an understanding of the nature of theatre which a rock audience denies almost by definition" ("David Bowie"). Dave Laing summarizes clearly the implications of these conflicting frames of reference for an artist who tried to bridge musical theater and rock:

> In contrast to musical theatre, much popular singing is heard within the space of the autobiographical: the skill of a singer or songwriter is judged by how far the audience is convinced of the authenticity of the emotion portrayed. . . . Hence, the ambiguity of Bowie's portrayal of Ziggy allowed the slide into autobiography for much of his audience. For them, he *was* Ziggy. (24)

Bowie's first album, replete with theatrical characterizations and Newleyisms, clearly was out of step with the times. As Bolan noted, 1967, the annus mirabilis for the hippie counterculture and psychedelic rock,[10] was "the wrong time" for an aspiring musician to produce an album of show tunes and music hall numbers ("Music Hall" 14). The next year saw Bowie venturing into the countercultural arena. With Hermione Farthingale and John "Hutch" Hutcherson, he formed a troupe called Feathers that "would attempt a combination of music, prose, dance and poetry" (Cann 47) and played at some important underground venues in London, includ-

9. These headlines are reproduced on the cover of the DVD edition of *Ziggy Stardust and The Spiders from Mars: The Motion Picture*.

10. For discussions of the importance of 1967 in the development of rock music, see Miles; Frith, "1967"; and Whiteley, *The Space* (61–81).

ing Middle Earth and the Roundhouse. In 1969, he and Mary Finni-
gan, a journalist who wrote for the countercultural *International
Times,* started the Beckenham Arts Lab, intended as an incubator
for artistic talent. That summer (the summer of Woodstock), Bowie
helped to produce the Beckenham Free Festival as an outgrowth of
the Arts Lab. By the end of the year, Bowie and his new wife,
Angela, would take up residence at Haddon Hall, a Victorian
townhouse; their flat evolved into a sort of commune for musicians
and other members of Bowie's growing entourage. His primary
stylistic influence during 1968 and 1969 shifted from Anthony Newley to Bob Dylan, and he became a hippie, at least sartorially.
Transsexual rock musician Jayne County, then Wayne County, one
of Warhol's transvestite acolytes, described one of Bowie's performances in London by saying, "We'd heard that this David Bowie
was supposed to be androgynous and everything, but then he came
out with long hair, folky clothes, and sat on a stool and played folk
songs. We were so disappointed with him. We looked over at him
and said, 'Just look at that folky old hippie!'" (qtd. in McNeil and
McCain 95).

"Join the Gang," a song on Bowie's first album, is a biting satire of
the way swinging London took up fashionable aspects of the counterculture: "Psychedelic stars / Throwing down cigars / They're
picking up the joints now that they've joined the gang." Executed
in a music hall style, with rolling drums and a barrelhouse piano,
the song is a diatribe against conformity disguised as nonconfor-
mity (a theme to which Bowie would return) that also mocks rock
music itself. During a verse on how expensive fashionable clubs had
become, the band ironically plays the opening bars of "Gimme
Some Lovin'" (1966) by the Spencer Davis Group, an exuberant
musical description of an exciting club scene, and the track ends
with a curious array of raucous buzzing noises that shift from side
to side of the stereo field in a parody of psychedelic "freak out"
effects.

"Join the Gang" is glib and condescending toward the counterculture. Keeping in mind Frith's dictum concerning the relationship
of the singer of character songs to his material, it is just as possible
that Bowie was acting the role of an irritable outsider taking pot-
shots at the underground as it is that he was expressing his own
perspective. Although Bowie's second and more successful album,

released in 1969 and known variously as *David Bowie: Man of Words, Man of Music;* and *Space Oddity*,[11] was as close as Bowie came to making a hippie record in a folk-rock vein, Bowie did not relinquish his stage actor's desire to play multiple roles in favor of portraying the consistent countercultural persona demanded by the culture of psychedelic rock. Rather, on this album, he portrayed a range of characters with very different, even opposing, relationships to the counterculture.

Two songs are positive portraits of different male countercultural avatars. "The Wild Eyed Boy from Freecloud," which I will discuss later in this chapter, depicts a gentle man-child whose espousal of the hippie values of freedom and authenticity puts him at risk in a hostile world. In the scenario of "Unwashed and Somewhat Slightly Dazed," a man harangues a wealthy young woman and tries to lure her away from her life of privilege to a bohemian existence. His identification with the hippie counterculture is implied first by his proudly antisocial self-presentation as an abject, unwashed visionary ("I'm the Cream / Of the Great Utopia Dream")[12] and, second, through his association with psychedelic imagery: he sees "electric tomatoes" and "credit card rye bread."

As described by the lyrics, the protagonist of this song may not seem very appealing, especially since much of the imagery is violent ("my head's full of murders"). But the music both suggests that his antisociality is superior to the woman's life of thoughtless privilege and reinforces the song's countercultural associations. The song begins quietly in a folk vein with a strummed acoustic guitar as the dominant instrumental sound. Bowie's voice, too, is quiet and meditative as he muses about the woman at the window and the probability that she will ignore his entreaties. As he becomes more assertive, drums and an electric guitar join the acoustic guitar and the song acquires a rock beat. I noted in my discussion of Bolan the association of the acoustic guitar and folk style with femininity in

11. *David Bowie* was the UK title for this album, while *Man of Words, Man of Music* was its U.S. title. It was rereleased in 1972 under the title *Space Oddity* to coincide with the U.S. release of the single version of the song of that name (which had been released in the UK in 1969). I have chosen to refer to the album here as *Space Oddity*.

12. Hippies were stereotyped as being dirty. The Bonzo Dog Band parodied this stereotype in the song "Busted" (1969): "I'm filthy, I'm hungry, I'm fed up to the teeth / I'm very revolutionary I haven't washed in weeks."

rock culture; Bowie uses that association here to make the protagonist seem vulnerable at first. The song remains in a folk style as long
as the protagonist presents himself as vulnerable to the woman's
rejection and moves to a rock style when he talks about his possible
impact on her complacent life as a haute bourgeoise, thus making
the connection between rock music, the counterculture, and masculinity. Bowie's voice becomes much stronger, more assertive and
aggressive—a rock singer's voice rather than a folk singer's.

In the first verse after the shift to rock, Bowie holds two syllables
(the pronouns "I" and "you") for several beats (approximately two
measures apiece), turning them into siren-calls at once inviting and
alarming. As the imagery becomes more violent, the rock beat shifts
to a loping Bo Diddley beat and the electric guitar moves to the
front of the mix. On the second Bo Diddley verse, a blues harmonica joins the instrumentation; there is a harmonica solo between the
penultimate and final verses. After Bowie has completed the lyrics,
a spirited blues-rock jam ensues. Driven by powerfully strummed
acoustic guitar, the jam begins with another harmonica solo
accompanied by modal runs on the electric guitar that lead into a
full-fledged guitar solo. At the end of the jam, a horn section playing soul riffs joins in.

I have described this performance in detail because it has a number of important features. For one thing, Bowie uses a rock style
that underpins the countercultural references in the lyric rather
than his pop/show music style of 1966–67. The various references to
black music through the Bo Diddley beat, blues harmonica, and
soul horns all reflect the way psychedelic rock used the blues and
black music to assert its own cultural authenticity. The combination of blues with an attitude of predatory male aggression is found
regularly in the rock of the 1960s; Bowie's song thus becomes a
cousin to the Rolling Stones' "Midnight Rambler" (1969), among
others, many of the Doors' songs (the violently lyrical protagonist
of this song also replicates Jim Morrison's *poète maudit* persona to
an extent), and Bo Diddley's own "Who Do You Love" (1957),
often covered by rock groups. At over six minutes, the length of the
track far exceeds that of standard pop songs and thus reflects the
priorities evident in psychedelic rock, whose practitioners often felt
hemmed in by pop conventions and wanted to express themselves
in longer compositions. That almost half of that time is devoted to
a blues jam that involves no singing is another departure from

Bowie's earlier pop style, one that typifies the emphasis on instrumental improvisation within psychedelic rock.

If the character Bowie portrays in "Unwashed and Somewhat Slightly Dazed" aligns himself with the hippie counterculture, the narrator of "The Cygnet Committee" questions it from the outside, though not in the flippant terms of "Join the Gang." "The Cygnet Committee" is a long (nine minutes), complex piece that expresses the difficulty of maintaining belief in the face of disillusionment. Bowie described it shortly before the album's release by saying it addressed "the more militant section of the hippie movement. The movement was a great ideal but something's gone wrong with it now" (qtd. in Cann 59).

The song focuses on three characters: the narrator, who is trying to sort out his feelings about what he sees going on around him; someone who facilitated a radical cause (though seems not to have been one of the radicals himself) only to end up feeling used and bitter; and the narrator's radical friends, who speak in a single voice. The recording begins with a decisive-sounding bass guitar line that is disrupted by an acoustic guitar strummed at a slower tempo and legato passages on the electric guitar that muddy the bass guitar's clear opening statement. The way a slow folk-rock melody emerges from this musical ferment may represent the difficulty of taking a firm position at a time of upheaval. The narrator's chief observation, which he states in verses that precede the introductions of the other two characters, is the melancholy "So much has gone and little is new"—the destructive part of the radicals' program has succeeded, but they have not managed to replace the old order with a new one.

The music turns from folk rock to rock at the start of the disillusioned supporter's testimony, largely with the entrance of drums playing a rock beat. Bowie repeats this transition in the next section of the piece: the narrator's dreamy, folk-rock accompaniment turns to heavier rock (marked again by the entrance of drums) as his friends recount their radical ambitions. Whereas the narrator's voice drifts into the mix surrounded by echo, the voices of the other characters are forceful and at the front of the mix. As in "Unwashed and Somehow Slightly Dazed," Bowie links rock style with countercultural portraiture.

Here, however, the portrait is unambiguously unflattering. The narrator's friends are the objects of the song's harshest commentary. They describe themselves by saying:

We . . . Stoned the poor on slogans such as
"Wish You Could Hear,"
"Love Is All We Need,"
"Kick Out The Jams,"
"Kick Out Your Mother,"
"Cut Up Your Friend,"
"Screw Up your Brother, or He'll Get You In the End."

The radicals' selfishness and self-righteousness are evident not only in the idea that all they have to offer the poor is slogans, but also in their distortions of well-known catch phrases. The postcard cliché "Wish you were here" becomes the smug "Wish You Could Hear." The Beatles' hippie anthem "All You Need is Love" becomes "Love is all *We* Need," while the MC5's exhortation to "Kick Out the Jams" takes an ugly turn toward violence against family members. (It is not absolutely clear whether Bowie's narrator is criticizing these groups and their music or suggesting that activists have misinterpreted their work and used it to their own ends or both.) The radicals' definitive statement of their attitude is "We Can Force You to Be Free," an echo of the critique of nonconformist conformity in "Join the Gang." In the end, the narrator is left confused. He deplores the violence to which the radicals have descended and has a nightmare vision of "a love machine . . . ploughing down man, woman" but retains the ideals for which they fought, declaring, "I Want to Believe."

"Unwashed and Somewhat Slightly Dazed" and "The Cygnet Committee" are polar opposites with respect to their representations of the counterculture. Whereas the former is an unembarrassed celebration of a certain type of self-righteous hippie (kin to Bolan's "Charlie"), the latter criticizes the movement's political tactics. Rather than develop a single persona with a single relationship to the counterculture (as did the vast majority of rock musicians in the middle and late 1960s) Bowie plays characters with enormously different attitudes to the underground. Although *Space Oddity* is stylistically very different from Bowie's first album in that it is a rock album rather than a pop album, Bowie approached both recordings like a stage actor playing multiple roles with which he cannot necessarily be identified rather than a film (or rock) star whose concern is to develop a consistent persona. Intentionally or not, this strategy implicitly challenged the "us and them" mentality of the counterculture. Although Bowie's characters could be defined as part of the solution or part of the problem from the counterculture's point of view, his own role was that of actor, not ideologue. As such, he could represent multiple positions without aligning himself clearly with any side.[13]

Prior to 1969, Bowie did not perform live as a musician all that much; it was mostly after the success of his recording of "Space Oddity" that he experienced significant demand as a concert attraction. When Bowie started performing music live on a more regular basis, he began a series of experiments that led to his development of Ziggy Stardust, a performance persona that constituted a physical analog of his vocal presence on record. Just as Bowie did not appear "as himself" on his early recordings but in a series of character roles, he did not appear "as himself" on stage, either. Ziggy Stardust, the bisexual alien persona that Bowie performed in 1972 and 1973, was both a figure who mediated between sexualities and a third term that triangulated the relationship between Bowie and the characters in his songs.[14] Ziggy, rather than Bowie, became the actor who impersonated the characters delineated in the songs, yet Ziggy was also a fictional entity enacted by Bowie. Revealed on stage, the "real person" who portrayed the characters in the recordings turned out not to be a real person at all. Just to make matters more complex, Ziggy was himself a character from one of Bowie's songs, meaning that Ziggy was sometimes singing about himself.

13. In an essay on Bowie's politics, David Buckley points out that Bowie's actorly stance has made it difficult to identify his actual political beliefs: "Superficially, Bowie's development has been from far right to soft left, though it has always been extremely difficult to pin him down on single issues" (207).

14. Bowie's Ziggy period began at the start of 1972 and lasted almost exactly two years till the beginning of 1974. During that time, Bowie released three albums: *The Rise and Fall of Ziggy Stardust and The Spiders from Mars* (1972), *Aladdin Sane* (1973), and *Pin-ups* (1973). He toured the UK twice, the United States twice, and Japan once. Although Bowie announced the retirement of Ziggy Stardust and the Spiders from Mars at the final concert of the second UK tour, that was not quite Ziggy's last performance. Bowie made *The 1980 Floor Show*, a special for U.S. television, in the Ziggy persona and with several of the Spiders at the Marquee Club in London in October 1973; it aired on NBC's *Midnight Special*. Although the Ziggy persona mutated somewhat over its two-year life span (the final tour was actually called the Aladdin Sane Retirement Tour), it remained fairly consistent. Bowie's new image early in 1974, associated with the song "Rebel Rebel," was a transitional variant on the Ziggy persona; by the spring of 1974, when he embarked on the Diamond Dogs Tour of the United States, Bowie's abandonment of Ziggy was definitive.

The performative experiments that contributed to the development of Ziggy Stardust centered on two issues: transvestism and the development of explicitly artificial performance personae. Very early in 1971, Bowie appeared on television "wearing a frock and playing acoustic guitar" (Cann 71). The frock in question was one of six Mr. Fish dresses Angela Bowie had bought for him;[15] he took several of them on a short publicity tour of the United States that began a week after the television appearance and was photographed in one for the cover of his album *The Man Who Sold the World* (which came out in April 1971).[16]

Bowie's interest in transvestism was fueled by several influences: his own earlier experiences performing with Lindsay Kemp, whose mime troupe was characterized by a flamboyantly gay sensibility; a theatrical production produced by Andy Warhol; and time spent at a disco. Around the same time that Angela Bowie acquired the Mr. Fish dresses for David, she also "introduced him to a club in Kensington High Street named the Sombrero. This prototype disco, with a mainly male, ambisexual clientele, had an immediate impact on Bowie. He spent hours on the neon-lit dance floor, or sitting craning to appraise the most *outré* extremes of hair and make-up" (Sandford 77).

During the summer of 1971, Bowie attended the London performances of *Pork*, a play based on tape recordings of conversations made by Warhol.[17] Bowie, who was already aware of Warhol and

15. Michael Fish was an offbeat fashion designer who began his own business in 1966 after working for other clothiers. He innovated the male dress in 1967; Mick Jagger wore one at the Rolling Stones' famous 1969 free concert in Hyde Park (Gorman 54).

16. The U.S. release of *The Man Who Sold the World* had a different, less provocative cover featuring a cartoon illustration.

17. *Pork*, directed by Anthony Ingrassia, opened for a two-week run at La Mama in New York City on May 5, 1971. The New York cast embarked on a run at the Roundhouse in London in August. According to the website www.warholstars.org, "*Pork* was based on tape-recorded telephone conversations between Andy Warhol and Brigid Berlin about her family's private life. Her mother Honey Berlin, a Fifth Avenue socialite who included the Duke of Windsor amongst her close friends, was livid when she found out about the play by reading a review of it in the New York *Times*. Brigid angrily called Andy and told him, 'You're nothing but a fucking faggot! You don't care about anyone but yourself! And your goddamn fucking fame! And your fucking Factory! And your fucking money!'"

the Velvet Underground, the rock group Warhol sponsored,[18] was very impressed with *Pork:*

> For Bowie, the New York scene looked far more decadent and enticing than London's. There was an element of danger there— in the movies of Warhol and the songs of Lou Reed—which was unknown in Britain.[19] New York was about drag queens and junkies, small-town freaks transforming themselves into gutter aristocrats as they revolted against America's repressive homophobia. Warhol had made these people "superstars," and the Velvets had hymned them in speed-freak anthems like "Sister Ray." (Hoskyns, *Glam!* 25)

Eventually, a number of people associated with *Pork* would join MainMan, the new management company that represented Bowie, and Bowie would work with Lou Reed, formerly of the Velvet Underground, on *Transformer,* Reed's second solo album. Jayne County was happy to take credit for Bowie's budding persona:

> Of course we influenced David to change his image. After us, David started getting dressed up. I'd gotten the shaved eyebrows thing from [transvestite Warhol superstar] Jackie Curtis, and David started shaving his eyebrows, painting his nails, even wearing painted nails out at nightclubs, like we were doing. He changed his whole image and started getting more and more freaky. (Qtd. in McNeil and McCain 95)

Alongside his developing interest in "ambisexuality," Bowie also experimented with artificial performance personae. The first experiment was the series of performances given by Bowie and his new band early in 1970 as the Hype. (The Hype consisted of some of the musicians who played on *Space Oddity* [guitarist Mick Ronson; bass guitarist Tony Visconti, who would work with both Bowie and Bolan primarily as a producer and arranger; and drummer

18. Bowie's interest in Warhol produced several artifacts: Bowie's own song "Andy Warhol" (1971) on his *Hunky Dory* album; Lou Reed's best-known song, "Walk on the Wild Side" (1973), a chronicle of the lives of Warhol's superstars, which Bowie produced; and Bowie's performance as Warhol in the film *Basquiat* (dir. Julian Schnabel, 1996).

19. If Bowie acknowledged Reed and the Velvet Underground as influences, that influence later proved to be reciprocal, as Reed's performance style in 1973 was clearly modeled on Bowie's version of glam rock. See Bockris (206).

John Cambridge] and was also the nucleus of the Spiders from Mars, Bowie's recording and touring band for the entire Ziggy period.) According to Mark Paytress, the Hype represented a new way of thinking about rock and rock performance:

> On the way out were worthiness and endeavour in favour of a lighter more mischievous attitude, and the name of Bowie's new band—The Hype—said it all. Hype: the word was a curse on the scene, cheaply purchased praise that masked a woeful lack of authenticity. . . . The Hype's real claim to pre-Glam infamy was a show they played on February 22 [1970] at London's premier underground Mecca the Roundhouse. "We decided to dress up," Visconti recalls. "David was dressed as Rainbowman in lurex, pirate boots and with all these diaphanous scarves pinned to his clothes. I was Hypeman in a mock Superman costume with a white leotard, crocheted silver knickers and big red cape with a collar. Ronson wore a gold lamé double-breasted suit and fedora, so he was Gangsterman. And John Cambridge was Pirateman wearing a kind of buccaneer's outfit." (*Bolan* 155–56)

Although this performance was not a success—the Roundhouse's hippie audience vociferously rejected the Hype and what it apparently stood for—it was nevertheless a significant preliminary attempt on Bowie's part to construct rock performance personae that were clearly presented as theatrical roles rather than manifestations of the musicians themselves. (The comic book fantasy aspect of these roles also anticipated the science fiction aspect of Ziggy Stardust, which anticipated, in turn, the comic book hero personae of Kiss.)

The other exercise in fabricated identities in which Bowie engaged was the formation of a group called Arnold Corns built around Freddi Burretti (who also called himself Rudi Valentino), an art student Bowie had met at the Sombrero. (In reality, the group was basically the Hype under a different name.) Several of the songs Bowie recorded with Burretti as Arnold Corns early in 1971 reappeared later in different versions on *The Rise and Fall of Ziggy Stardust and the Spiders from Mars*. Arnold Corns was also associated with Bowie's experiments in transvestism: "During the summer of 1971 David and Freddi turned up in dresses for an interview in a Carnaby Street pub, not unnaturally turning the heads of the regulars" (Cann 77).

Conceptually, the synthesis of transvestism and an approach to rock performance based in theatrical characterization that gave rise to Ziggy Stardust was already present in Arnold Corns. But Bowie had not yet refined the identity and physical appearance of his persona. That development took place rapidly in the first months of 1972 and can be seen in Bowie's televised performances during that time. In a series of performances broadcast on BBC television in February 1972, after Bowie had done only one concert of his Ziggy Stardust material and just before he embarked on a concert tour of the United Kingdom, Bowie appeared in an olive green jumpsuit with an open front showing his bare chest. He no longer had the flowing tresses seen on the cover of *The Man Who Sold the World;* instead, his haircut was a mullet. The first shot of the television performance of "Queen Bitch" was of Bowie's huge, red, plastic boots laced-up with clashing green laces. The camera traveled up his legs toward the twelve-string acoustic guitar he held, offering a glimpse of codpiece along the way. Close-ups of his face revealed that he was wearing eye makeup and offered a clear view of his distinctive eyes, which are of different colors (one brown, one blue), giving him a somewhat otherworldly countenance.[20] The bold, rectilinear pattern on his jumpsuit was reminiscent of a circuit board. Guitarist Mick Ronson appeared in a gold lamé open jumpsuit similar to Bowie's, his long, golden blond hair cut in a shag. Bowie's movements and his interplay with Ronson were typical for rockers: legs apart, guitars brandished. When they sang together at the same microphone, they looked at each other but did not touch.

A performance of "Starman" filmed for the BBC program *Top of the Pops* about two months later shows the further development of these images. Bowie and Ronson again appeared in jumpsuits— Bowie's featured a colorful zigzag pattern in bold yellow, blue, and red, while Ronson's was again gold lamé (though not the same one as on the earlier program). Trevor Bolder, the bass player, wore a shiny black vinyl top and a long, dark black version of Bowie's mullet. Bowie's hair was a more extreme version of his earlier style—the sandy brown color replaced by flaming red and his hair lacquered into an improbable upsweep. He wore two shades of eye makeup, a pale powder base, and lipstick. Bowie looked directly and seductively into the camera. When he and Ronson sang at the

20. This difference of color between Bowie's eyes is the result of a youthful injury. As his biographer Christopher Sandford notes, it has sometimes been proffered as evidence of his ostensible extraterrestrial origins (20).

David Bowie as Ziggy Stardust, ca. 1973. © MichaelOchs Archives
.com.

same microphone, he put his arm around the guitarist's shoulders and touched Ronson's arm. These gestures evoked both male camaraderie and a more sexualized homosociality. In the course of the ensuing months, as Bowie and his group toured, the physical interaction between Bowie and Ronson would become more and more explicitly sexual—during a concert in the summer of 1972, Bowie famously simulated fellatio on Ronson by "going down" on the guitarist's instrument as he played. This routine and variations on it became staples of the Ziggy Stardust concerts.

Bowie's management circulated the cover photographs for the album *The Rise and Fall of Ziggy Stardust and the Spiders from Mars* for six months before the album was released in June 1972; the audience thus saw the embryonic Ziggy persona in print and on television and the stage well before hearing the album. These photographs, along with the other manifestations of the Ziggy image, were often seen as suggesting that Ziggy was an extraterrestrial (Bowie himself frequently described Ziggy as a Martian). The hand-colored front cover image is of Bowie clad in his chest-revealing jumpsuit with an electric guitar slung over his left shoulder, purple boots, and greenish blond hair, perched outside the door of a building on a London side street, next to piles of trash. The rear cover provides a closer view of the same figure posing languorously, hand on hip, inside a telephone booth, bathed in a yellow-green glow. The hand coloring exaggerates the strangeness of his appearance and makes Bowie seem not to belong to the urban landscape in which he appears. On the front cover, Bowie is stationed immediately under a large commercial sign reading "K. West," a pun that lends itself all too obviously to the interpretation that Ziggy is an alien arrived on earth on a quest.[21] (A bit less obvious are the signs to the right of the doorway describing the companies inside the building. The fact that they are dress manufacturers alludes to the other main traits attributed to Ziggy, his transvestism and bisexuality.)[22]

In suggesting that Ziggy Stardust was an extraterrestrial, Bowie borrowed a trope from psychedelic rock only to reverse its ideological polarity. References to outer space, space travel, and space aliens abound in psychedelic rock, to the point that "space rock" is

21. Bowie played just such a character in his first major film, *The Man Who Fell to Earth* (1976), directed by Nicholas Roeg.

22. The K. West sign was not fictional—it belonged to a furrier whose business was in the building where the photo was shot. The choice of a building associated with the rag trade evokes Bowie's Mod past.

sometimes nominated as a rock subgenre.²³ Artists who have dab-
bled in various versions of space rock include the Byrds, Jimi Hendrix, Pink Floyd, Jefferson Airplane/Starship, Amon Düül II and
other German groups, Mu, H. P. Lovecraft, Hawkwind, and a
great many others.²⁴ Space takes on several meanings in psychedelic
rock. A voyage into outer space, an unknown and unpredictable
realm, made a good analogy for drug experience, particularly LSD
trips (Whiteley, *The Space* 23); a journey into outer space is thus
metaphorically equivalent to a "Journey to the Center of the
Mind," to quote the Amboy Dukes. Extraterrestrials are usually
represented in psychedelic rock as benign beings in sympathy with
the hippies' desire to make a new society or world. Sometimes, it is
suggested that such a utopian world might exist on another planet
or be built in space; in other cases, aliens are depicted as benefac-
tors (or even the founders) of the human race.²⁵

Bowie had a long-standing interest in space travel: it was one of
his preoccupations while growing up and, in the late 1960s, he
recounted his UFO sightings in interviews and wrote of them for a
UFO enthusiasts' magazine in London (Sandford 70).²⁶ The songs
on the Ziggy Stardust album were not his first compositions to

23. Rock was not the only musical genre to employ space tropes. For a brief
discussion of space tropes in jazz and art music, see Braun (115–17). For an
analysis of space-age music in the 1950s, see Taylor (72–95).

24. For an entertaining and idiosyncratic brief overview of space rock, see
Jon Savage.

25. In the psychedelic imaginary, the depths of the ocean constituted a
utopian space very similar to the reaches of outer space. This is reflected in
such songs as the Jimi Hendrix Experience's "1983" (1968), and the Beatles'
"Yellow Submarine" (1966) and "Octopus's Garden" (1969). Donovan suggested in "Atlantis" (1969) that the sources of human civilization are to be
found underwater, while Spirit's "Water Woman" (1968), which begins and
ends with aqueous sound effects, seems to propose suicide by drowning as a
way of accessing a better world. Reynolds and Press devote two chapters to the
intersections between "cosmic rock" and "oceanic rock" (181–210).

26. Some rock musicians took the preoccupation with space travelers further than Bowie. The members of Mu, for instance, moved from California to
Hawaii to be closer to sites where extraterrestrials were likely to land. According to their own accounts, they were rewarded with the opportunity to witness
several landings (Irwin). In a 1972 interview with the *New Musical Express,*
Robert Fripp, the guitarist for King Crimson, declared, "You know, spirits
from other places can take on physical bodies on this planet. Examples of people from other places? Jimi Hendrix, Marc Bolan, David Bowie . . ." (qtd. in
Stable 14). Turning once again to the Bonzo Dog Band for parody, we find that
in "Beautiful Zelda" (1968), a 1950s-style teenage lament, the extraterrestrial
girlfriend turns out to be as faithless as any earth woman.

address these themes.[27] Both the first song and the last song on *Space Oddity* make significant use of them, once again in ways that allowed Bowie to play roles with different relationships to the counterculture.

The opening song of this album is "Space Oddity," one of Bowie's best-known songs and his first hit (it reached number five on the UK charts in September 1969). Inspired by Stanley Kubrick's film *2001: A Space Odyssey* (1968) and the disaster that befell the Apollo 8 astronauts, the song tells the story of Major Tom, an astronaut who ends up stranded in space, presumably facing death. It expresses something of the counterculture's reservations about technology and the military-industrial complex. Although Theodore Roszak argues that an opposition to the dominant culture of "technocracy" was the hippie generation's "paramount struggle" (4) and Paul Willis refers to the hippies' deep suspicion of "technological rationalism" (91), the counterculture was not unified in its view of technology. The struggle against technocracy manifested itself in two distinct ways: the technophobia of back-to-the-land communards on the one hand and a quest for ecologically sound alternative technologies on the other (Kirk 354). Inasmuch as Major Tom ends up stranded as the result of the failure of high technology, Bowie's song reinforces the technophobic position. A sense that the technology is in the hands of people who do not have Major Tom's best interests at heart emerges when the first thing he is asked after entering orbit is to endorse a brand of shirts; here, the song reflects the counterculture's general suspicion of commodity culture and its relationship to the military-industrial complex (the drumming during the takeoff sequence is a military tattoo). The consequence is that Major Tom is rendered helpless to address the world's ills: sitting in his capsule, he muses, "Planet earth is blue / And there's nothing I can do."

By contrast, the last verse of "Memory of a Free Festival,"[28] the

27. In an interesting bit of glam revisionism, Bowie made videos in 1972 and 1973 featuring the Ziggy persona for rereleases of some pre-Ziggy songs. Both "Life on Mars" (from the 1971 album *Hunky Dory*) and "Space Oddity" included space references. An earlier video for "Space Oddity," made when the song was first issued in 1969, featured Bowie as a Pierrot. The later one shows the Ziggy Stardust persona at a sound studio console that looks like Mission Control.

28. "Memory of a Free Festival" belongs to the rock genre of songs about music festivals. Many of the songs in this category were occasioned by the

final song on the album, in which Bowie commemorates the Beckenham Free Festival he helped to organize in the summer of 1969,
refers to a vision of extraterrestrials experienced by the festival
crowd: "We talked with tall Venusians passing through." The song
represents the hallucinatory experiences and utopian yearnings that
space aliens represented to the hippies by having Venusians drop in
on the festival (in this, Bowie actually anticipated an unachieved
plan hatched in the early 1970s, at John Lennon's behest, "for a
Peace Festival [in Toronto] that would include guest shots by
extraterrestrial beings" [Morthland 338]). But the encounter is a
failure: "And Peter tried to climb aboard but the Captain shook his
head / And away they soared." Whereas the extraterrestrials in
"Mr. Spaceman" (1966) by the Byrds or "On Our Way to Hana"
(1972) by Mu are only too happy to take people for rides in their
flying saucers to show them a better world, and the alien represented in Hendrix's "Up From the Skies" (1968) has returned to rub
shoulders with the human race, these Venusians remain aloof,
interested enough to swoop down for a look but finally keeping
their distance. Whatever promise they represent remains unattain-
able.

The alien in "Starman," the one song on *The Rise and Fall of
Ziggy Stardust and the Spiders from Mars* that refers directly to
extraterrestrial life, is similarly diffident. In the song, an alien communicates with the song's protagonist, a teenaged rock fan,
through the radio and television. On one level, the song wittily
equates the space alien with rock music itself: the alien speaks
through the mass media; his audience is the young—he frightens
adults ("Don't tell your poppa")—and he expresses himself in
musical terms that recall rock and roll's debt to black music. The
alien declares, "Let all the children boogie," undoubtedly a reference to John Lee Hooker's famous blues "Boogie Chillen" (1947).

But like the other aliens Bowie depicts, the starman is a bit reti-
cent. The first three lines of the chorus are "There's a starman waiting in the sky / He'd like to come and meet us / But he thinks he'd

---

Woodstock Music and Arts Festival that took place at the same time as the
London event; these include "Woodstock" (1970, written by Joni Mitchell and
recorded by both Mitchell and Crosby, Stills, Nash, and Young), Melanie's
"Lay Down (Candles in the Rain)" (1970), and Creedence Clearwater Revival's
"Who'll Stop the Rain" (1970). "Monterey" (1967) by the Animals, which
commemorates the 1967 Monterey International Pop Festival, is an earlier
entrant into this category.

blow our minds"—like the Venusians at the Free Festival, the star-man is keeping his distance. In his performance of the song on *Top of the Pops,* Bowie waggled his finger at the audience in a gesture of admonishment during this line, as if to suggest that it would be unwise for his listeners to approach the starman too closely. It has often been noted that in this song, Bowie borrowed a guitar riff from the Supremes' recording of "You Keep Me Hanging On" (1966) and part of the melody from Harold Arlen and E. Y. Har-burg's "Somewhere Over the Rainbow" (1939). The specific significance of these two allusions has gone unnoticed, however. Both are songs about a desire for escape or transcendence that seems unlikely to be fulfilled: the lover in the Supremes' song shows no sign of releasing the narrator but "just keep[s] me hangin' on," while in "Somewhere Over the Rainbow" the narrator observes birds flying where he or she would like to go but cannot. These allusions suggest that despite the song's exuberance, the protagonist of "Starman" sees in the alien a chance for escape that is unlikely to be realized.

Philip Ennis makes the provocative claim that the success of the U.S. space program in placing astronauts on the moon sealed the doom of the counterculture:

> It is probably not hyperbole to assert that the Age of Aquarius ended when men walked on the moon [in July 1969]. Not only was the countercultural infatuation with astrology given a strong, television-validated antidote of applied astronomy, but millions of kids who had not signed up for either belief system were totally convinced. A significant proportion became part of a new genera-tional pulse, moving toward the imperatives of the space age rather than toward the politics of the rock era. (360)

Although I think Ennis underestimates the extent to which psyche-delic music (and earlier forms of rock) had claimed space-related tropes well prior to the moon walk,[29] his analysis suggests a perti-

29. As Ken McLeod points out, "Rock and roll developed roughly contem-poraneously with the era of space exploration and the concomitant boom in science fiction. . . . Indeed, the association of space and alien themes with rock 'n' roll rebellion is found throughout rock's history and has had an impact on nearly all its stylistic manifestations" (340). An early example is "Flying Saucers Rock and Roll," a piece of rockabilly from 1957 by Billy Lee Riley and his Little Green Men.

nent historical context for Bowie's performance as Ziggy Stardust. Taking the moon walk as a defining point in the transition from the countercultural moment of the 1960s to the 1970s, we can see that rock musicians aligned themselves on one side or the other of the divide.

On one side were those who reclaimed outer space for the counterculture following the moon walk. The cover art for Canned Heat's album *Future Blues* (1970), for instance, depicts the members of the group, dressed as astronauts, planting an American flag on the moon. That they are posed like the famous Iwo Jima figures equates the moon landing with a military mission, a negative connotation in countercultural terms. In a gesture of protest, the flag is upside down. Paul Kantner and Jefferson Starship's *Blows Against the Empire* (1970), a continuous suite of six songs, presents an unrepentantly activist view of outer space. The underlying narrative premise is that the government has built a starship that is hijacked by a group of hippies who take it out into space to create a utopian community: "free minds, free bodies, free dope, free music." Although there is a hint of disillusionment in the suggestion that since the situation on earth is hopelessly repressive, hippies must take to the skies if they are to achieve their dreams ("you gotta let go you know"), Jefferson Starship maintains the counterculture's faith in outer space as a potential utopia.[30]

Ziggy Stardust, by contrast, as a figure, implies a rejection of values central to the hippie ethos and therefore falls on the post-countercultural side of the divide. As I discussed in chapter 1, the governing assumption for the counterculture was that psychedelic rock musicians emerged from the hippie community and spoke to and for that community. In a dialogue with the Beat novelist William Burroughs published in *Rolling Stone* in 1974, a few months after Bowie had put the Ziggy persona to rest, Bowie repudiated hippie communitarianism: "The idea of getting minds together smacks of

30. *Blows Against the Empire* has an interesting relationship to Kirk's point that the counterculture had a dual relationship to technology. On the one hand, the album sides with the advocates of alternative technologies by suggesting that the hippies can put technologies created by the dominant culture to utopian use. Although Jefferson Starship uses electric instruments to evoke the technologies of space travel, the primary sound of the album is acoustic: strummed acoustic guitar and acoustic piano are the dominant instruments. This gives the music an organic, folky feel that suggests the values of the back-to-the-landers more than those of the hippie technophiles.

the flower power period to me. The coming together of people I find obscene as a principle. It is not a natural thing as some people would have us believe" (qtd. in Copetas 109). Although it is probably wise not to take this statement purely at face value, since the dialogue as a whole suggests that Bowie and Burroughs were trying to out-curmudgeon each other, it does reflect on the difference between Ziggy Stardust and the performance personae of psychedelic rockers. Whereas the onstage images of most underground musicians resembled their audiences (and each other), thus helping to foster a sense of community, Bowie constructed Ziggy Stardust to be visibly different from his audiences. Ziggy was a figure of alterity, not authenticity. Certainly, there was no extant community within rock culture from which Ziggy emerged and of which he was an expression. In an inversion of hippie ideology, Bowie's audiences emulated Ziggy by showing up at concerts dressed in homemade Ziggy costumes, makeup, and hairstyles. To the extent that these fans, known as "Bowie boys" and "Bowie girls," constituted a community, that community formed around Ziggy Stardust—it expressed him rather than the other way around.

In an essay on space-related tropes in popular music, Ken McLeod defines musical performers' adoption of alien personae as intrinsically critical of the ideology of authenticity: "By drawing on the fantastical, at least improbable, possibility of alien existence, such artists actively subvert and negate notions of authenticity. . . . By employing metaphors of space, alien beings or futurism, metaphors that are by definition unknowable, such artists and works constantly 'differ' the notion of 'authentic' identity" (339). In his discussion of Bowie, however, McLeod recuperates the trope of alienation for the discourse of authenticity: "Bowie's alien persona was emblematic of his bi-sexual alienation from the heterosexual male-dominated world of rock music" (341).[31] By treating Bowie's sexual

31. From my point of view, it is equally possible that the glamorous personae tinged with science fiction alienation adopted by both Bolan and Bowie referred to an aspect of their identities other than sexuality: their Jewishness. Bowie is only technically Jewish: although his mother was Jewish, the religion in which he has taken the greatest interest is Buddhism (he is hardly the first person of Jewish descent to be attracted to Zen!). Bolan grew up in a Jewish family, though he did not specifically identify himself as Jewish. Nevertheless, I can hear echoes of dahvening and Yiddishkeit in the incantatory quality of some of his early songs (including, ironically, "Iscariot") and the "dye dye

identity as known and stable and making Ziggy Stardust metaphoric for that identity, McLeod suggests that the alien is an authentic (in the sense of being faithful to an underlying personal reality) representation of a real social experience.

In fact, Bowie's performance of Ziggy's bisexuality was a good deal more complex than such an account suggests. There is no doubt that Bowie-as-Ziggy, especially in his visual manifestations, was perceived, both positively and negatively, as androgynous and sexually deviant. A teenaged female fan reported on the first time she saw Bowie on television:

> My parents were reading newspapers and I was sitting directly in front of the television as I always did then, watching. Suddenly this colourful man or perhaps it was a woman, I really couldn't tell, was in the centre of the TV.
>
> I was amazed. I turned to my parents and demanded to know more about this thing.
>
> "Oh . . . that's David Bowie," replied mother, "He's gay." (Qtd. in Vermorel and Vermorel 73)

Bowie was alternately vilified and celebrated for his queer public image. Another fan said that since "my parents didn't like him at all—and since they spoke about him as though he was some sort of monster I began to think of him as something really evil!" (qtd. in Vermorel and Vermorel 73). A pair of sociologists accused him of having "emasculated" rock music (Taylor and Wall 116). On the other hand, his fans clearly appreciated his androgynous appearance and intimations of queer sexuality; one fan (whose sex is unidentified) wrote in a letter: "Dear beautiful David I could make love to you, beautiful wo-man me too honey I'm a wo-man myself you ought to see me dressed up I'm sexier than you beautiful god-

---

dyes" and, occasionally, "oi oi ois" that appear in the vocal jams I discussed in the previous chapter. It would be reasonable to argue that Bolan's and Bowie's respective changes of name and creations of new personae could relate to the intertwined sense of difference and desire to assimilate that are so much a part of the Anglo-American Jewish experience, not to mention the sense of belonging to a tiny minority among rock musicians. Although Bowie's Jewish roots remain an unexplored issue, Bolan has been claimed as a Jewish rocker—he is profiled in Scott R. Bernade's *Stars of David: Rock 'n' Roll's Jewish Stories,* and John Zorn produced a CD of Bolan's music as performed by a roster of downtown New York musicians as part of the Great Jewish Music series on his record label Tzadik.

dess" (qtd. in Vermorel and Vermorel 25). A *Gay News* review of Bowie's concert at the Royal Festival Hall in July 1972, entitled "Gay Rock," concluded with this laud: "David Bowie is the best rock musician in Britain now. One day he'll be as popular as he deserves to be. And that'll give gay rock a potent spokesman" (Holmes 78).

It is worthy of note that whereas McLeod conflates Ziggy Stardust's identity as an alien with Bowie's putative identity as a bisexual man, at least some of Bowie's fans saw the two things as separate aspects of the persona. Androgynous sexuality and extraterrestrial origin seem to have provided two different points of identification for Bowie fans: whereas some were taken with his wo-manliness, others were struck by his spaciness. As one fan reports, "From an early age I was interested in science fiction and spacy things like paranormal beings. And Bowie was a personification of that kind of thing" (qtd. in Vermorel and Vermorel 63). Another has almost exactly the same thing to say: "I thought he was so extraordinary that he couldn't possibly be human. He was paranormal almost. . . He was science fiction personified. . . . I really believed he was an alien of some kind. I didn't think he was at all normal, human" (qtd. in Vermorel and Vermorel 99).

Bowie went beyond the visual construction of Ziggy Stardust in performing queer sexuality. In a now-legendary interview with Michael Watts published in *Melody Maker* in January 1972, Bowie declared: "I'm gay . . . and always have been" (49). Seven months later, during a press conference at the Dorchester Hotel in London, Bowie presented Lou Reed to the British public:

> It was at this moment that Lou Reed minced officially into glitter rock, entering in his Bowie-influenced Phantom of Rock persona, made-up and sparkling in Bowie's designer's jumpsuit, six-inch platforms, and black nail polish. With studied deliberation, the Phantom deposited his two cents into the gay-liberation kitty by tottering across La Bowie's suite and firmly planting a kiss on Bowie's mouth. (Bockris 204)

The crucial thing about these episodes is not what was said but the way it was said. In his article, Watts clearly implies that he did not take Bowie's declaration at face value:

David's present image is to come on like swishy queen, a gorgeously effeminate boy. He's as camp as a row of tents, with his limp hand and trolling vocabulary. "I'm gay," he says, "and always have been, even when I was David Jones." But there's a sly jollity about how he says it, a secret smile at the corners of his mouth. . . . The expression of sexual ambivalence establishes a fascinating game: is he, or isn't he? (49)

In discussing the constitution of gender identities, Judith Butler argues that "gender attributes . . . are not expressive but performative," meaning that "these attributes effectively constitute the identity they are said to express or reveal" (141). Extending Butler's analysis to sexual identities, I argue that Bowie's presentation of his sexuality on these occasions suggests a perception of such identities as performative, not expressive. His performance of a gay or bisexual identity did not express some essential quality of his person; it was, rather, a performance of signs that are socially legible as constituting a gay identity. In Butler's terms, the question "is he, or isn't he?" is the wrong question because it cannot be answered: "If gender attributes and acts [or, here, attributes and acts associated with sexuality], the various ways in which a body shows or produces its cultural signification, are performative, then there is no preexisting identity by which an act or attribute might be measured" (141).

Bowie's performance of gay sexuality was multiply subversive. On the one hand, it flew in the face of rock culture's traditional heterosexual imperative. On the other hand, it did so without simply asserting gay rock as an equal alternative—Bowie, who had subverted rock's ideology of authenticity through his insistence on rock performance as theatrical role-playing and his use of multiple voices and subject positions, did not perform "authentic" homosexuality or bisexuality. Rather than raising questions about his own sexuality, Bowie threw the sexuality of rock into question, not only by performing a sexual identity previously excluded from rock but also by performing that identity in such a way that it was clearly revealed *as a performance* for which there was no underlying referent (as did Reed when he crossed the room to kiss Bowie "with studied deliberation"). As Butler suggests, Bowie's pointing to the performativity of queer identity brought "into relief the utterly constructed status of the so-called heterosexual original" to imply that the heterosexuality considered normative in rock culture is no more foundational than any other sexual identity (31).

Butler's analysis also sheds light on aspects of Bowie's music at this moment. For all the discussion of Ziggy Stardust as a bisexual alien, the album bearing his name contains relatively few songs that refer overtly either to extraterrestrial identity or queer identity. Aside from the phrase "space invader" and some futuristic language in "Moonage Daydream," "Starman" is the only song to evoke outer space in direct terms. The only song to suggest homo- or bisexuality is "Lady Stardust," a song about a musical performer (probably Bolan).[32] The singer, Lady Stardust, who is described as wearing makeup, is identified with masculine pronouns; he attracts the attention of his male and female spectators equally. The narrator of the song, whose voice is masculine, coyly admits to having a sexual attraction to the singer on which he feels he cannot act: "I smiled sadly for a love I could not obey." In all the other songs on the album, sexual references are couched in heterosexual terms in which the masculine voiced singer refers to the objects of his lust by using feminine pronouns.

Two such songs are "Hang on to Yourself" and "Suffragette City." Their placement on the album is significant. The second side of the original LP constitutes a six-song cycle on the theme of rock stardom as seen from a variety of perspectives: an audience member's, a would-be rock star's, a successful musician's band mate's, and others. "Hang on to Yourself" follows immediately after "Star," the song about an aspiring rock star that ends with his saying, "Just watch me now." "Hang on to Yourself" thus becomes his rock performance. "Suffragette City" is in the same position with respect to "Ziggy Stardust," which describes the rise to success and disastrous fall of a rock star. Both of these songs serve as emblematic rockers performed by the musicians described in the preceding songs. As such, they are prototypically upbeat, masculinist rock-and-roll songs (the music on this album is the closest Bowie came to emulating Bolan's fifties inflections) about sex that objectify their female love objects.

And yet, as recorded, these songs are not entirely representative rock expressions of male heterosexual desire: they are played overly

32. Bowie "performed ['Lady Stardust'] at the Rainbow in August [1972] while an image of Bolan was projected behind the band" (Paytress, *Bolan* 218–19).

fast, sung in mannered voices, and convey sexual urgency in almost parodic terms. "Hang on to Yourself" features a hyperactive bass line that mirrors Bowie's overstuffed lyrics: "She wants my honey not my money she's a funky-thigh collector." Bowie's vocal mannerisms range from prissy-sounding emphases of certain words, to chuckling pseudodetachment as he brags about his and his partner's sexual prowess ("we move around like tigers on Vaseline"), to a squeaky, imploring tone as he urges his lover to "come on." The song ends with ever more beseeching repetitions of that phrase punctuated by heavy breathing.

The scenario of "Suffragette City" involves the protagonist's explaining to a male friend, Henry, that he cannot stay over at the protagonist's place that night because he is expecting a visit from a woman ("There's only room for one and here she comes"). As the protagonist begs for his friend's understanding, his voice is high and somewhat pinched; when he talks about his potential lover, it descends to deep machismo: "she's all right." The voice becomes almost cartoonish when trying to convey to Henry just how desirable the woman is ("she's a total blam-blam"). For his part, Henry is represented by repetition of the comically laconic "Hey man," his inarticulate attempt to make the case that his friend should prefer their friendship over sexual conquest. (Part of the song's humor comes from the fact that "Henry" shifts in the mix from the left side of the stereo field to the right between verses, making it seem that he is hovering around his friend trying to get him to change his priorities.) As the woman (and the promise of sex) comes closer and closer, the protagonist's voice becomes more and more urgent and shrill; by the crowing, crude climax of "Wham Bam Thank You Ma'am!" the voice has acquired an edge of hysteria.

In discussing gender parody and subversion, Butler refers to "the replication of heterosexual constructs in non-heterosexual frames" (31); this seems to me a good description of what Bowie is up to in these songs. Like most rock songs, they reflect the social behavior and attitudes of heterosexual men, but Bowie's performances of a queer alien identity on television, in print, and on stage for six months prior to the album's release constituted the "non-heterosexual frame" within which he placed male heterosexuality. Butler mentions hyperbole as a tactic in this context; the overly fast tempi and often squeaky, imploring, exaggeratedly urgent voices on these recordings can be heard readily as hyperbolic representations of male heterosexuality pushed to the edge of hysteria. "The replication of heterosexual constructs in non-heterosexual frames brings into relief the utterly constructed status of the so-called heterosexual original" (Butler 31). If Bowie's public performances of bisexuality can be said to have emphasized the socially constructed status of gay sexual identities, then his framing of rock heterosexuality through that identity reveals the extent to which rock's normative sexuality is also constructed through and by the music itself. Like Bowie's performance of a queer public identity, these recorded performances raised questions about sexuality in the context of rock culture and the cultural norms by which behavior is assessed and policed.

Bowie's concert performances as Ziggy Stardust were the culmination of the three intertwined tendencies I have been discussing: his continual challenges to rock's ideology of authenticity, his desire to theatricalize rock performance, and his engagement in complex representations of gender and sexuality. To a far greater extent than Bolan, who retained the relative informality of the rock concert but inserted anomalously self-conscious images into it, Bowie reconceived the rock concert as an obviously designed and choreographed theatrical event. Bowie's Ziggy concerts, as represented by the final one at the Hammersmith Odeon on July 3, 1973, captured by documentarian D. A. Pennebaker, flouted the ideology of authenticity. Whereas the hippie counterculture expressed its commitment to presentism and authenticity through musical performances that deemphasized theatrics, Bowie treated the rock concert as a monument to glittering artifice.

Although *The Rise and Fall of Ziggy Stardust and The Spiders from Mars* has often been called a concept album or even a rock opera, Bowie's performances in his Ziggy persona were nevertheless *concerts*, not musical theater. As opposed to the Kinks' *Preservation*, which the group performed in 1974 as a staged opera in which they and their backup singers and musicians "took on various identities to portray the characters . . . and performed the opera from start to finish" (Dalton), Bowie's Ziggy Stardust concerts had no continuous plot or characters (apart from the musicians' performance personae). The music played at these concerts was not limited to the *Ziggy Stardust* album; it was drawn from Bowie's work from 1969 on, and included songs by other composers, including Jacques Brel, Lou Reed, and Mick Jagger and Keith Richards.

In his concerts, however, Bowie made use of all the means available to the theater: sets (fairly minimal ones constituted primarily by large, hieratic symbols of a lightening bolt in a circle), lighting, makeup, and costumes. As a comparison with a more conventional concert that occurred around the same time shows, the lighting was used specifically to create dramatic effects. The concert at Madison Square Garden that served as the basis for Led Zeppelin's film *The Song Remains the Same*—which also took place in July 1973—was bathed in atmospheric washes of light that allowed all the members of the group to be equally visible at most times. The Ziggy Stardust lighting was virtually the opposite: the concert was staged in the dark. Whereas psychedelic rockers used darkness to promote a meditative concentration on the music, Bowie used it to create a dramatic effect as individual spotlights picked out the four members of Ziggy Stardust and the Spiders from Mars. The full performing group actually included five other musicians who were hidden in darkness. Another example of the dramatic use of lighting came at the end of the performance of "Changes." Bowie made a downward sweeping gesture with both hands as if he were signaling for quiet. This gesture was the cue for a saxophone solo—after making it, Bowie turned his head very deliberately toward the left as the saxophonist appeared out of the darkness in a spotlight.

The concert abounded in such clearly staged moments at which music, gesture, and other theatrical means combined to present spectacular images and effects. During the long instrumental section of "Width of a Circle," for example, bass guitarist Bolder and guitarist Ronson engaged in a kind of ritual combat while playing a duet. Initially, Bolder advanced on Ronson, driving him across the stage and eventually onto the floor, where he continued to play while lying on his back. Struggling heroically to his feet, Ronson fended off the attack and pressed Bolder back to his side of the stage. The victorious Ronson raised his hands in a gesture of triumph identical to those used by professional wrestlers. This kind of showmanship, which clearly evoked the byplay of such 1950s rock and rollers as Bo Diddley and Jerry Lee Lewis, was wholly different from the emphasis on inwardness and seriousness characteristic of psychedelic rockers.

Like his interviews and recordings from this era, Bowie's concerts raised issues of gender and sexuality. In analyzing how these images were constructed, I will borrow from the conclusions of sociologist Erving Goffman in his *Gender Advertisements*. In that book, Goffman develops a semiotics of gender performance by

identifying and analyzing the postures, gestures, and facial expressions that seem to be coded as "feminine" within Western indus-
trial societies by looking at representations of women, and their
visual relationships to men, in advertisements and other commercial photographs.[33] (It is fortuitous that since Goffman originally
published his findings in 1976, many of his examples come from the
years during which glam rock was at its height.)

I will expand on Goffman's analysis by suggesting that behaviors
coded as feminine can be enacted by men as well as women. Goffman's emphasis on the socially constructed nature of gendered
behavior and his insistence that there is no intrinsic connection
between coded displays of masculinity and femininity and the biological state of being male or female are salutary in the context of
Bowie's performative treatment of gender and sexuality. I shall
argue that Bowie's performance as Ziggy Stardust reflected a complex interplay of masculine and feminine gender codes enacted by
male performers. Part of this complexity derived from Bowie's individual performance, in which he frequently performed femininely
coded gestures and poses yet sometimes reverted to more masculine
ones. This complexity also derives from a clearly identifiable,
though not altogether stable, gendered division of labor between
Bowie and lead guitarist Ronson, with whom he shared the stage
and interacted extensively during the concert. Even though Bowie
sometimes exhibited masculine coding in his performance and there
were ways in which Ronson was feminized, the primary staged
relationship between them was one in which Bowie embodied femininity and Ronson masculinity, a relationship made very explicit at
some of the more overtly erotic moments of the performance.

The opening song of the concert, a rendition of "Hang Onto
Yourself," established these images and relationships immediately.
Bowie appeared in a long glittery tunic and sang while smiling
ingratiatingly at the audience. Goffman identifies this kind of smile
as a "ritualistic mollifier," and "more the offering of an inferior
than a superior." This kind of smile is also coded as a feminine
expression, inasmuch as "women [are represented as] smil[ing]
more, and more expansively, than men" (48). In and of itself,
Bowie's smile might not be interpreted specifically as feminine, but

33. Goffman does not provide the sources for the many images he uses in
the book. Though most appear to be North American, some clearly are Western European. Essentially all of the images are of Caucasian women and men.

I argue that in the context of his staged relationship with guitarist Ronson, it should be. Bowie ceded the stage, retiring to the back, while Ronson played a guitar solo. Although Ronson was thoroughly "glammed up" in glittering costume, shag haircut, eye makeup, and lipstick, his position in the gender economy of the performance was clearly the masculine one. Although Bowie plays several instruments, he appeared initially only as a singer, a feminine position in rock since women have participated in the music far more frequently as singers than instrumentalists (Bayton 37). As lead guitarist, Ronson occupied a position that is coded as masculine within rock culture. Ronson made a great show of his guitar solo, strutting, showing off his instrumental virtuosity by playing the guitar with one hand, stalking across the stage with his body in a wide-open stance that contrasted sharply with Bowie's more feminine, closed stance as he sang at the microphone.

In all these respects, Ronson was the very embodiment of the rock guitar hero. As Steve Waksman describes it, the figure of the guitar hero encompasses virtuosity, power, and flamboyance in "a ritual that validates masculine prowess" (249). Crucially, Ronson did not smile as he performed this ritual; in fact, while Bowie smiled frequently at the audience throughout the concert, Ronson never did. Bowie, the feminized "girl" singer, ingratiated himself to the audience (and his guitarist), while Ronson, the masculine guitar hero, demanded recognition through domination.

Bowie's feminized deference to his guitarist carried over from his absenting himself during Ronson's solos into the moments at which they interacted, frequently in overtly erotic ways. During the song "Moonage Daydream," when Bowie and Ronson shared a microphone while singing, Bowie gazed fondly and smilingly at the guitarist, and gave him an affectionate kiss. (The song itself is a space-age love song, including romantic lyrics like "Press your space face close to mine, love" and the more phallic and sexual "Put your ray-gun to my head.") This flirtation was consummated during the song "Time."

At this point in the concert Bowie wore a feather boa and adopted a Marlene Dietrich–like persona appropriate to the cabaret-style song. After sashaying around the stage manipulating his boa and singing, Bowie turned toward Ronson, breathing heavily. The guitarist literally leapt toward the singer, who fell submissively to the floor in a prone position suggesting sexual rear entry of either the heterosexual or homosexual variety. Ronson straddled

Mick Ronson *(top)* and David Bowie *(bottom)*, 1973. © MichaelOchs
Archives.com.

Bowie while playing his guitar solo, thrusting his guitar toward Bowie in an unmistakably phallic fashion. They rose and fell together in a copulatory rhythm just prior to a blackout.

At one level, this scene can be understood as a dramatization of the often sexually charged relationship between male singers and guitarists in rock groups. Susan Fast, discussing Led Zeppelin, proposes that Robert Plant, the group's singer, performed "a feminine musical persona" to guitarist Jimmy Page's masculine persona (44). In her analysis of the musical and verbal interplay between the two musicians, Fast points to moments at which Page was cast "in the role of receiver of sexual pleasure during intercourse, the 'woman' who is asking for more, thus strengthening his role as feminine other to Page" (45). Clearly, Bowie and Ronson's performance made literal and visible that which is generally only implied in the interactions between rock singers and guitarists: in doing so, they transgressed the carefully policed border between homosociality and homosexuality (Sedgwick 15).

But even at this level, the scene is not devoid of ambiguity, in large part because of Ronson's particular way of performing the role of guitar hero. Although Page, for example, is a flashy guitarist who runs, jumps, engages in large gestures with his arms, and is generally an animated and energetic player, he does not offer himself as an object of display to the audience to the same degree as Ronson did. Ronson—glistening in his spotlight like a golden statue with blond hair, gold lamé clothing, and a burnished gold guitar—took every opportunity to hold his body in a wide-open stance directed at the audience. His gestures were overstated; his facial expressions indicating musical concentration and effort were distorted by his makeup into larger-than-life grimaces. His portrayal of the guitar hero was, in a word, excessive, even for a role that is intrinsically overstated. His performance style italicized all of his guitar hero gestures and mannerisms for the audience. As psychoanalyst Jacques Lacan famously observed, "in the human being, virile display itself appears as feminine" (qtd. in Owens 214). By making such a spectacle of being a macho guitar hero, Ronson uncovered the gender ambiguities latent in that role itself. Whereas the "sex scene" between Bowie and Ronson seemed to be premised on the idea of Ronson as "masculine" and Bowie as "feminine," Ronson's masculine status was called into question by his spectacular overplaying of the role of guitar hero.

The scene is also ambiguous on a dramatic level: What exactly was being represented? Ronson and his guitar performed sexual aggression. But on whom was he aggressing? Was Bowie, in his cabaret singer guise, to be understood as a straight woman or a gay man? The simulated sex act provided no suggestion of a physiological answer to this question. The polyvalence of Bowie's and Ronson's performances of gender and sexuality created the "hyperbole, dissonance, internal confusion, and proliferation" Butler identifies as strategies for destabilizing normative representations (31). There was also ambiguity as to whether Ronson's sexual aggression toward Bowie was that of a lover or a rapist. Although Ronson's tackling Bowie at the start of this sequence could be read as a sexual assault, the final image of this sequence suggested more that his aggression was welcome. The song ended with another blackout; when the lights came back up, Bowie and Ronson were posed in a tableau, with Bowie behind and above Ronson, head turned passionately to his right, his left hand reaching down to touch the strings of Ronson's guitar right over the guitarist's genitals.

At the end of "Hang On To Yourself," Bowie had the first of many costume changes. This one occurred onstage: after the spotlights came back on from a blackout, hands darted out from both sides of the darkness surrounding Bowie's circle of light and snatched away an outer layer of clothing, revealing a different costume beneath. This routine, which Bowie used again at the beginning of his *1980 Floor Show* (1973) television special, clearly positions Bowie as an object of display. In the course of a two-hour performance, he wore five different costumes that actually seemed to be seven because two of them featured a cape or tunic that was removed to reveal the outfit beneath. All of these costumes, designed either by Freddi Burretti or the Japanese designer Kansai, were feminine in one sense or another. They featured oversized earrings and bracelets, a see-through top, hot pants, leotards, and so on. The performance was almost as much a fashion show, with Bowie posing and parading in different outfits, as it was a concert. This concept, too, reappeared in the *1980 Floor Show,* in which Bowie-as-Ziggy wore a different costume for each song he performed.

Bowie's performance persona changed along (though not necessarily in synch) with his costumes in the course of the concert, from rocker to folkie balladeer to torchy cabaret singer to his incarnation as a Mick Jagger–type figure who stalks back and forth across the stage during "Let's Spend the Night Together" while wearing a decidedly feminine see-through sheer black top. (Bowie dedicated his performance of the Rolling Stones' song to Jagger, the original icon of sexual ambiguity in rock, who is a recurrent figure in Bowie's career.)[34] Like the costumes themselves, these changes of outfit and persona are coded as feminine, according to Goffman:

> Men are displayed in formal, business, and informal gear, and although it seems understood that the same individual will at different times appear in all these guises, each guise seems to afford him something he is totally serious about, and deeply identified with, as though wearing a skin, not a costume. . . . Women in ads seem to have a different relationship to their clothing and to the gestures worn with it. Within each broad category (formal, business, informal) there are choices which are considerably different from one another, and the sense is that one may as well try out various possibilities to see what comes of it—as though life were a series of costume balls. Thus, one can occasionally mock one's own appearance, for identification is not deep. (51)

This observation sheds important light on Bowie's performance. Not only were Bowie's costumes feminine, his frequent changes of costume read as the feminine lack of commitment to a single identity Goffman describes. While Ronson remained onstage for the entire concert, working hard and unsmilingly in his role as rock guitar hero, the feminine Bowie had the freedom to leave the stage and reappear in new outfits and new guises. (These moments revealed a fundamental difference between Bowie's performances and those of psychedelic rock. The fact that Ronson had to play for long enough to allow Bowie to change costumes indicates that the music served the spectacle rather than the other way around.)

Goffman's point is important for another reason, too, for it suggests that the very strategies by which Bowie coded himself as feminine simultaneously allowed him to assert the artificiality of that coding. His frequent changes of costume suggest a feminine lack of

34. Robert Duncan describes Mick Jagger as glitter rock's grandfather: "before Alice Cooper and David Bowie and the New York Dolls . . . there was Mick Jagger, rock 'n' roll's foremost androgyne, Woodstock nation's leading homo-hetero" (105). Bowie referred frequently to Jagger in interviews; in 1985, they recorded "Dancing in the Streets" together and made a video to go along with the record.

identification with any particular outfit or persona. The fact that the outfits and personae he passed through were themselves coded as feminine further suggests that he did not identify deeply with a feminine image of himself and did not expect his feminine representations to be taken seriously. Rather, Bowie took aspects of feminine gender display and used them in what Goffman calls "a quotative way" (3). Bowie treated gender identity in the same way he treated sexual identity: as performative and, therefore, lacking in foundation.

A medley of three of his songs Bowie performed at the Odeon is well worth examining for the way it charted both Bowie's own career and a transition in rock masculinity. The first song of the medley is "Wild Eyed Boy from Freecloud," a 1969 ballad from the *Space Oddity* album expressing countercultural values. The song concerns the boy of the title, a free-spirited "missionary mystic of peace/love" who is threatened with execution by the people of a village, who fear what they see as "the madness in his eyes." When he is about to be hanged, Freecloud, his mountain home, destroys the village with an avalanche, much to the boy's chagrin. The boy from Freecloud exemplifies the countercultural version of masculinity: gentle, innocent, opposed to violence, misunderstood by a convention-bound society.

Bowie sang the song intently, but with a distant expression on his face of the kind Goffman refers to as "licensed withdrawal," a feminine mood in which women are depicted as "remove[d] . . . psychologically from the social situation at large, leaving them unoriented in it and to it" (57). Bowie enacted versions of licensed withdrawal frequently in the concert, most notably during his performance of "Space Oddity," when he seemed completely abstracted from the audience and his situation on stage. For "Space Oddity," Bowie assumed the role of female folkie, similar to the image Bolan presented with Tyrannosaurus Rex: he sat, drifted into licensed withdrawal, and strummed his acoustic guitar. Although "Space Oddity" comes after "Wild Eyed Boy" in the concert, it is clear that Bowie's performance of the latter song evokes the same image of the woman folk singer.

In fact, the feminine-coded acoustic guitar was the only instrument Bowie played in public during his Ziggy years even though he appeared on the cover of *The Rise and Fall of Ziggy Stardust and The Spiders from Mars* with an electric guitar and played multiple instruments on the recordings. The character of Ziggy Stardust in the song of that name is described as a guitar hero; the first and last lines of the song are "Ziggy played guitar."[35] Perhaps depicting Ziggy as an electric guitarist while only playing acoustic guitar was a means for Bowie to distinguish himself as a performer from his character. One of the signs that Bowie had moved on from the Ziggy persona was that in 1974, around the time of his *Diamond Dogs* album, a bright red electric guitar became part of his new image.

The Wild Eyed Boy's mantra concerns existential authenticity: "It's so hard for us to really be / Really You / And Really Me." Bowie did not sing the whole song in the medley; he stopped after the first chorus and moved on to the next song, the glamthem "All the Young Dudes." In moving from the first song to the second, Bowie recapitulated the transition from countercultural masculinity to glam masculinity that he undertook as a performer and that glam rock institutionalized. Bowie's juxtaposition of the two songs suggested that what it means to be "really me" is, ironically, expressed by the overtly artificial feminine masculinity of glam rather than what the counterculture considered to be a naturally androgynous masculinity. Bowie's performance style shifted radically as he moved from the first song to the second. He abandoned licensed withdrawal and inserted himself fully into the situation, smiled, swung his head and hips, and really seemed to be enjoying the song in a way he did not enjoy the first one, suggesting that the transition from the masculinity represented by the wild-eyed boy to that represented by the young dudes is liberatory.

The third song in the medley, "Oh You Pretty Things" (from *Hunky Dory*), consolidates these themes rather than adding to them. Originally written to commemorate the birth of David and Angela's son, Zowie, in 1971, the song takes on a different meaning in the context of the medley. In this context, the chorus of the song—"Oh You Pretty Things / Don't you know you're driving your / Mamas and Papas insane"—refers not to newborns, but to

35. "Sweet Head," a song recorded during the Ziggy Stardust sessions but not included on the album (it is available as a bonus track on the 1990 CD reissue), is sung from Ziggy's perspective. He celebrates his own prowess as a guitarist and makes an explicit analogy between the bobbing of the head that may result from listening to his music and the listener's performing oral sex on him. It is not possible to discern the sex of the listener from the lyrics.

teenagers who have adopted glam's androgynous style to the chagrin of their elders. At the Odeon, Bowie sang this part of the medley directly to the audience. This song makes the transition from
rock masculinity to glam masculinity charted by the first two songs
seem teleological, for the lyrics refer explicitly to concepts of evolution and natural selection. The last verse states, "Homo sapiens
have outgrown their use," and the lines of the chorus that follow
the ones I just quoted are "Let me make it plain / You gotta make
way for the Homo Superior." In the context of the medley, the
young dude and the homo superior are clearly one and the same,
and, though I am reluctant to belabor the obvious, it is clear that
the word "homo" is being used punningly. In this medley, Bowie
celebrated the triumph of glam over the counterculture: Glam Man
is presented not just as superior to Countercultural Man, but as the
evolutionary successor to *Homo sapiens*.

On December 4, 1974, Bowie sang "Young Americans" on *The
Dick Cavett Show*. He wore a light brown suit with exaggeratedly
padded shoulders and high-waisted trousers from which a long
chain looped down, zoot suit style, on his right side; white shoes; a
blue shirt; and a tie. His hair was bright orange, but no longer in
Ziggy Stardust's overstated mullet.

If Ziggy's voice was a high, somewhat nasal, head voice, this
singer's voice was deeper, huskier, throatier. Whereas Ziggy's posture was erect yet relaxed, this singer seemed to carry tension in his
shoulders, his head jutting from his shoulders like a vulture's. Ziggy
stood simply and easily at the microphone—this singer leaned
toward it, sometimes grasping it in the manner of a lounge singer.
If Ziggy's countenance was relaxed, often in an easy smile, every
muscle in this performer's face seemed tensed, making his sharp
features prominent. Whereas Ziggy's movements were often expan-
sive—he would stride from one side of the stage to the other, sometimes lowering himself toward the floor—this performer kept his
arms locked forcefully by his sides, sometimes raising them in
vaguely Latin dance movements, his eyes tightly closed.

The music was not rock music, exactly, but a version of African-
American soul and disco. None of the Spiders from Mars was there;
the singer was accompanied largely by African-American musicians
and a sextet of backup singers.

This performer's persona was as carefully constructed and managed as Ziggy's, yet different from Ziggy in almost all respects. This persona, the white, British soul boy living out a fantasy of being black, was Bowie's next role.[36]

36. Bowie's frequent transformations of persona are the hallmark of his career strategy: as I have discussed here, he moved from Mod to hippie to Ziggy Stardust to Ziggy's second incarnation as Aladdin Sane. The replacement for the soul boy persona that succeeded Ziggy was the Thin White Duke, named for a song on *Station to Station* (1976). This was arguably the last of his well-defined personae. Although Bowie's music would undergo several more stylistic transitions, as from the avant-rock of *Low* and *Heroes* (both 1977) to the dance-pop of *Let's Dance* (1983), he did not cultivate performance personae as explicitly as he had earlier on but emerged as an avuncular elder statesman of rock with keen interests in visual art and the Internet. Looking back on this aspect of his career in 1993, Bowie told *Rolling Stone:* "It has been gnawing at me, the idea of one more time developing a character. I do love the theatrical side of the thing—not only do I enjoy it, I also think I'm quite good at it. But for the time being I'm *quite* happy being me" (qtd. in Wilde 216).

5. Inauthentic Voices

Gender Bending and Genre Blending with Bryan Ferry and Roy Wood

The idea was that Roxy Music could be any kind of music,
could do anything.
—Bryan Ferry (qtd. in Frith, "Bryan Ferry" 31)

I know that there's been a load of letters written to the musical papers
accusing me of plagiarism—but if someone says any of our records
sound a bit like Phil Spector's that's O. K. by me, 'cause
Phil Spector is the greatest producer of them all.
—Roy Wood (qtd. in Carr, "Who's" 21)

The grammatical concepts of the indicative and subjunctive moods take on particular meanings in the context of performance studies, meanings established by the anthropologist Victor Turner. Turner used the idea of the subjunctive to characterize the liminal phase of transformational rituals, a phase he otherwise described as a state of being "neither here nor there . . . betwixt and between [known] positions" (qtd. in Schechner, *Performance Studies* 58).[1] He defined the subjunctive as "a world of as if . . . it is 'if it were so' not 'it *is* so'" (Victor Turner 83). Because "the cognitive schema that give

1. Folklorist Arnold Van Gennep formulated the idea that rituals entail three phases, the preliminal, liminal, and postliminal in *The Rites of Passage* (1908). Van Gennep identified the liminal phase as the one in which the ritual transformation actually takes place. During the preliminal phase, the ritual subjects are removed from their present lives and identities; during the postliminal phase, they are restored to their social groups and take up the new identities conferred on them as a consequence of the ritual. The liminal phase is thus the transformative phase during which the ritual subjects no longer possess their original identities but also have not yet achieved their new ones.

sense and order to everyday life no longer apply" in this phase, the subjunctive is for Turner a space of potential "cultural innovation" in which "new meanings and symbols may be introduced" (84–85).

Susan Fast has applied Turner's concept of the subjunctive to music by suggesting that musical experience is analogous to the liminal phase of ritual in the sense that it transports the listener to an experiential realm different from that of everyday life, a realm in which daily norms are suspended and new meanings proposed (129). Fast thus uses Turner's distinction between the subjunctive and the indicative in one of the ways Turner himself used it: to distinguish performance from ordinary behavior. But Turner also used this dichotomy in another way: to distinguish different types of performance from one another. Although the liminal phase of ritual involves subjunctivity and engagement with the "world of as if," another kind of cultural performance, which Turner calls *ceremony,* "constitutes an impressive institutionalized performance of indicative, normatively structured social reality" (83). Applied to music, this aspect of Turner's analysis would suggest that whereas some musical performances carry their listeners into the subjunctive to explore the imaginative terrain of the "as if," others remain in the indicative mood by reifying and celebrating what *is.*

The vocabulary of indicative and subjunctive, ceremony and ritual, provides a useful way of describing the relationship between psychedelic rock and glam rock. The centrality of the ideology of authenticity to the counterculture means that, as mood music, psychedelic rock is in the indicative. To emphasize authenticity is to place a high value on what *is;* the link between authenticity and the indicative mood is indicated by the primary nongrammatical meaning of the word *indicative:* "showing, suggesting, or pointing out that something exists or is true" *(Encarta World English Dictionary).* Keir Keightley observes that "musical experiences considered 'authentic' are . . . those which highlight or nourish individual identity, or signal affinities with the smaller communities and subcultures which sustain that identity" (134). One of the criteria for authenticity in rock is that performances point to a grounding reality, whether the reality of the musician's individual psyche or that of an existing cultural identity.

It is quite clear from the way the hippie counterculture saw rock music as a direct emanation of itself that the performance of psychedelic rock was more akin to ceremony, the indicative form of cultural performance in which existing realities are affirmed and celebrated, than to the liminal, subjunctive phase of ritual in which those realities are completely suspended and subject to radical redefinition. Glam rock, by contrast, celebrated the subjunctive and the liminal through its play with ambiguous gender and sexual identities and overtly constructed personae. Whereas the performance of psychedelic rock referred to and was thought to reflect directly the offstage social reality of which it was a part, glam rock treated the stage as a liminal space in which things could happen that had no necessary counterpart in external reality. Identities could be explored in the subjunctive mood: David Bowie, for instance, could perform rock star identity *as if* he were a bisexual space alien.

Glam rockers of the first wave, among whom Marc Bolan and Bowie were the most prominent, innovated the performance of musical personae that were both transgressive with respect to gender and sexuality and self-consciously constructed. By 1972, glam rock was an established stylistic option and other performers, whom I refer to as the second wave, took it up and interpreted its impulses in their own ways. In this chapter, I discuss the work of two second-wave glam artists, Bryan Ferry and Roy Wood, both with and apart from the groups of which they were members. Their work reflected the defining characteristics of glam and its resistance to the ideology of authenticity, but also extended that challenge further into the realm of musical style and vocal expression.

There is a direct link between authenticity and musical style in rock culture. Commitment to a particular musical style is thought to be a direct expression of an artist's sensibility; as such, it is expected to remain relatively stable—radical changes of musical direction are not often welcomed. Vocal style is considered to be a performer's signature and a manifestation of that performer's individuality. Ferry and Wood challenged these aspects of rock's ideology by creating groups with multiple and shifting stylistic commitments that made music whose genre identity changes from song to song and sometimes within single compositions. As singers, Ferry and Wood performed in overtly artificial voices that went beyond even Bolan's highly stylized singing in asserting that a singer's voice is not necessarily an authentic expression of identity.

Roxy Music emerged fully formed in mid-1972, at the high point of glam when T. Rextasy was in full swing and Bowie had hit his stride as Ziggy Stardust. Unlike Bolan and Bowie, however, Bryan Ferry, the group's leader, singer, keyboardist, and main songwriter, had not spent years striving at the edges of the music business. He sang with a northern soul group called the Gas Board while at Newcastle University, where he earned a fine arts degree. Arriving in London in 1969, he found the underground music scene to be "dull"; two years later he set out to create a group that would have at least a chance of succeeding quickly. "The average age of this band is about 27," Ferry told journalist Richard Williams, an early supporter, in 1971, "and we're not interested in scuffling."

Inevitably, a group that came out of nowhere, made up of musicians with no previous track record, was regarded with suspicion by the remnants of an underground scene that valued both musical virtuosity and the aura of authenticity conferred by a history of dues-paying prior to success. Roxy Music challenged both precepts. One founding member, Brian Eno, directly contested notions of virtuosity since he did not play any conventional musical instruments but engaged in electronic bricolage using tape recorders, synthesizers, and homemade equipment. One of his main functions in the group was to manipulate sounds produced by the other musicians. Ferry, for his part, openly repudiated the ideology of dues paying: "People think that to be a success you've got to have served your apprenticeship on the road. That's completely bogus" (qtd. in Steve Turner, "Roxy Music").

Ferry also rejected the underground's commitment to a low-key, antitheatrical performance style as an expression of authenticity: "I've never had any time for this theory that if you go out onstage wearing denims, you're for real" (qtd. in Nicholl 48); "I've always thought that if you're going to present yourself on stage you should dress up" (qtd. in Steve Turner, "Roxy Music"). If Bowie sought to counter psychedelic rock's suspicion of spectacle with theater, Ferry pursued a different direction by melding music with fashion, particularly through an alliance with designer Antony Price, who styled Ferry and other members of the group.[2] The group's first album, *Roxy Music* (1972), which one critic later described as being

2. The alliance between Ferry and Price continues to this day: Price designed Ferry's stage outfits for his 2000 tour, for example. Ferry has conspicuously supported other British designers as well, including Sir Paul Smith and Mark Powell.

"as stunning visually as it was musically" (Coon), featured an inner gatefold image of the five group members, all holding guitars (which only one of them played on stage) and dressed in Price's extravagant outfits. The front cover, designed by Ferry, featured former Mary Quant model Kari-Anne Moller displayed like a pinup girl in a distinctly retro dress also by Price (models Amanda Lear and Jerry Hall, as well as *Playboy* centerfold Marilyn Cole, all posed for the covers of Roxy Music albums). To emphasize the importance of visual style to Roxy Music, the album's liner notes included credits for "clothes, make-up & hair" alongside of more conventional lists of musicians and recording personnel.

Like Bolan's and Bowie's respective looks, Roxy Music's style caught on with fans, who attended concerts dressed in emulation of band members, their album covers, or other appropriate styles. Like Bowie, Ferry continually changed his image (Caroline Coon cataloged them in *Melody Maker* as "the White Tux, the Gaucho, the Country Squire, Hitler's cousin, the sleazy Fifties Mohair"). But whereas Bowie's transformations entailed changes of persona, Ferry's were transformations of style akin to the arrival of new collections with each fashion season. His persona as a fashion-conscious aesthete from an earlier era remained fairly constant across these changes.

Roxy Music's image was not ancillary to its music: "every last detail of their visual image matched their music, a retro/futuristic concoction which blended honking '50s rock 'n' roll with systems music and '40s crooning" (Gorman 103). In fact, the range of musical styles the group exploited on their first album was even broader, extending to country music, jazz, society dance band sounds, hard rock, and a crooning style associated with the popular music of the 1920s and 1930s. The close relationship between musical style and visual presentation in Roxy Music is clearly shown in a 1973 performance for the German television program *Musik Laden*. Ferry placed himself squarely in the retro category: he embodied a lounge crooner by wearing a white suit with a black shirt open at the collar, his hair slicked into "a wet-look take on the Fifties elephant trunk" (Sims 176). Saxophonist Andy Mackay had an even more explicitly fifties-style haircut and wore an outfit that combined a satin version of the Rocker's muscle shirt with padded pants to form a futuristic look strongly resembling some of Bowie's Ziggy Stardust costumes, including large donut-like bracelets and a stuffed codpiece. Phil Manzanera, the guitarist, wore very tight pants and a puffy-sleeved dark blue collarless shirt that looked like

Publicity shot of Roxy Music, ca. 1972. *Back row, from left to right:*
Phil Manzanera, Bryan Ferry, Paul Thompson. *Front row, from left to
right:* Brian Eno, Andrew Mackay. © MichaelOchsArchives.com.

a couturier's fantasy of the psychedelic rocker's typical denim garb.
Musical bricoleur Eno was dressed exotically in a black vest that
sprouted huge feathers and revealed his bare chest. Slender and visibly made-up, his was the most overtly feminized presence in the
group *(The Best of Musik Laden)*.

This array of musical and sartorial styles was matched by the
variety of performance conventions to which the musicians
referred. Whereas Manzanera behaved in the typically circumspect
manner of a psychedelic rock guitarist, Mackay played his saxophone like a 1950s rhythm and blues honker, leaning back, away
from the microphone, playing his sax showily with one hand while
keeping the other raised in the air, and playing it upside down.

Ferry moved in a stylized way reminiscent of a cheesy lounge singer. Even when moving across the stage, his torso faced the audience. His gestures were sometimes overly literal illustrations of the song lyrics, sometimes drawn from 1960s social dances such as the twist, and sometimes show-biz clichés like the "jazz hands" gesture originated by blackface minstrels.

Roxy Music's ability to traverse a broad terrain of musical styles is attributable in part to its unusual instrumentation and the diverse interests of its members. While Ferry cited musical influences that include Charlie Parker, girl-groups of the 1960s, the Inkspots, Lotte Lenya, Ethel Merman, and Billie Holiday ("Whatever Turned Me On"), Mackay is a classically trained oboist with strong interests in rock-and-roll saxophone styles, electronic music, and experimental composition. Eno, too, was interested in electronics and radical approaches to composition and performance.[3] Ferry recruited Mackay and Eno specifically because of their interest in electronic music (and their ownership of electronic equipment) so that the latest sounds and technologies would be in the group's mix alongside references to past styles. Consequently, Roxy Music is the only group associated with glam rock to make extensive use of synthesizers and other advanced musical technologies, as well as the only one to have a wind player as one of its major soloists. The other two members who made up the initial core of the group, Manzanera and drummer Paul Thompson, are highly accomplished, if basically more conventional, rock musicians who brought that strength into the fold.

Roxy Music was not the first rock group to employ multiple musical styles, but their particular way of doing so queried the identity of rock music as a genre and the concept of a rock group as an entity committed to a particular kind of music. Rob Chapman describes the group's first album by saying that it sounds like "half

3. Two of the experimental music groups with which Eno was involved were the Portsmouth Sinfonia and the Scratch Orchestra, founded by the British composer Cornelius Cardew. Eno sometimes performed with these groups and was instrumental in producing their recordings. Both groups were founded in the late 1960s and questioned the professionalization of music by inviting a wide range of participants. Eno described the Portsmouth Sinfonia by saying, "The philosophy of the orchestra was that anybody could join. There was no basis of skill required for joining. The only condition was that if you joined you should attend rehearsals and take it seriously. It wasn't intended as a joke—though it was sometimes extremely funny. The orchestra only played the popular classics, and it played only the most popular parts of these popular classics, the bits that everyone knows" (qtd. in "Portsmouth Sinfonia").

a dozen separate bands clamoring for attention" ("Roxy Music"). Not only did the group's style vary significantly from song to song, it would often change dramatically midsong, sometimes more than once. "If There is Something," from *Roxy Music,* for instance, begins as a country song, with twangy guitars and a drawled vocal. An early indication that all is not as it seems, however, is that Ferry's voice is sometimes surrounded by an echo effect foreign to country music production (not the slap-back echo used in rocka- billy recordings). The lyrics to this first section, which express exis- tential uncertainty bordering on paralysis, are not at all like those of country songs, which are typically assertive even when the char- acter depicted is in a bad way.

The first instrumental break initially maintains the feeling of country or country rock; the guitar solo is closely backed by a country piano. At the end of the guitar solo, however, a new motif enters, played on saxophone and guitar, that evokes progressive rock (with a hint of jazz) much more than country. Ferry abandons his initial vocal twang in favor of a pleading lover's voice that becomes more and more imploring as he promises to perform incredible feats (climb mountains, swim oceans, walk great dis- tances, and so on) to impress the object of his desire. The fervor with which Ferry sings this section is undercut somewhat by the strong vibrato he employs at the ends of lines, which makes his emotional intensity seem artificial. His ardor is also hard to take seriously because of the way the lyrics parade clichés of pop song- writing that become ever more absurd as the character seemingly becomes more desperate. By the end of this section, he promises to grow "potatoes by the score" as part of a picture of the bucolic domesticity he offers to his loved one. Despite this ironic distanc- ing, the ferocity of Ferry's performance is emotionally affecting. After an instrumental section dominated by the saxophone that returns to the "progressive rock" motif and wrings variations from it, the song changes style again. When Ferry returns, he sings in an almost screamed, soul-inflected style backed by male harmony singers and a rock guitar. This section, in which the chorus repeats the line "when you were young" many times, is elegiac in feel and evokes the innocence attributed to youth.

The shifts of musical style in "If There is Something" underline shifts in perspective and attitude from section to section of the song; it is, in fact, like three different songs joined together. The relationships between style and tone are neither direct nor uniform: the use of a country style to describe a character in existential crisis seems ironic, while the use of soul and rock styles in the final section, while self-conscious, does not. Though the overstated romanticism of the middle section is clearly parodic, it still has emotional impact. In the end, these shifts of style and mood make it impossible to classify the song in terms of either genre or tone. They create a liminal identity for Roxy Music by remaining betwixt and between a number of musical styles (country, rock, soul), emotional states (despair, nostalgia, exultation), and attitudes (sincere, parodic) without settling on one or another. Implicit in the idea of the subjunctive as the realm of "as if" is the idea that no identity is stable—it is always possible to move from one performative position to another.

The open-endedness of the subjunctive is further suggested by the structure of "Strictly Confidential" from the second Roxy Music album, *For Your Pleasure* (1973). Like "If There is Something," the song incorporates several different styles, beginning with Ferry singing in a high-pitched, breathy, and tremulous voice that comes very close to resembling Tiny Tim's. Like Tiny Tim, Ferry uses this voice to evoke a pop crooning style from the 1920s. "Strictly Confidential" is epistolary in form: the narrator, on his deathbed, promises to reveal all his secrets to the listener in a letter; this premise, like the singing style and the title of the song, is deliberately old-fashioned, evoking the manners and mannerisms of a period well before the rock era. As the narrator describes his inability to sleep by using the phrase "rolling and turning," however, there is an abrupt shift of style to a rock sound dominated by drums, particularly tom-toms. This sound evokes the style of jazz-influenced psychedelic rock drummer Ginger Baker. (It is not coincidental, I suspect, that Baker's group Cream recorded a famous version of the blues "Rollin' and Tumblin,' " a well-known blues with a long history often associated with Muddy Waters, also about sleeplessness, in 1967. In a version of word association, aspects of Cream's style are brought into play through the appearance of a phrase that resembles the name of one of their songs.)

After this brief excursion into a more rock-oriented style, the antiquated crooning of the first verse reappears. But with the entrance of an electric rock guitar sound after four more lines, the overall style shifts into heavier rock, and Ferry moves somewhat gradually into rock singing: his voice becomes less whispery, more of a chest voice. This heavier rock sound persists for four verses. In the last two verses, the protagonist's voice alternates with those of a male chorus that seems to represent deliverers of death ("Tell us are you ready now"). When this dialogue is completed, the song returns to the first, Cream-like rock style for one last verse before ending. The song thus passes through three distinct musical styles in two different genres (pop crooning and rock) in an A-B-A-C-B sequence. (It is worth noting that whereas the first appearance of the progressive rock style refers obliquely to blues-based rock, the lyrics during its second appearance mention a "magical moment" and a spell, as if it had strayed into Tyrannosaurus Rex's territory, though both actually refer to the moment of death.)

This sequence of stylistic shifts shows how the song's structure creates expectations it then frustrates. The A-B-A sequence at first suggests a design for the whole song in which the crooning style will alternate with a psychedelic rock style in a verse/chorus pattern. The appearance of a third style that actually dominates the song throws that implied design into a chaos that is only compounded when the song returns to, and ends abruptly with, the B-style, which had seemed earlier to be transitional. The song is far from incoherent: it is built on a dramatic arc in which the narrative of the speaker's impending death climaxes with the arrival of the otherworldly chorus. Ferry's singing becomes more intense and the music becomes heavier rock as the performance approaches that moment. Nevertheless, the deployment of musical styles in "Strictly Confidential" is irregular and unpredictable, leaving the impression that the song could take on any stylistic identity at any moment.

Ferry and Roxy Music sometimes exaggerated and satirized the musical and performance conventions of the styles they employed, particularly when they evoked the music favored by the hippie counterculture. Manzanera observes that "there was a lot of humour . . . a lot of piss-taking of heavy rock" (qtd. in Chapman, "Roxy Music"). But just as Ferry can simultaneously sing highly emotively and make fun of highly emotive singing, these moments often prove to be ambivalent rather than simply satirical. On his first solo album,[4] *These Foolish Things* (1973), Ferry performs Bob Dylan's "A Hard Rain's A-Gonna Fall," an apocalyptic song from

---

4. Ferry began his solo career about a year after Roxy Music's emergence and functioned simultaneously as a solo artist and group leader for the duration of the group's existence. He commented on this dual musical identity in 1975: "Songwriting is still the most important thing. The solo career is pure style, imposing my style on a ready-made content. I have two careers now, I extend myself in different directions" (qtd. in Nicholl 50).

Dylan's early folksinger phase. Ferry, who is on record as preferring Dylan's later, more rock-oriented electric music to his earlier folky work ("Whatever Turned Me On"), performs the song in a manner antithetical to Dylan's own style, treating it as an up-tempo pop song complete with a prominent backbeat, strings, electric guitar fills, and gospel-style female backup singers. On the third verse, a sound effect follows each of Dylan's vivid images: a storm effect comes after the reference to "the sound of thunder that roared out a warning," whispering sounds after "ten thousand whisperin' and nobody listenin,' " and hearty laughter follows the mention of people laughing while someone starves. These overly literal, even cartoonish illustrations of the song seem campy and mocking, as if to point out and undermine the portentousness of Dylan's lyrics. (Roxy Music often used this strategy of employing aural asides to deflate the potential pomposity of its own compositions, too.) The performance as a whole, however, does not simply make fun of Dylan's brand of seriousness because it also works as an effective interpretation of the song. This is due largely to the fact that Ferry takes the song at a faster tempo than Dylan did. The tempo, Ferry's interaction with the backup singers, and the density of the arrangement and production all give the performance a sense of urgency that is entirely appropriate to the song even though it contains many elements that seemingly "take the piss" with respect to Dylan and everything he represented to the rock culture of the 1960s.

Even more complex in its relationship to the counterculture is "In Every Dream Home a Heartache" from Roxy Music's *For Your Pleasure*. The song's narrative is from the point of view of a protagonist who is apparently so steeped in suburban anomie that he prefers the company of an inflatable sex doll to that of real women.[5] The implication that this predilection is the outcome of suburbanization (the lyrics include a compendium of real estate sales terms: "Open plan living / Bungalow ranch style") is harmonious with a countercultural perspective that would see the emptiness of the materialistic suburban lifestyle as breeding consumerist perversity. But several features of the recorded performance make it difficult to take that message at face value.

5. Ferry's song anticipated Neil Innes's "Randy Raquel" (1977), a similar paean to an inflatable sex doll. It is also interesting that at least one such doll was used as a model at designer Tommy Roberts's Mr. Freedom, one of the trendiest London clothing stores of the early 1970s (see the photograph in Gorman [102]).

The first is that Ferry's voice sounds very much like that of another singer: Eric Burdon. Burdon, who grew up, like Ferry, in Newcastle, was the singer for the Animals, one of the first Newcastle rock groups to achieve more than regional success, reaching number one on the British charts in 1964 with "House of the Rising Sun." Burdon's vocal style was basically that of a blues shouter: loud, raspy, powerful, and relatively uninflected. By the later 1960s, however, he became a staunch advocate of the counterculture, praising its epicenter in "San Franciscan Nights" (1967) and celebrating the Monterey International Pop Festival, where he performed with a revised version of the Animals, in "Monterey" (1968). Although he continued to sing in his earlier aggressive fashion, he also resorted to a quieter, more restrained voice during his psychedelic period ("San Franciscan Nights" exemplifies the latter style). The timbre of Ferry's voice on "In Every Dream Home" closely matches Burdon's; because he sings in a similarly raspy but restrained style and does not disguise the Geordie accent he shares with Burdon, he sounds as if he were Burdon.

It is funny to think of the anaesthetized suburbanite of Ferry's song being portrayed by the robust, psychedelicized Burdon, though Ferry's laid-back, almost monotone performance of the character also suggests psychological disturbance (in the *Musik Laden* performance, he stood perfectly still while singing, bathed in blue light and staring off into the distance over the heads of his audience). The evocation of Burdon was the launching point for what may be Roxy Music's most exuberant piss-taking at the expense of psychedelic rock. After singing (really almost chanting) the lyrics, Ferry speaks the lines: "I blew up your body / But you blew my mind." (The presence of the latter phrase, uncharacteristic for Ferry but of which Burdon was inordinately fond, contributes to the impression that Ferry is evoking Burdon.) Immediately after that, Manzanera roars in with a fast, hard rock guitar solo that leads to a false fade-out, a device found on many recordings of psychedelic rock. Ferry's allusive lyrics and mannered vocal are replaced by a repeated chorus of "Oh those heartaches / Dream home heartaches" sung in a straightforward rock style.

When the guitar-heavy music returns after the fade, it is adorned with phase shifting, a special effect used repeatedly in recording psychedelic rock (and that Burdon used extensively on his hit recording of "Sky Pilot" [1968]) that was, by 1973, clearly recognizable as a generic cliché. By singing in a voice that was clearly not his own, Ferry questioned the notion that individuality and authenticity reside in a distinctive singing style. By using the voice of an iconic psychedelic rocker, Ferry turned "In Every Dream Home" into a parody of the genre whose domination of the London music scene he had found so dull upon his arrival there.[6] For the *Musik Laden* performance of this song, Ferry atypically played an electric guitar. In keeping with his distanced attitude toward the conventions of rock, he used a white guitar that matched his white suit; he thus employed the guitar, the quintessential rock instrument, to make a fashion statement rather than to establish his authenticity as a rocker.

Although Roxy Music's kaleidoscopic approach to musical style was distinctive, earlier albums by other groups also made use of radical shifts in musical style, among them *The Turtles Present The Battle of the Bands* (1968) and the Beatles' *Sgt. Pepper's Lonely Hearts Club Band* (1967). In both of these cases, however, extreme musical eclecticism is contained within a metanarrative frame that allows the group both to show off its versatility and retain a clear identity. The Turtles' album is organized around the idea of a competition among bands; the outside cover shows the members of the group wearing tuxedos as if to serve as emcees for the competition, while the inner gatefold image shows the Turtles dressed up as a series of different groups, each with its own humorous name (The Quad City Ramblers is the country-and-western group, for instance, while the Atomic Enchilada is the psychedelic rock

6. There is more to be said about the connections between Burdon and Ferry. On one hand, they share a tendency to look back and a propensity for the elegiac. This is apparent in Ferry's ambivalent use of outmoded musical styles and his commitment to a version of sartorial elegance that evokes the 1940s and in Burdon's songs, such as "Good Times" (1967) and "When I Was Young" (1967). It is also quite likely that "Sky Pilot" (1968), Burdon's antiwar song, is the direct or indirect model for "The Bob" on the first Roxy Music album. Both are long by rock standards (Burdon's is over seven minutes long, while Ferry's is almost six minutes in duration), and each has a long middle section that juxtaposes the sounds of warfare with musical sounds. On the other hand, there is a sense in which Ferry is the anti-Burdon. Both men come from working-class Newcastle families; both turned to music (and, in Ferry's case, art and higher education) as an alternative to life as a coal miner; both achieved considerable success. But whereas Burdon celebrates his working-class roots and identity, Ferry has suppressed his in favor of conspicuous displays of wealth and elegance without, it must be said, repudiating or denying his background.

group). The first track, "The Battle of the Bands," explains the album's concept in much the same way that the song "Sgt. Pepper's Lonely Hearts Club Band" suggests that the Beatles are assuming the guise of a fictional brass band for the duration of that album. On both albums, the groups show off their mastery of a dizzying array of musical styles while also maintaining a distance from them through the mediation of metafictional groups.[7] In the case of the Turtles, satire was part of the motive (as it was for other hyper-eclectic artists of the countercultural moment, such as the Mothers of Invention). In the Beatles' case, the narrative conceit comes in and out of focus and the album overall contains enough hallucinatory imagery, sound collage, drug references, invocations of Eastern mysticism, and other countercultural elements to satisfy the psychedelic rock audience that the Beatles belonged to them.

Whereas these two albums were clearly framed as special projects for which known groups took on identities other than their own, Roxy Music's use of many, sometimes incompatible musical styles was the paradoxical heart of the group's identity from the beginning. Along with the group's designed appearance and exaggerated performance personae, this refusal of a settled stylistic commitment made Roxy Music seem artificial by the standards of rock authenticity, as if it were a metafictional group unmoored from the real musicians who had created it (as if, in other words, Sgt. Pepper's band took on a life apart from the Beatles). When the Turtles and the Beatles explored the subjunctivity of performance by recording as if they were other bands, their explorations were anchored by their original group identities. Roxy Music, by contrast, had no clearly defined anchoring identity: theirs was always a liminal musical identity that seemed to border on all sorts of stylistic categories without truly belonging to any of them. Much has been made of Ferry's love of cinema and his choosing the group's name from a list of movie theaters he compiled with saxophonist Mackay, but I hear the name differently. To me, it evokes the group's self-consciously ambivalent approach to musical genre: its music was rocks-y (or rock-ish)—like rock music, but not quite.

Roxy Music's performances of gender and sexual identity were consonant with their approach to musical style. Whereas both

7. For further discussion of the concept of a metafictional rock group, see Auslander, "Good Old Rock and Roll."

Bolan's and Bowie's performances centered on a single ambiguous figure, Roxy Music offered a range of gendered musical identities. Although the group's rhythm section (Manzanera, Thompson, and, in the *Musik Laden* performance, bassist John Porter) dressed far more extravagantly than most of the men in their audiences, their onstage behavior conformed to rock performance conventions. Manzanera looked only at this own hands when playing a solo, an expression of seriousness and concentration on his face; he also sang along quietly with his own playing, a sign of how immersed he was in the musical moment. Manzanera, Porter, and Mackay turned to face Thompson or each other when jamming, sometimes turning their backs to the audience as they did so. Their performance of normative musical conventions was implicitly a performance of the normative masculine identity associated with rock.

These four musicians were flanked on either side, however, by two others who performed distinctly nonnormative versions of masculinity: the excessive, effeminate Eno and the more restrained, elegant Ferry. Eno, heavily made up and typically dressed in lavish outfits of feathers or glittering spangles, was showily effeminate. When singing behind Ferry (as on the *Musik Laden* performance of "Editions of You") he emulated female backup singers by swinging his hips to the beat and engaging in patterned arm movements while standing in place at the microphone. His feminine demeanor was further reinforced by delicate hand gestures and self-touching, identified by Erving Goffman as belonging to the vocabulary of feminine gender performance (31).

Eno's status as a synthesizer player is intriguing in terms of gender performance. Whereas instruments like the acoustic and electric guitars were clearly gendered in rock culture, the synthesizer was not well established enough in rock music to have a clear gender identity (at the time of Roxy Music's emergence, rock musicians had been using synthesizers for only about five years). On the one hand, synthesizers clearly belonged to the male-dominated tradition of electronic tinkering associated with the *Popular Mechanics* crowd. And, as Mavis Bayton notes, male musicians have often used technical knowledge and jargon as means of excluding women (42). Early synthesizers, which were technically demanding, high-maintenance machines, could have been assimilated to this tendency as well. But because the synthesizer did not have a clear gender identity, it was a liminal instrument whose meaning could be pushed in one direction or another through performance.[8] Whereas Keith Emerson of Emerson, Lake and Palmer used the ribbon controller for his Moog synthesizer in a way that reproduced "all the cultural and gender symbolism that the guitar as 'technophallus' in rock music evokes" (Pinch and Trocco 63), the synthesizer could also be associated with keyboard instruments that occupied a more feminine gender position. In Eno's case, the synthesizer's ambivalence with respect to gender seemed congruent to the musician's own hybrid gender performance.[9]

For his part, Ferry enacted still another version of masculinity, steeped in a sense of elegance as defined by Hollywood films of the 1940s (the song "2HB" on *Roxy Music* is a tribute to Humphrey Bogart). Although there was nothing specifically feminine or effeminate about this persona or the way he enacted it, his concern with image, stylishness, and fashion were perceived as homosexual in the context of a rock culture that prized none of these things. Indeed, it was often remarked in the music press that Ferry preferred to move in social circles made up of fashionistas and gay men rather than those around rock music. In her 1975 *Melody Maker* interview, Coon queried Ferry repeatedly about this preference, pointing out that the flashy models who appeared on Roxy Music's album covers "are as close to being men in drag as it's possible to get" and seemingly trying to get Ferry to admit to being gay. Arguably, this imputation of a homosexual identity to Ferry was an accurate judgment in a cultural sense. Fashion designer Price noted, "Bryan had a big gay following from very early on. He looked like a male model . . . he thinks gay, acts gay but is in fact straight. . . . his credibility in the fashion business is much higher than any other male singer because they know he knows" (qtd. in Chapman, "Roxy Music"). Ferry thus can be credited with importing aspects of a gay sensibility into the performance of rock music.

It is worth noting that the various versions of masculinity Roxy

8. It is noteworthy in this context that one of the most important musicians to publicize the Moog synthesizer, Wendy Carlos, started out in life as Walter Carlos.

9. Jason Middleton makes the point that in the New Wave music of the later 1970s, the synthesizer (as opposed to the guitar favored by punk rockers) stood for an ideology that inherited glam rock's blurring of gender distinctions and combined it with a parallel blurring of the line between human and machine (par. 16).

Music presented did not interact very much. Those members of the group who performed normative rock masculinity tended to interact with each other, while Eno and Ferry performed largely as individuals adjacent to, yet apart from, the others. Just as the group juxtaposed multiple musical styles rather than combining them, the members of the group juxtaposed an array of images of masculine gender and male sexuality as if alluding to possibilities rather than presenting a defined identity, a strategy Ferry also employed in his vocal performances. Ferry varied the pitch and timbre of his voice considerably from song to song and within songs. To a large extent, this was a function of his portraying different characters: the high-pitched, breathy voice of the letter-writer in "Strictly Confidential," who is dying in the grand manner, sounds very different from the regionally inflected but flat and relatively affectless voice of the perverse suburbanite of "In Every Dream Home a Heartache." In addition to providing character development, however, Ferry's use of many voices has implications for both gender representation and the concept of authenticity.

In "Sea Breezes," from *Roxy Music,* Ferry sings in two different voices. The first voice is a high-breaking near-falsetto that sounds ethereal at first but becomes more earthbound (and lower) as the lyric becomes more forlorn. In the second part of the song, when the arrangement turns percussive through the switch from electric piano to piano and the addition of drums, Ferry uses a deeper, more forceful chest voice that seems just as mannered as the earlier falsetto because of a stilted, strangely accented rhythm that isolates words rather than allowing them to flow easily into sentences. The final verse of the song is a repeat of the first that involves a return to the higher voice. Both voices express a sadness that verges on desperation, but in a melodramatically overemotional way that distances the listener. (The way Ferry sings "down duh duh down" at the end of the second section, in what seems to be an intentionally awkward emulation of a rhythm and blues vocal trope, contributes to this effect because it seems arbitrary and out of place.)

Ferry's use of two voices in this performance constitutes a vocal version of glam rockers' transvestite play with visual signifiers of gender and sexuality in their costuming and makeup. As I noted in my discussion of Bolan's singing, the falsetto is traditionally characterized as an "unnaturally" feminine male voice that intimates "deviant" sexual inclinations. Ferry's use of the falsetto, like Bolan's, thus functions as one of the many ways that glam rock teased its audience with suggestions of queer sexuality.[10] Elizabeth Wood, in her account of music and lesbian desire, describes what she calls the Sapphonic voice, a woman's voice with a very broad range that crosses the border between registers traditionally considered male and female. By moving from falsetto to chest voice and back again, Ferry demonstrates his own wide vocal range. Hoping to be forgiven for applying terms of a feminist analysis developed to describe a female opera singer to a male rock singer, I will venture to say that Ferry's voice can be heard as a male version of the Sapphonic voice, a voice that, like other aspects of glam rock, "challenges the polarities of both gender and sexuality as these have been socially constructed" (Elizabeth Wood 32).

Because it is considered an "unnatural" voice, the falsetto also challenges rock music's ideology of authenticity. Since vocal techniques such as falsetto, vibrato, and tremolo require "long discipline, work, and training to produce" (Elizabeth Wood 31), they cannot meet the ideology of authenticity's requirements for spontaneity and immediacy, for the use of such a synthetic voice inevitably implies premeditation. Whereas Johan Fornäs describes the authentic voice as "the genuine or the honest expression of a subject [as] implied in the words '*your* voice'" (99), the falsetto is thought to be a depersonalized voice. The nineteenth-century composer Isaac Nathan described it as "a species of ventriloquism," "an inward and suppressed quality of tone, that conveys the illusion of being heard at a distance" (qtd. in Elizabeth Wood 31). This is a good description of the quality of Ferry's voice as he sings in falsetto at the start and end of "Sea Breezes," an effect emphasized by the way his voice was recorded. The echo around his voice and the fade at the end of the first falsetto section make it seem that his voice is receding into the distance; the contrast between the disappearance of the falsetto and the strong entrance of Ferry's chest voice in the second part of the song also reinforces the effect of distance. Far from serving as the "genuine or the honest expression of a subject," Ferry's voices in "Sea Breezes," as in most of his perfor-

10. Sparks, a second-wave glam rock group, made the most extensive use of falsetto. The group's founding members were Ron and Russell Mael, Americans from Los Angeles who found their initial audiences in the United Kingdom. Russell Mael sang almost exclusively in falsetto, while Ron composed songs that pushed the limits of his brother's vocal range. Their song "This Town Ain't Big Enough for Both of Us" reached number two on the British charts in the spring of 1974.

mances, are marked as mannered and artificial. (I hasten to add, however, that this does not mean that his performance is unaffecting—"Sea Breezes," like much of Roxy Music's work, is simultaneously heartbreaking and hilarious.)

On his solo album *These Foolish Things*, for which he recorded only the work of other songwriters, Ferry performs vocal identities suggestive of gender and sexual identities that contrast from song to song. In keeping with his musical tastes, the material Ferry selected is eclectic. In addition to songs associated with such linchpins of rock as Dylan, Elvis, the Beatles, the Rolling Stones, and the Beach Boys, Ferry included two Motown songs; the title song, a pop and jazz standard that comes from a stage musical of the 1930s; and four pop songs associated with female singers. Steve Bailey, who places Ferry's album in the context of a trend in the 1970s in which rock artists recorded collections of older songs, observes that Ferry's performed relationship to his material is atypical. Whereas most such recordings were made in tribute to the earlier music and performers rockers perceived as their historic roots, Ferry's take on the rock songs he performed was more critical and ironic (as I noted earlier in my discussion of his performance of "A Hard Rain's A-Gonna Fall"). Bailey also points out that since he treats the pop songs on the collection, which would be considered trivial from the point of view of rock culture, "with considerably more respect [than the rock songs] (at least in terms of fidelity to the original), Ferry is able to question the conventional mode of rock aesthetic evaluation" (148).

Bailey does not address the gender politics of Ferry's strategy, however. Part and parcel of the low status accorded to pop music within rock culture is its association with women performers and a predominantly female audience (Coates 52–53). By making an album in which pop material is treated more respectfully than the grand old men of rock, Ferry implicitly made a bid to redress that imbalance. Bailey argues that Ferry's versions of rock songs hold up for scrutiny some of rock's more embarrassing pretensions (e.g., "the rather silly Satanic image of the Stones" [147]). I argue that the album as a whole points to many of the gendered conventions of popular music in a similarly self-conscious fashion. For instance, Ferry performs both "River of Salt" and "Tracks of My Tears." Both songs are associated with African-American singers (Ketty Lester and Smoky Robinson, respectively), both center on the same image of crying over the loss of a lover, and Ferry performs both in a fairly straightforward, respectful fashion (his reading of "River of Salt" is particularly moving). The presence of two such similar songs on the same album cannot be coincidental; their juxtaposition serves to point up the differences in how popular music conventionally represents masculine and feminine emotional experience and expression. Whereas the (implicitly female) narrator of "River of Salt" speaks of endless, uncontrollable crying, the (implicitly male) protagonist of "The Tracks of My Tears" makes it very clear that he hides his true emotions behind a veneer of bonhomie and bravado. Although the relationship of these representations to cultural assumptions regarding differences in the emotional lives of men and women is readily understandable from each song in isolation, it becomes that much more apparent when the two songs are presented in the same context.

Ferry's pairing of two other songs, both from the rock-and-roll era, addresses the representation of female gender performance in rock and roll. The first song, "Don't Ever Change," originally recorded by the Crickets in 1962, describes a woman who presents herself in a masculine fashion: she never wears dresses or make up and is uninterested in dancing. The second song, Elvis's "(You're So Square) Baby I Don't Care" (1957) describes the opposite kind of woman, one who performs an entirely normative femininity by professing disinterest in such masculine pursuits as hot-rod racing and rock-and-roll music. Hearing these two songs near each other on the same album, one is struck by how similar they are even though they ostensibly celebrate women who perform gender identity in opposing ways. The crucial similarity is that in both songs, the women in question reveal their true femininity in their sexual behavior with men. "Your kisses let me know you're not a tom boy," declares the narrator of "Don't Ever Change," while part of the adorable "squareness" attributed to the woman in "You're So Square" is that she would rather "park" with the narrator than do anything else.

At one level, the juxtaposition of these songs suggests that rock and roll did not represent desirable women monolithically: the masculine woman of one song is just as desirable as the ultrafeminine woman of the other. But just beneath the surface, the differences between the two women disappear when both are characterized as desirable chiefly because of their sexual availability to men. Although Ferry performs "You're So Square" in a fairly straightforward emulation of rockabilly style, he performs "Don't Ever

Change" in a way that implies a different frame of reference. Although the recording features handclaps, a drum style, and organ playing one might find on a pop record of the mid-1960s, on the chorus it evokes cabaret more than rock and roll with Liberace-esque piano playing. Ferry frequently employs his rich vibrato and sings in a manner insinuating enough to suggest that there is just a chance that the "tom boy" in question is not a girl, thus complicating the song's referent.

In performing "Piece of My Heart," a song written by male composers but associated with female singers (it was originally recorded by Erma Franklin [Aretha's sister] in 1967 and, famously, by Janis Joplin in 1968), Ferry foregrounds the song's emphasis on female romantic masochism through the simple device of expressing those sentiments in a male voice. Ferry sings in a light, somewhat high-pitched voice that could appropriately be described as feminine but is unquestionably male sounding. Hearing that voice express the sentiments articulated in the song places the listener in the position of having to come to terms with the idea of a man enacting a submissive, stereotypically "feminine" role in a relationship, thus throwing that role into relief. Ferry makes a similar, if less subtle, gesture with his "gay" version of Leslie Gore's "It's My Party" (1963), which he performs without altering the lyrics. (On "River of Salt," Ferry refers to his lost love using the feminine pronoun, while his version of the lyrics for "Piece of My Heart" is gender-neutral.) The song's depiction of hotheaded female jealousy is thus transposed to a male protagonist, and the situation described becomes more complex in relation to sexuality. In Gore's version of "It's My Party" a woman expresses anger at the fact that her boyfriend has apparently taken up with another woman on her birthday. In Ferry's hands, it becomes a song in which a gay man is deserted on his birthday by his boyfriend (Johnny, in both cases) who not only has taken a new lover but is now apparently seeking his romantic partners among women.

Another of Ferry's choices, the Beach Boys' "Don't Worry Baby" (1964), is inherently somewhat complex in its depiction of gendered behaviors and attitudes. Because of the narrator's proclivity for machismo he must participate in a car race or risk losing face. Recognizing the foolishness of the posturing that got him into this predicament and feeling insecure, he turns to his supportive girlfriend, who bolsters his male ego. Although this scenario is fundamentally conventional in its representation of gender roles (the male as active and a bit overaggressive; the female as passive, supportive, and patient), the song's gentle tempo, sweetly rising melody, and the Beach Boys' luscious harmonies all work against hearing it as a simple expression of male dominance. Ferry brought the "femininity" implicit in these aspects of the Beach Boys' performance to the fore by actually rewriting the song's lyrics. He excised all references to the car race and replaced them with a new verse in which the male protagonist's insecurities are shown to stem from his uncertainty about the relationship with the woman, not from self-doubt about being overly aggressive toward other men. Shorn of all references to stereotypically masculine interests and behaviors, the song becomes purely romantic and, in that sense, feminine even as it represents the thoughts and actions of a heterosexual male protagonist.

Ferry's selection of material for *These Foolish Things* and his treatment of that material constitute an exploration of representations of gender and sexuality in popular music. In some cases, particularly those of "It's My Party" and "Don't Ever Change," he performs the songs against their original grain, making them expressive of gender positions and sexualities they were not originally intended to represent. In other, somewhat more subtle cases he points up the gendered assumptions underlying specific songs and the musical genres to which they belong through the creation of alienation effects in which music and sentiments conventionally gendered as feminine are conveyed through a male voice. Ferry performs a range of male gender identities that extends from the more or less normative masculine voice of "Baby I Don't Care" and "Tracks of My Tears" to the highly mannered, epicene Satan of Ferry's version of "Sympathy for the Devil" to the apparently gay but not overtly effeminate male voice of "It's My Party" to the "soft boy" romanticism of the rewritten "Don't Worry Baby." Along the way, he also occupies a number of more ambiguous, liminal positions such as those suggested by the feminized male voices of "River of Salt" and "Piece of My Heart." Like *Roxy Music*, *These Foolish Things* provides Ferry with an opportunity to move among musical styles and sing in multiple voices.

Although Bryan Ferry and Roy Wood are very different as performers, they have more in common musically than it may first appear. Their differences are evident in their respective backgrounds and public personae. Whereas Ferry presented himself as the art-school grad and aesthete who appeared on the London scene with almost no previous musical history and traveled in circles devoted to art and fashion, Wood portrayed the hardworking professional rock musician who had been plugging away in the musical hinterland of working-class Birmingham since the early 1960s before achieving success in 1967 as a member of the Move. Whereas Ferry came on as a somewhat chilly and effete fashion plate and trendsetter, Wood was an exuberant performer who always seemed to be enjoying himself. If the look of Roxy Music was self-consciously designed, the look of Wood's group Wizzard was more in the DIY spirit of glam bricolage: tacky, incongruous elements thrown together for pleasure rather than refinement. But the similarities between them are as striking as these differences. They share the ability to sing in a wide variety of voices and a chameleonic tendency to disappear into the sonic spaces they create (though Wood disappears much more completely than Ferry). Both are profoundly interested in working in the liminal spaces between musical styles, composing songs and constructing groups and recordings that continually shift ground and refuse stable musical identities.

The Move, founded in Birmingham in 1965 as an alliance of the best musicians from a variety of local groups, was one of the success stories of the London music scene in the late 1960s, placing ten singles on the British charts between 1967 and 1972, all but three in the top ten. The group performed regularly at the Marquee Club and other Mod venues. Although the Move has been accurately described as purveying "mod-pop-psychedelia" (Unterberger, "The Move" 639), I argue that it should be seen as a protoglam group. The Move admittedly did not anticipate glam's gender-bending personae, and its extravagant, often violent stage shows were not direct precursors of glam theatricality. But as the group's chief songwriter, Wood already displayed the penchant for playing with and combining musical styles that would become the hallmark of his work in the early 1970s with his glam rock group, Wizzard, and as a solo artist.

Wood regularly wrote songs for the Move in the styles of other composers, particularly John Lennon and Paul McCartney. "Wave Your Flag and Stop the Train" (1967) is a case in point.[11] The song

---

11. Except where otherwise noted, all recordings by the Move discussed here are available as part of the *Movements* CD box set.

is a pastiche of the Beatles' style circa 1964 with elements that strongly resemble specific songs: the melody recalls "She's a Woman" (1964) while a solo bass guitar motif is similar to the defining riff of "Day Tripper" (1965). Although the song is more an emulation of the Beatles than a parody, the lyrics about a woman attempting to commit suicide by leaping from a train are somewhat anomalous. In the context of 1967, the highpoint of psychedelic rock and the year of *Sgt. Pepper,* there is something prankishly retrograde in the Move's revival of the Beatles' earlier style. The song was originally issued as the B-side of "I Can Hear the Grass Grow," a major hit that seemingly referred to synaesthetic drug experience by a group not associated with the underground or known for its commitment to psychedelia.[12] The single suggested that the Move was operating in the realm of the subjunctive by performing on one side as if they were an up-to-the-minute psychedelic rock group and on the other as if they were the prepsychedelic Beatles.

The Move returned to the Beatles' evolving styles several more times. "Blackberry Way" (1968) was clearly a revision of "Penny Lane" (1967), while "This Time Tomorrow" (1969), in an arrangement dominated by acoustic guitar and bongos, recalled "I'll Follow the Sun" (1964) with vocal harmonies reminiscent of both Lennon and McCartney and Peter and Gordon (for whom McCartney wrote several hits in the mid-1960s). "The Minister" (1971), written by Jeff Lynne, another adept of the Beatles' style who joined the Move in its final incarnation, looked back to "Paperback Writer" (1966). The Move borrowed as well from groups other than the Beatles: Lynne's "No Time" (1971) could easily be mistaken for a Bee Gees song, and the verses of his "What" (1970) again suggest the Bee Gees, while the choruses echo the Beatles' "I Am the Walrus" (1967). Wood's "California Man" (1972) opens with a precise rendition of Jerry Lee Lewis's vocal and boogie-woogie piano styles.[13] Although most of these recordings were treated as stylistic experiments and released as album tracks or the B-sides of singles, "Blackberry Way" and "California Man" were both hits in the United Kingdom, the former reaching number one on the charts, the latter number seven.

12. See Whiteley's discussion of this recording and the Move's status as an ersatz psychedelic rock group (*The Space* 69–70).

13. "The Minister," "No Time," "What," and "California Man" are on the album *Split Ends.*

Fornäs asserts: "Authenticity can be thought of as a special relation between style and identity. The authentic style is particularly
well anchored or rooted in an identity, or at least foregrounds such
style/identity homologies" (100). The Move repeatedly demonstrated the opposite: that musical style can be detached from the
underlying identities that lend it authenticity, whether the identity
of particular performers or that of the subculture associated with a
specific style such as psychedelic rock. Wood and the Move treated
musical styles, even those very clearly associated with other artists,
not as vocabularies specific to particular creative subjectivities but
as languages in which anyone may choose to speak. In the group's
hands, both compositional and performance styles functioned sub-
junctively rather than indicatively: they did not point back reliably
to an originating source but pointed, rather, to performative gestures enacted under the sign of "as if."

The Move's stylistic experiments took forms other than the
direct emulation of other groups' compositional and performance
styles, particularly on their second album, *Shazam* (1970), which
represented a conscious effort on the group's part to shed their
image as a source of clever hit singles by becoming "heavier." (The
title, which refers to Captain America, and the cover illustration of
the group dressed in superhero costumes presumably refer to this
transformation.) The album has some characteristics seemingly
designed to appeal to an underground audience: it contains only
six, relatively long performances (as compared with the thirteen
shorter songs on the group's first album, *The Move* [1968]) and produced no successful single. The songs are punctuated eccentrically
by sound effects and spontaneous-seeming studio conversations.
There are also, however, snippets from man-in-the-street interviews
about pop music that suggest a level of irony and self-consciousness
not usually present in "head" music. The Move achieved heaviness
in part by performing against the grain of some of the material they
chose: "Don't Make My Baby Blue," for example, a pop song originally recorded by Cliff Richard and the Shadows in 1965, became
a piece of guitar-driven rock in the style of the Jimi Hendrix Experience. The most radical experiment, which points clearly toward
Wood's later preoccupations, is "Cherry Blossom Clinic Revisited"
for which the group rerecorded a song from their first album concerning a man who has been committed to a mental institution.

The first verse is performed entirely differently in the two versions. In the earlier rendition, the first part of the story, in which the

narrator describes the circumstances of his commitment, is sung as a series of rhymed couplets. The later version recasts it as a prose narrative containing the same details but spoken, rather than sung, by a heavily accented male voice accompanied by a solo acoustic guitar. The second verse is performed in much the same way in both versions, though the later one is a bit slower in tempo and emphasizes the "heavy" sounds of distorted electric guitars, bass, and drums. On the last two lines of the chorus in this version, however, the style shifts abruptly to barbershop quartet harmony not present on the earlier recording. Whereas the original version has string and brass arrangements (by Tony Visconti), the latter features voices pretending to be brass instruments. The relationship between the two versions implies that "Cherry Blossom Clinic" is not a stable text, neither as written nor as recorded. That which was originally verse might just as well be prose; that which was originally sung might just as well be spoken; passages originally scored for instruments could be performed by human voices.

Although the first half of the recording features abrupt stylistic shifts from acoustic guitar to heavy rock to barbershop quartet and back again, it is dominated by the heavy rock style from which the others seem to be temporary deviations. The whole piece undergoes its most radical and destabilizing transformation in its second half. After all the verses of the song have been performed, the final barbershop quartet indicates the end of that portion of the performance. A brief interlude for two acoustic guitars punctuated by percussion leads to the next section, which begins with electric guitar, strummed acoustic guitar, and drums playing an introduction that sounds very much like the opening bars of the overture to *Tommy* (1969), the Who's rock opera. It turns instead into a rendition of J. S. Bach's "Jesu, Joy of Man's Desiring" played on acoustic and electric guitars accompanied by drums—classical music with a backbeat.[14] The remainder of the track is devoted to variations on Bach, including a section in which a vocal chorus sings "Jesu, Joy of Man's Desiring" in a somewhat manic version of the Swingle Singers' wordless syllables.

Robert Walser identifies three different uses of classical music in rock. He describes progressive rockers like Emerson as wanting "to

---

14. The Move's grafting of *Tommy* onto Bach could have served as the inspiration for Apollo 100's "Joy," a hit single from the winter of 1972 based on the same classical source that sounds very similar.

confer some of [classical music's] prestigious status and seriousness" on rock but goes on to suggest that some uses of "classical
resources" in popular music have more to do with "expand[ing its]
rhetorical palette" than with a bid for prestige (62). He also
describes heavy metal guitarists as having "fused [classical
resources] with their blues-based rock sensibility" (59). None of
these descriptions fits the Move's use of Bach precisely. The second
description is perhaps the closest, since it is certainly the case that
Wood was very interested in expanding the expressive palette of
rock by incorporating orchestral instruments such as the French
horn, oboe, bassoon, and cello (all of which he learned to play). But
rather than using these instruments to bring classical elements into
the music, Wood often played rock on them: in "Rock Down Low"
from his first solo album, *Boulders* (recorded in 1969 but released
only in 1972), for instance, Wood plays spirited rock solos on bassoon and cello. Wood even observed that the first cello he acquired
was particularly well adapted for playing rock because of its tone:
"It didn't sound like a sweet, mellow cello, especially the way I was
playing it. I was doing all these Jimi Hendrix riffs on it. It sounded
really quite wild" (qtd. in Sharp).

Although Wood plays Bach well on "Cherry Blossom Clinic
Revisited" (his initial rendering of the piece on acoustic guitar
would hold its own in a classical recital), it is doubtful that his purpose was to elevate the cultural status of "Cherry Blossom Clinic"
by associating it with Bach. If anything, it may have had more to do
with bringing Bach "down" to the cultural level of rock music, as
he did with orchestral instruments. More to the point, the idea that
classical music confers cultural prestige accords it a certain privilege. For Wood, by contrast, classical sounds are just one of many
musical vocabularies and are no more privileged than barbershop
quartet harmonies or any of the other styles he uses.

By 1971, the final version of the Move consisted of only three
people: Wood, Lynne, and drummer Bev Bevan. This trio was actually two groups, for in addition to recording as the Move they also
began recording as the Electric Light Orchestra (often referred to as
ELO). This latter group was meant to provide an avenue for
exploring the rock/classical connection. Ben Edmonds has pointed
out, however, that although "ELO has been called a classically-ori-
ented project . . . such labels stem more from the instruments . . .
than from the actual product. More than anything else, ELO is an

attempt to find new means of expression for *rock and roll*" ("Time Capsule").

It is also crucial that "Cherry Blossom Clinic Revisited," and much of the music Wood went on to make after the Move and ELO, does not really *fuse* rock and classical styles, as Walser says of heavy metal. Rather than melding the two styles, Wood presents them side by side—the classical section begins only after the original song is over. Classical and rock styles are not so much fused or synthesized as juxtaposed in a compartmentalized structure that keeps them largely apart from one another (though rock sound admittedly bleeds into the classical section in the form of electric guitar and drums). "Cherry Blossom Clinic Revisited" thus anticipates both Roxy Music's sequential juxtaposition of musical styles in such pieces as "If There is Something" and Wood's own future musical strategies.

Wizzard, the glam rock group Wood founded after his brief tenure with ELO, was the vehicle through which he continued the stylistic play begun with the Move, including his propensity for writing and recording in other people's styles and voices, his interest in playing rock on classical instruments, and his inclination to work in multiple musical styles simultaneously. Wizzard was made up largely of members of a Birmingham-based group called Mongrel, founded by bassist and guitarist Rick Price, who had previously been in the Move, that Wood refashioned, in part through the addition of two reed players, cellist Hugh McDowell, and pianist and horn player Bill Hunt, both of whom had been in ELO. For two years, from late 1972 through 1974, the group issued seven singles all but one of which reached the top ten in the United Kingdom. Two reached number one, and "I Wish It Could Be Christmas Everyday" (1973) became a seasonal favorite.

Wizzard assumed an intentionally ambiguous stance with respect to musical genre. Wood has said, "I always feel that you should keep singles as commercial as possible so that the people can walk down the road and whistle a song. But on the other hand on albums I think you can afford to show people what you can do" (qtd. in Sharp). Wizzard's singles were consistent in strategy if not style— all were pastiches of earlier rock and popular musical styles. Wood's plan for Wizzard's first album, which he saw as a double disc, reflected his idea of displaying the group's full range: "One side will be classical, one jazz, one country and one rock" (qtd. in Benton, "Wizzard" 43). It is not at all surprising that this album never came to fruition, given the rigidity of music industry sales categories (despite Wood's saying that he "want[ed] Wizzard to appeal to all markets").[15] But the album produced in its stead, *Wizzard Brew* (1973), reflected this impulse by featuring songs in several different genres (including hard rock, brass band, rockabilly, and symphonic rock) and some that switch genre identification from moment to moment.

"Buffalo Station—Get on Down to Memphis," from this album, is a case in point, not least because it is actually two songs joined together, as the title suggests. Wood did not construct a conventional medley from them in that he made no effort to join the two songs smoothly and make them stylistically harmonious. Rather, one simply ends and the other begins after a short transitional passage. "Buffalo Station" begins with a brief cello introduction but is otherwise a piece of hard rock with an active horn section. The cello remains a significant voice throughout the piece as well, providing rock licks that might otherwise be played on a guitar. The transitional section consists of a riff borrowed from King Crimson's 1969 "Twentieth-Century Schizoid Man" (perhaps in acknowledgment of the piece's split identity) played on the cello, followed abruptly by a short percussion jam and the beginning of "Get on Down to Memphis."

The second song is in a hard rock style similar to the first, albeit with a Dixieland clarinet replacing the cello as a secondary voice. A brief section of Dixieland played by the entire group follows the first chorus. After the second chorus, the rock style disappears, replaced first by Dixieland, then by Elvis-style rockabilly. The third verse is sung in an Elvis-like voice accompanied by boogie-woogie piano that is recorded with a slap-back echo that sets it apart from the rest of the song. On the chorus to the third verse, the original

15. The only example of an album of this kind of which I am aware is David Amram's *No More Walls* (1971). The first disc of this double LP is devoted to Amram's symphonic compositions, which he conducts. The other disc contains Amram's work in jazz, folk, and world music (before it was known by this name) in which he draws on mid-Eastern styles and instrumentation. Amram appears on this disc as a performer as well as composer and conductor, playing piano, French horn, guitar, and bouzouki. It is interesting that the CD reissue of this album features only material from the second disc, thus limiting Amram's claim to have transcended genre barriers.

rock style returns and persists till the end of the track. The total effect is of a series of very different musical styles replacing one another abruptly and without meaningful transitions. Even though the Dixieland clarinet is present from the beginning, it does not blend with the rock style but stands out conspicuously as something different. Rather than a synthesis of rock and Dixieland, the song sounds like a rock band trying to drown out a Dixieland band that nevertheless manages to surface and make its presence known at certain points. The Elvis-like style is a completely unanticipated surprise that appears suddenly for the duration of one verse and disappears just as suddenly. The piece as a whole is stylistically digressive: it returns frequently (though not regularly) to its basic hard rock style but also departs from that style abruptly to undergo multiple unanticipated mutations.

The only song on *Wizzard Brew* to resemble the group's singles is the rock-and-roll pastiche "Gotta Crush (About You)," an up-tempo, horn-driven boogie with an echo-enhanced vocal that sounds like Eddie Cochran. Like this track, each of the singles evokes an earlier musical style from the 1950s or early 1960s. "Ball Park Incident" (1972) and "Are You Ready to Rock" (1974) evoke primal rock-and-roll styles: the former is in a taut Chuck Berry mode, while the latter partakes of an earlier jump band style. Whereas these songs call the 1950s to mind, several others employ a much denser, early 1960s production style resembling Phil Spector's famous "Wall of Sound." These recordings feature strings as well as horns, large choirs of backing singers, and layers of percussion, including the tympani, xylophones, and castanets Spector used so often. "See My Baby Jive" (1973) includes a direct quotation from Spector's recording of the Crystals' "He's a Rebel" (1962) to drive home the reference.

Collectively, these singles and Wizzard's first album presented the group as an entity with no fixed identity in terms of style, genre, sound, or voice. Although some of the album tracks suggested that the group had a distinctive sound, its identity on the singles derived entirely from its ability to forge other artists' identities. This continual shifting of identity can be traced through the changing uses of saxophones and the mutations of Wood's own singing voice in the recordings. "Ball Park Incident" features an alto saxophone solo in the hard, chattering style of King Curtis; in "Rock and Roll Winter" (1974), one of the Spectoresque compositions, the saxophones are soothing and syrupy, with a breathy, mellow tenor solo presented against a wash of strings. In the boogying "Are You Ready to Rock," the saxophone section pushes the tempo, and a leaping baritone solo is interrupted by interjections from an impatient tenor. The changing musical identities portrayed by the saxophonists (always Nick Pentelow and Mike Burney, with Wood himself sometimes joining in) are matched by the shifting sound of Wood's singing voice. Whereas his voice is a rough rock shout in "Ball Park Incident," it becomes the relaxed voice of a hep cat in "Are You Ready to Rock" and turns into a shriller head voice in "See My Baby Jive." On "Rock and Roll Winter," Wood's voice explicitly becomes that of another performer: Neil Sedaka, whose tone, accent, and enunciation Wood captures expertly (the pizzicato violin sound associated with Sedaka's recordings is also present).

Wizzard's second album, *Introducing Eddy and the Falcons* (1974), was much more continuous with the group's singles than their first album had been. The cover represents the surface of a red-and-white checked tablecloth covering a table in a cheap diner. Laid on the table are an ornate business card, an ID bracelet, a greasy comb, and a number of photographs. The business card indicates that Eddy and the Falcons are a group native to Birmingham, where they are available to play at social functions, dances, and weddings. (In fact, the Falcons were the first group Wood played with in Birmingham in the early 1960s.) The ID bracelet next to the card has "Wizzard" engraved on it, revealing the identity of the group that actually made the album. The gatefold photographs recount a narrative in which Eddy and the Falcons, dressed as Teddy Boys and Rockers, enter the diner. A conflict develops and the members of the group assault one of their own number. Although the movie posters on the wall of the diner (for *The Buccaneer* [1958] and *Rebel Without a Cause* [1955]) and the group's attire suggest a 1950s setting, the members of Eddy and the Falcons have the long hair and beards of 1970s rock musicians. The idea of rock musicians' revisiting the rock-and-roll past and its attendant subcultural identities is thus put into play, as it was so many times during the early 1970s.

Wood's version of 1950s revivalism was quite different, however, from those of his fellow glam rockers or such artists as John Lennon and Sha Na Na, whose return to the earlier era I discussed in chapter 1. The music on the recording covers a variety of styles, from rock and roll to rockabilly to teen ballads to Spector's "Wall of Sound." Wood's songs are frequently pastiches that sound very similar to other, well-known songs. "Everyday I Wonder," for example, borrows the well-known organ riff from Del Shannon's "Runaway" (1961) and bears a strong resemblance to the earlier song (the famous organ solo from Shannon's recording reappears in an arrangement for double reeds). Similarly, "Come Back Karen" strongly resembles Neil Sedaka's "Oh Carol" (1961). Other artists Wood emulates on this recording include Paul Anka, Bobby Vee, Dion, Duane Eddy, Gene Vincent and the Blue Caps, and Carl Perkins.[16] Wood's use of pastiche has the curious effect of robbing Eddy and the Falcons of authenticity even though their music accurately reflects styles of the 1950s and early 1960s. Because Wood's songs sound like other songs but are not those other songs, they seem inauthentic even in comparison with Sha Na Na's repertoire, which consisted, after all, of real 1950s music.

The final song on the album, "We're Gonna Rock and Roll Tonight," seems to depart from the project of stylistic re-creation because it sounds contemporary. Alan Niester observes in his review of the album that the song

> sounds as if Wizzard is dropping the Falcons persona . . . and celebrating "Good Old Rock 'n' Roll" . . . but anyone aware of

---

16. There was some critical disagreement as to exactly which earlier artists Wood evoked on *Introducing Eddy and the Falcons.* Both Alan Niester, who reviewed the album for *Rolling Stone,* and Roy Carr, who reviewed it for the *New Musical Express,* agreed that Duane Eddy, Del Shannon, and Gene Vincent were referenced. But whereas Niester hears one song as suggesting Bobby Vee, Carr hears that same song as Dion. Niester identifies a rockabilly number as a replication of Carl Perkins, whereas Carr hears it as Elvis. Such differences are due to several factors, including critical error (Niester is simply wrong to suggest that "Come Back Karen" is "a rewrite of Paul Anka's 'Diana'"; Carr is correct in identifying it as a remake of Neil Sedaka's "Oh Carol"). The more important point is that Wood so skillfully evokes musical genres and styles as well as specific performers that a particular performance might reasonably be attributed to different artists within the same genre. Both Niester and Carr point out that one song, "This is the Story of My Love, Baby," communicates the essence of a genre without precisely evoking any single performer (though they agree that it is in Phil Spector's production style). Niester describes it as "what might have happened had Phil Spector discovered that Scott Walker and Annette Funicello had fallen in love in his living room, and celebrated their consummation in a song." Carr suggests very much the same thing, but with a different pairing: "Jeez, you can almost imagine Sandra Dee and Troy Donahue holding sweaty hands and pledging Colgate fresh fidelity to one another over a malted milk while Phil Spector plays gooseberry."

Wood's previous work with the Move or Wizzard will quickly realize that the clichéd lyrics, off-key vocals, and pedantic, one-note solos are all done purposely and therefore the song serves as a nifty sendup of all the Seventies glitter bands who feel the need to celebrate the Fifties but end up helping to bury it.

As Niester suggests, even the more authentic-seeming song for which the group apparently drops their masks does not actually express Wood's or Wizzard's "real" musical identity any more than the other, more obvious pastiches do.

Like Marc Bolan, Wood borrowed directly from identifiable songs and artists of the 1950s and reworked them into his own music. But Wood's way of doing so inverted Bolan's: whereas Bolan reshaped his rock-and-roll sources to fit his own voice and persona, Wood assumed the voices and personae implied by the songs. He altered the range, timbre, and accent of his voice (all of the various accents he uses are American) in keeping with the conventions of each musical genre he emulated. He shaped his voice to the particular style of each song rather than interpreting the songs in a manner that stamps them with his performance persona.

Much the same can be said about Wood's earlier solo album *Boulders*. In the context of rock ideology, the solo album is considered an opportunity for a musician primarily identified as a member of a particular group (as Wood was at the time he recorded it in 1969) to present a truly authentic, personal expression not possible in the group context (solo performers do not make solo albums!). *Boulders* has the earmarks of a very personal project. Wood wrote all the songs and played all the instruments on the recording. Although it partakes of a few musical gestures one might consider experimental—such as using a bucket of water as an instrument and playing the instrumental solos of a hard rocking tune on cello and bassoon—the album is musically conventional and very accessible. But it gives no access to a consistently defined identity one could call Roy Wood. As on *Eddy and the Falcons*, the songs are stylistically very different from one another, and Wood sings in different accents, employs different parts of his range, and alters his voice electronically. While the trappings of the solo album encourage the listener to perceive *Boulders* as Wood's personal expression—it certainly provides ample testimony to his skills as a multi-instrumentalist and musical conceptualist—the recording itself produces Wood as more of an absence than a presence.

Wood's performance persona with Wizzard differed from those

of most glam rockers in ways that parallel his relationship to the music of the 1950s. Although Wizzard gave spectacular performances both live and on television, these performances did not serve to define specific and continuous personae in the way that Ferry's and Bolan's did but created different images for different songs. Wood describes his image with Wizzard as originating in a late television performance by the Move that anticipated glam rock:

> We had to go on and do "Brontosaurus" [1970] and we had a rehearsal and we were all in the dressing room and I had this long sort of coat which was made of black and white triangles of material. I was a bit nervous. It was the first time I'd ever been the lead singer on TV properly. I was thinking that it was time for a new image. The guys went to the bar and I put this jacket on and it looked like there was something missing that should have went with the jacket. So I got my comb and I combed my hair out so it looked really wild. I went down to the makeup department and borrowed some black and white makeup and I made my face up to match the coat with triangles around the eyes and I put a star in the middle of my forehead and this was the creation of the Wizzard image really but I did it then. (Qtd. in Sharp)

Wood thus created a distinctive look that he ultimately used in his performances with Wizzard, but that look did not suggest a specific persona or character the way that Bolan's, Bowie's, and Ferry's manipulations of image did.

Just as Wood's voice is different on each song, so his and Wizzard's images changed from song to song in their television performances. A video of "Ball Park Incident" showed the band dressed in candy-colored versions of the Teddy Boy apparel they displayed on the cover of *Introducing Eddy and the Falcons* but not doing anything to suggest a particular image or set of personae beyond that: their movements were slightly exaggerated versions of conventional rock performer gestures. The video for "I Wish It Could Be Christmas Everyday" (1973), by contrast, was an extravaganza keyed entirely to a seasonal theme. The opening shot was framed to suggest a Christmas card and the members of the group dressed in red and white outfits against a background of glistening white snow. Although the saxophone players still looked a bit like festive Teddy Boys, one drummer appeared as a tin soldier, Rick Price dressed as a schoolboy on holiday, and Wood himself portrayed either the spirit of winter or a snowman. He wore a long white wig

Roy Wood performing with Wizzard, ca. 1974. © MichaelOchs Archives.com.

with his face and beard frosted in white and his nose tipped with red. Midway through the performance, a group of children appeared on the stage, each playing a toy instrument. Although this was a lip-synched performance and the children did not actually sing, they represented the children's chorus that joins Wizzard on the recording and constituted a miniature version of the group.

The television performance that probably came closest to reflecting the group's live performances was the video for "See My Baby Jive." Here, Wood appeared in his basic Wizzard guise with long, matted, multicolored hair and his face made-up in geometric patterns.[17] He stood downstage center, amid the other musicians,

17. According to Wood, the makeup he developed for his Wizzard persona influenced the American group Kiss: "When we eventually toured with Wizzard in America we did a few gigs supporting KISS and I did this radio interview; me and Gene Simmons did the interview together. I think it was in Detroit or something like that and he actually admitted on the air that they had been influenced by my makeup to get the band on the road, which I thought was nice of him to say in public" (qtd. in Sharp).

holding a French horn that he never actually played (or pretended to play since this was another lip-synched performance). Although he moved to the music, his primary gestures were those of a conductor, which he made with his right hand. The five female backup singers upstage right were dressed in gray as if to avoid competing with the more colorfully dressed male musicians, all of whom wore extravagant outfits. One was dressed as an angel in a white tunic with large wings; two figures appeared in gorilla suits holding guitars and dancing.[18] As the performance progressed, the scene became more and more anarchic—the gorilla-suited men launched cream pies, one of which landed on the angel's face. Wood observed the action around him with an amused expression but did not take part, concentrating instead on "conducting" the band and lip-synching the vocal. Interviewer Ken Sharp later reminded Wood that "a lot of people described Wizzard as being like a traveling rock 'n' roll circus," a characterization with which Wood concurred. If so, Wood's role was to look like a clown but act like a ringmaster.

Wizzard's performances were undoubtedly spectacular, but the spectacle was arbitrary (like Wood's French horn) and undertaken for its own sake rather than to delineate specific performance personae. On record, Wizzard's identity as a group was no more consistent with respect to musical genre than Wood's singing voice. If one had to identify a single persona for either Wizzard or Wood, it would be a protean persona able to assume a wide range of different identities, including some belonging to other performers. Bowie was similarly protean, but whereas Bowie marked different phases of his career by assuming different personae, Wood moved from identity to identity within a single phase. If glam rockers of the first wave questioned rock's ideology of authenticity by constructing overtly artificial performance personae, Wood took that impulse a step further by asserting both the artificiality and the arbitrariness of performing personae. Arguably, by constructing a persona whose very identity resided in its lack of identity, Wood parodied glam rock even as he participated in it.

Wood's only top-ten hit as a solo artist, "Forever" (1973), shares salient characteristics with his earlier recordings in that Wood nei-

---

18. Wood mentioned to interviewer Ken Sharp that for some live performances Wizzard "had the roadies dressed as gorillas," which suggests that the figures in gorilla suits in the video were not actually musicians.

ther composed nor sang it in his own voice. Although all of the voices on the recording literally belong to Wood, they re-create styles and sounds specifically associated with other artists: initially the Beach Boys, then Neil Sedaka. As the song switches from one stylistic reference point to the other and back again, the melody remains constant, as does the basic rhythm track. But the vocal styles change completely, as do the details of the arrangement: Wood's vocal tone when singing as the Beach Boys' Carl Wilson is much more relaxed than when he is singing as Sedaka, at which point his voice becomes more strident and laden with echo; his accent and diction also change. The backing vocals undergo a similar transition: the Beach Boys' Southern Californian surfer version of doo-wop gives way to the brittle New York Brill Building sound associated with Sedaka. Whereas the Beach Boys–style backing vocals provide full support and background for the lead vocal, the backing vocals in the Sedaka-style sections are reduced to interjections. The pizzicato violin sound Wood used to suggest Sedaka's style on "Rock and Roll Winter" reappears as well. Because "Forever" juxtaposes multiple styles, it is more like "Buffalo Station— Get on Down to Memphis" than the other Wizzard pieces discussed here, each of which has one dominant style. The evenhanded way Wood moves back and forth between two equally present voices makes the stylistic identity of "Forever" even more equivocal than that of the earlier song. To return to the circus metaphor, Wood serves here in a triple capacity, as two different acts and, implicitly, the ringmaster who directs audience attention first to one, then the other.

Wood re-creates the sounds of these artists with an almost scholarly meticulousness. His rendition of the Beach Boys' style, for example, is not a stereotype—it refers to a specific moment in their stylistic development: the post–Pet Sounds Beach Boys, circa 1967. This precision is important because it suggests that Wood is not just evoking the Beach Boys in his recording but *embodying* them through his vocal performance, a notion Wood confirms in his description of the actorly approach he took to making the record: "When I was putting down the vocal tracks on 'Forever' I had to visualize that, for the moment, I was those people—otherwise I'd never have been able to come anywhere near the sound I wanted" (qtd. in Carr, "Who's" 21). By re-creating the Beach Boys' voices, Wood re-created the Beach Boys' bodies as well, as they existed at a particular moment in time.

The concepts of the indicative and the subjunctive provide useful touchstones for thinking about singers' appropriations of other singers' voices. When blues singer Taj Mahal, for example, borrows Howlin' Wolf's rasp, he usually does so only after singing in a voice we take to be Mahal's own.[19] This voice serves as a baseline, a performative norm from which Mahal departs when he borrows other voices and to which he returns after each stylistic quotation. When Mahal sings in his "own" voice, he performs in the indicative mood. His quotation of another singer's style moves his performance into the subjunctive: Mahal sings *as if he were* Wolf.[20] But the overall mood of these performances remains in the indicative because Mahal's positing of a normative voice points to his own presence as the one doing the quoting. The key formal difference between Wood's quotative strategy and Mahal's is that Wood does not establish a baseline voice from which his stylistic quotations deviate. In his recording of "Forever" and his earlier work with Wizzard, Wood himself disappears into his vocal embodiments of other artists. Even though we know the recording to be the product of an entity named Roy Wood, there is nothing there for the listener to identify as the distinctive voice or presence of Roy Wood. On these recordings, Wood sings *only* in borrowed voices; the subjunctive is thus the only mood of these performances.

The opening section of "You Sure Got It Now," from Wood's second solo album, *Mustard* (1975), combines an electronic sound reminiscent of both a telephonic busy signal and the *Twilight Zone* theme with a classical-sounding passage overlaid with windlike electronic noises. The diversity of sounds here—some recognizably musical, some noise—and the passage's lack of definition with respect to musical style and genre suggest that Wood is welcoming

19. I am not suggesting that this voice is Mahal's "real" voice, only that it functions as the normative voice for a particular performance. Like many singers, Mahal has multiple "real" voices that vary according to the genre and emotional tone of the songs he performs.

20. Mahal uses Howlin' Wolf's voice quite frequently. One good example is Mahal's recording of "Blues with a Feeling," in which he sings the penultimate line as Wolf. This is an interesting case since the song is associated with Chicago bluesman Little Walter, who wrote and recorded it. Mahal enters the liminal space of the subjunctive to give a sense of what Wolf, Walter's contemporary, would have sounded like singing it. Mahal sometimes frames his borrowing of another's voice explicitly as a tribute to the other singer, as he does with Muddy Waters on "Blues Ain't Nothing," a recording on which he also briefly imitates Wolf's voice.

us into a chaotic realm where anything is possible—a musical Twilight Zone, or the realm of subjunctivity. This characterization of the opening is borne out in the body of the song: each section reflects the stylistic conventions of a different genre of music. The opening section is in the World War II era style of the Andrews Sisters (whom Wood also imitates on the album's title track); Wood's voice is multitracked and electronically altered so that he sounds like three women singing in harmony. This section is punctuated by an instrumental rendition of the melody in the style of an acoustic blues band that continues into the next section. There, Wood almost speaks the (now slightly different) lyrics in a deep male voice perhaps intended to suggest an African-American blues singer. In the final section, Wood sings yet another version of the lyrics in a voice that sounds like that of a female blues-rock belter, perhaps on the model of Janis Joplin (the horn and electric-guitar-laden arrangement of this section is reminiscent particularly of *Kozmic Blues* era Joplin, ca. 1969).

Wood sustains the subjunctive mood by switching among different styles and vocal identities, sometimes clearly assuming the identities of recognizable artists, sometimes singing in voices that typify a musical genre rather than a particular person. Identities posited in the subjunctive mood are open to perpetual revision: since Wood is no more Neil Sedaka than he is the Beach Boys, no more the Andrews Sisters than Janis Joplin, he can assume any and all of these identities and move among them at will.

This fluid approach to musical identity is also reflected in the way Wood constituted his groups. I already mentioned that he, Lynne, and Bevan were simultaneously the Move and the Electric Light Orchestra for a period in 1971. In December 1973, Wood released "Forever" and "I Wish It Could Be Christmas Everyday" within a week of each other. Given that both recordings are pastiches of earlier styles and artists, there is no discernable reason why one should be considered the work of the group and the other that of an individual.[21] Their almost simultaneous release also meant that Wood

21. Todd Rundgren's album *Faithful* (1976) raises similar questions. The second side consists of Rundgren's near-perfect re-creations of famous recordings by the Beatles, Hendrix, Bob Dylan, the Beach Boys, and others. On a later recording, *Deface the Music* (1980), Rundgren and his group, Utopia, perform a whole album of songs written in various styles associated with the Beatles. The album as a whole traces the Beatles' stylistic development chronologically. These recordings whose purpose is to sound like other recordings throw

was effectively competing with himself on the charts in two different guises (both recordings did well: "Forever" reached number
eight while "I Wish It Could Be Christmas Everyday" peaked at
number four). This deliberate blurring of the lines distinguishing
performing entities flies in the face of rock ideology, which generally assumes that musicians will maintain a single group
identification. (Rock is different in this respect from both jazz and
classical music, in which is commonly accepted that individual
musicians may belong simultaneously to a number of different
groups or ensembles.)

Wood's recordings with Wizzard and after reflect what Richard
Schechner calls "performance consciousness," which he describes
as a state of mind that "is subjunctive, full of alternatives and
potentiality." Performance consciousness "activates alternatives:
'this' and 'that' are both operative simultaneously." Schechner further observes that "during rehearsals especially, alternatives are
kept alive, the work is intentionally unsettled" (*Between Theater* 6).
This idea of rehearsal is an apt metaphor for what Wood does on
these recordings. I am not suggesting, of course, that Wood's
recordings are anything other than thoroughly realized, polished
productions. But the multiple musical styles, genres, and voices in
which he renders his songs keep his performances forever unsettled
and leave open multiple options for both the song's style and the
artist's identity. One can easily imagine a much longer version of
"You Sure Got It Now" in which Wood would go on performing
the song in a growing profusion of different styles, adjusting the
lyrics to each, without any style seeming definitive.

Through his assertion of performance consciousness, Wood
assumes a quizzical relationship to rock's ideology of authenticity.
As Fornäs suggests, "The authentic as the genuine or honest expression of a subject is implied in the words '*your* voice'—a symbolic
expression of precisely your own creative subjectivity" (99). As we

---

into question the authenticity of Rundgren's own songs on the first side of
Faithful. Where are we to locate his artistic identity—in his overt stylistic
appropriations or his supposedly "original" songs, which inevitably also
reflect other people's musical ideas? Rundgren also voids his own identity and
that of his group, Utopia, by indiscriminately labeling some records as his own
solo albums and others as the group's, even though all are made by the same
personnel and there is no apparent reason why the re-creations of 1960s music
on *Faithful* should be identified with Rundgren and the Beatles pastiches on
Deface the Music should be identified as the work of Utopia.

have seen, Wood frequently sings in voices that are obviously not his own, voices that even belie his sex, race, national origin, and historical era.[22] Nevertheless, these voices do express Wood's "creative subjectivity." Paradoxically, part of what makes Wood distinctive as a creator of rock music is his recombinant approach to composition; he is an auteur whose signature is his very lack of signature or his appropriation of the signatures of others.

I hasten to add that Wood's choices of styles and the transitions he makes between them are not at all arbitrary. As I already hinted, by alternating stylistically between the Beach Boys and Neil Sedaka on "Forever," Wood travels wittily through time and space by bouncing back and forth between sounds associated, respectively, with the East Coast of the United States in the very early 1960s and with the West Coast during the psychedelic era. The sequence of styles in "You Sure Got It Now" arguably constitutes a brief history of blues-based American popular music that moves chronologically from the 1940s (the Andrews Sisters) to the 1950s (the highwater mark of African-American blues recordings) to the 1960s (blues rock); the changes in the lyrics correspond to each era and style.

"Rock Medley," from *Boulders*, functions similarly: each section evokes a different moment in the development of rock music, presented in chronological order. The first part lies stylistically on the border between country crooning and rockabilly. The second specifically re-creates the Everly Brothers sound, another style that helped bridge country music and rock and roll (Phil Everly would later sing on *Mustard*). The third part, called "The Locomotive," moves into the sound of 1970s hard rock while also recalling "The Locomotion," a dance song from 1962 (it thus curiously anticipates Grand Funk's 1974 recording of "The Locomotion").[23]

22. As Simon Frith suggests, the relationship between voice and identity is always tenuous: "The voice . . . may or may not be a key to someone's identity, but it is certainly a key to the way we change identities, pretend to be something we're not" (*Performing Rites* 197).

23. It is again worthwhile to mention Rundgren's musical re-creations in the context of Wood's practices. Steve Bailey describes the first side of Rundgren's *Faithful* as "an act of willful pointlessness" that "reflects a response to the exhaustion of art rock as a genre" and thus "anticipates key aspects of the punk/new wave movement" (154). This is a plausible position, but I suggest that the same evidence can lead to an opposite reading. All of the songs on the first side of *Faithful* were originally released between 1966 and 1968; four of the six are from 1966. They are presented in chronological order, which can be

I do not want to create the impression that Wood never sings in his own voice—he does. At least, there is a voice on his recordings that we experience as Wood's own voice in part because it is familiar from his days with the Move and also because it does not sound obviously like anyone else's, a phenomenon that itself raises some trenchant questions about the links between voice and identity. The crucial point is that on such solo albums as *Boulders* and *Mustard,* Wood sometimes sings in his own voice, sometimes in those of others. He thus implies that his own voice is akin to the musical styles he employs: it is but one of many available to him and neither it nor the identity it indexes enjoys any privilege in his performance practices. Sometimes he sings as if he were the Andrews Sisters or the Beach Boys, and sometimes he sings as if he were Roy Wood.

Even more explicitly than Ferry's falsetto, Wood's electronic manipulation of his voice to sound like several female voices on "You Sure Got It Now" constitutes a form of vocal transsexualism that parallels glam rock's transvestism. Crossing back and forth between "male" and "female" registers, Wood's voice, like Ferry's, is a male version of the Sapphonic voice, though Wood's vocal transsexualism is more obviously technologically enhanced. And, like Ferry's, Wood's vocal practice challenges a tenet central to the ideology of authenticity by severing the link between individual creativity and individual voice.

Both Ferry and Wood sing in multiple voices without suggesting that any one of them is the "real" voice from which the others are to be distinguished. In Ferry's case, it is actually difficult to find a voice to call his "real" voice—as I suggested earlier, the deeper chest voice on "Sea Breezes" sounds just as mannered and artificial as the falsetto. Listening to Ferry sing on the first Roxy Music album (on which "Sea Breezes" appears), I hear many voices, some of which correspond to the numerous musical genres Roxy Music combined and hybridized. In addition to the falsetto and chest

---

read as the gesture of a rock historian as much as that of an ironist. Rundgren's remaking these recordings from what many would consider to be rock's most fertile era in 1976, year one of the punk revolution, does not necessarily suggest punk iconoclasm: it can also be read as an homage to the rock predecessors being trashed by punk. In this interpretation, the word *faithful* stands unironically for Rundgren's ongoing fidelity to the rock counterculture (even as he helped usher in a new era by producing the New York Dolls' first album in 1973).

voices already discussed, there is the highly mannered, vibrato-laden voice of the hit song "Virginia Plain"; a pleading lover's voice; a 1950s rock-and-roll voice; a drawling, stereotyped country singer's voice; a hard rock voice; a jaunty pop voice; and a variety of voices associated with versions of night club, cabaret, or music hall singing. It is impossible to identify any one of these as Ferry's "natural" or spontaneous voice against which his various vocal mannerisms might be measured.

This proliferation and confusion of voices recalls Jonathan Rée's account of "natural" and "funny" voices. Describing an attempt to leave a message on a telephone answering machine, Rée anticipates performance anxiety at the thought that one's voice will sound funny and unnatural. Rather than leave the message, his subject "hang[s] up in panic" and is faced with a dilemma:

> When you try to get back to your natural voice, you may discover that you have no idea where to look for it. Is it big or small, classy or common, stagy or intimate? You will be plunged into an elementary philosophical experience: feeling absolutely certain of something but unable to tell what it is or how to lay your hands on it. . . . You glimpse the possibility that it is quite arbitrary to mark off certain of your vocal performances and nominate them as one voice, the voice that really belongs to you: do you really possess an ownmost, innermost voice which has the power to clamp quotation marks around the others and shrug them off as "funny"? (1052–53)

In addition to questioning conventional representations of gender and sexuality in rock music and the idea that the voice is a vehicle for the singer's existential authenticity, the inauthentic voices of glam rock allude to this larger philosophical problem. Vocal practices that assert the artificiality of the singer's voice place quotation marks around all voices, suggesting that all are equally "funny" and leaving little room for the possibility of a natural or authentic voice.

6. suzi quatro wants to be your man

Female Masculinity in Glam Rock

I'm a girl and it's wonderful
It fills my heart with joy
But sometimes, yes sometimes
I wish I were a boy.
—"I Wish I Were a Boy" (Recorded by Leslie Gore, 1964)

Dressed in a black leather jumpsuit accessorized with black leather bracelets and a studded leather dog collar, surrounded by three large, hirsute male musicians in black pants and black muscle shirts, Suzi Quatro crouches at the vocal mike. Her fingers thump out notes on her bass guitar as she sneeringly shouts the seemingly nonsensical and virtually unintelligible lyrics to her first number one hit, "Can the Can." The bass guitar is suspended low against her hips; she stomps her feet to the rhythm and thrusts her pelvis forward, against the bass, and back in a humping motion. With each cry of the lead guitar on the bridge, she thrusts herself toward the microphone with growing urgency as her vocals rise in pitch to climax finally at the chorus.[1]

When introducing the Spiders from Mars during his final Ziggy concert at the Hammersmith Odeon, David Bowie presented one musician by saying, "No, it's not Suzi Quatro—on lead guitar, we got Mick Ronson!" Bowie was presumably comparing Ronson's

1. All descriptions of Quatro's performances in this chapter are based on materials in a bootleg video anthology of about nine hours' worth of Quatro's collected television and live concert appearances. Because the tapes are not annotated, exact dates and sources of these performances are unknown, though I have provided educated guesses.

unisex shag haircut to the very similar one sported at the time by Quatro, but he was also tacitly acknowledging Quatro, a recent arrival on the glam rock scene, who had hit number one on the British pop charts just two months earlier, in May 1973, with her recording of "Can the Can." Quatro, an American from a musical family in Detroit, began her career in an "all-girl" garage band, Suzi Soul and the Pleasure Seekers, formed with two of her three sisters in 1964. While playing with a later version of the Pleasure Seekers, now renamed Cradle, Quatro was seen in 1971 by the British record producer Mickie Most, who was in Detroit recording British guitarist Jeff Beck. He offered to help establish Quatro as a solo artist if she were willing to move to the UK, which she did at the end of that year.

After a false start with a failed single and group, Quatro began working with Nicky Chinn and Mike Chapman, the highly successful songwriting and record-producing team known collectively as Chinnichap, who helped Quatro put together a working band made up of male musicians, with whom she both recorded and performed live. "Can the Can" (recorded with studio musicians) was Quatro's first single release under Chinnichap's guidance; between 1973 and 1983, she charted in the UK with sixteen songs, including two number ones and five in the top ten. Although Quatro was profiled in *Rolling Stone*'s very first issue for 1975 and appeared on the cover, she never enjoyed the same level of success in the United States, where her only top forty record was "Stumblin' In," a 1978 duet with Chris Norman, the lead singer of another Chinnichap group, Smokie, that reached number five on the U.S. charts early in 1979. In a parallel career as an actress, however, Quatro achieved some popularity in the United States by playing Leather Tuscadero, a character based on her rock persona, in several episodes of the *Happy Days* television show.[2]

Quatro's membership in the Chinnichap stable of artists, her status as an habitué of the London glam rock scene, and her masculine performance persona made her identification as a glam rocker almost inevitable in the early 1970s. Because of her diminutive stature (just over five feet tall), hyperenergetic movement style, and fondness for 1950s rock and roll, she was sometimes called "the

2. For a more detailed account of Quatro's early days in Detroit, see Tom Hibbert. For a fuller career biography, see Frank Oglesbee. I have also drawn on Gaar (218–21), Stambler (546–47), and Unterberger, "Suzi Quatro."

female Bolan" (Benton, "Suzi Q!" 3). As Arthur Davis explains, her persona could readily be understood as a female response to glam's transvestite male images: "Since many male glam rockers wore mascara and dressed as women . . . Suzi would wear very little make-up and—from a distance—looked somewhat like a man in her leather catsuit" (2). In some published remarks, Quatro positioned herself as the butch female response to glam rock's male androgynes: "You know the men are prettier than the women these days. Take Bowie for instance, he makes me feel real ugly" (Benton, "Suzi Q!" 3). Consequently, Quatro has been nominated as the sole female glam rock performer.

For all of glam rock's play with unconventional gender performances, virtually all glam rock performers and producers were male. In these respects, glam rock was entirely in line with the conventions of rock music as a traditionally male-dominated cultural form. Simon Frith and Angela McRobbie describe the situation clearly in an essay originally published in 1978:

> Any analysis of the sexuality of rock music must begin with the brute social fact that in terms of control and production, rock is a male form. The music business is male-run; popular musicians, writers, creators, technicians, engineers and producers are mostly men. . . . The problems facing a woman seeking to enter the rock world as a participant are clear. A girl is supposed to be an individual listener; she is not encouraged to develop the skills and knowledge to become a performer. (373, 376)

As I argued in chapter 2, glam rock clearly transcended one of the limitations Frith and McRobbie attribute to "rock's sexual ideology" when they argue that "rock offers a framework within which male sexuality can find a range of acceptable, heterosexual expressions" (375). Nevertheless, glam was absolutely typical of rock in its exclusive emphasis on male participation and concerns. Suzi Quatro is the only female musician to be included in the glam canon; apart from her contribution, the main role glam rock offered to its female participants was that of fan, as Frith and McRobbie's analysis would predict.

Women were important in the creation of glam rock, but always behind the scenes. There is no question but that June Bolan and Angela Bowie were crucial in the development of their respective husbands' innovations—each served as a combined muse, social secretary, manager, and stylist. Glam masculinity reflected a number of cultural influences, but it was in the immediate sense largely the creation of individual women. Chelita Secunda, T. Rex's publicist, took Marc Bolan shopping for women's clothes; it was either she or June Bolan who sprinkled glitter on his face before his landmark performance on *Top of the Pops.*[3] Angela Bowie is credited with introducing David to London's gay bar scene and creating his androgynous look. Johnny Thunders, the lead guitarist of the New York Dolls, was dressed in women's clothing and makeup by his girlfriend, Janis Cafasso. Brian Eno's costumes were designed by the woman he lived with, sculptor Carole McNicol (Hoskyns, *Glam!* 18, 22, 61, 69). Even Texas rocker Edgar Winter attributed his brief flirtation with glam to his wife's desire "to see what I looked like with all the makeup and stuff on" (qtd. in Alterman 3).

The feminized image affected by glam men was, at least to some extent, constructed by women. It appealed to female fans both as a style they could adapt for themselves and as a desirable male image: "the more camp and androgynous you looked in 1973, the more girls fancied you" (Hoskyns, *Glam!* 64). Eno, the most flamboyantly effeminate member of Roxy Music, proposes that heterosexual women were attracted to men who actively rejected the traditional image of masculinity: "It's the feeling that here is someone who is other but who is not threatening, who has surrendered their authority and their ability to command by strength. If you're gay or you're androgynous, you're not playing that usual male role of 'I'm the tough one here.' She knows that this guy isn't *playing the male*" (qtd. in Hoskyns, *Glam!* 64). It reflects no credit on the glam genre world that some performers used their attractiveness to female fans as a means of sexually exploiting them as groupies.

Nevertheless, glam rock's gender-bending did open a space for unconventional performances of female gender just as it did for male gender, even if only one musician claimed that space. Quatro took advantage of the upheaval into which glam had thrown rock's gender norms to produce performances that destabilize those norms as effectively as Bowie's, albeit using somewhat different tactics. At the same time, the mere fact of Quatro's being a woman

3. There are actually three different stories concerning Bolan's use of glitter on *Top of the Pops*. One is that he decided to use it himself. According to Hoskyns, it was the idea of his publicist, Chelita Secunda (*Glam!* 18). A third version, in which June Bolan put the glitter on Marc's face, appears in Novick and Middles (22).

means that analysis of her work must be framed in somewhat different terms than that of the male musicians discussed here. Rock was a male-dominated cultural form in the 1960s and 1970s (and continues to be one today, to a very large extent), and male glam rockers used their normative gender position to launch unconventional gender performances. As a female rocker, Quatro was an anomaly to begin with.

In the early 1970s, Suzi Quatro was unique. Although there were many women in rock by the late 1960s, most performed only as singers, a traditionally feminine position in popular music. At the time of Quatro's emergence in 1973, no other prominent female musician worked in rock simultaneously as a singer, instrumentalist, songwriter, and bandleader.[4] As I discussed in chapter 1, the international hippie counterculture was primarily masculinist in orientation and often overtly sexist. Psychedelic rock, as one of the counterculture's primary modes of expression, participated fully in the marginalization of women, as Sheila Whiteley suggests:

> both the counter culture and progressive rock[5] were largely dominated by men who were reactionary in their attitude towards women. Inscribed [in the lyrics of rock songs] as de-sexualized earth mothers, fantasy figures and easy lays, there was little real opportunity to either take control or enjoy the prestige afforded to male artists. Indeed, while the more challenging stance of progressive rock offered a new arena for experimentation, the opportunities for women performers remained largely conventional in that they were not encouraged to compose or become instrumentalists. Further, the emphasis on image remained. Front-line performers were expected to *look* feminine. (*Women and Popular Music* 51).

One of the primary obstacles faced by women rock musicians is sexual objectification and a concomitant lack of interest in their

4. For a discussion of the situation of women in rock contemporaneous with Quatro's emergence, see Michael Gray's series of three articles in *Melody Maker,* published on consecutive weeks in the spring of 1974. In the first, Gray discusses the ways rock is gendered as male in terms that anticipate Frith and McRobbie's later, more formal discussion. The second article addresses representations of women in the lyrics to rock songs, while the third takes up the question of women's status in the music business.

5. Whiteley uses the phrase *progressive rock* to denote the same musical subgenre I call *psychedelic rock*.

abilities as musicians. Quatro complained of being called upon by members of her audience to strip (Benton, "Suzi" 13), a phenomenon experienced by female rock performers well into the 1990s (Bayton 46). Robot A. Hull's review of Quatro's first album for *Creem* magazine represents a closely related and equally egregious form of objectification. In an ostensibly positive review, Hull proposes that his (male) reader use Quatro's work as the basis for masturbatory fantasy: "So, sport, if yr hungry for some good things and need something to make ya really hard, then pleeze don't be no fool run out and pounce on Suzi's debut album. It beats those life-size rubber dolls any day" (65). (It is conceivable that Hull intended his overheated diatribe as satire. Even if so, it still exemplifies the treatment of female rock musicians as mere sex objects rife in rock culture and rock criticism.)

Despite the systematic discouragement of female participation in rock, a plethora of "all-girl" garage bands similar to Suzi Soul and the Pleasure Seekers appeared across the United States, beginning in the mid-1960s.[6] A notable example was a group called She, from Sacramento, California, whose leader, Nancy Ross, set out, also in 1964, to create a female version of the Rolling Stones. Ross, a guitarist and singer, wrote the group's songs, scathing social critiques reflecting the attitude of a highly intelligent and disaffected adolescent woman, which She presented very assertively in live performances. She was active for about eight years, but the group's career was largely limited to playing high schools, air force bases, and college fraternity houses, not venues in which young women were likely to be appreciated primarily for their musicianship (Quatro and her group toured American military bases in Southeast Asia). Although She recorded fairly extensively, only one single was ever released, with no commercial success.[7] The story of She is typical of

6. "The garage bands of the late 1960s, so called as exponents made the music in the garage or basement, were especially prominent in the United States, where they responded to the British Invasion of the American market. . . . Garage rock's musical characteristics were 'a premium on sheer outrageousness, over the top vocal screams and sneers, loud guitars that almost always had a fuzztone.' The genre was the province largely of white, teenage suburbanites. It first emerged around 1965, predominantly on tiny, local record labels, linked to strong regional scenes (especially Texas and California), each with a distinctive style. The genre declined in 1967–68 with the impact of the Vietnam War draft and college attendance on band members, and the performers' general lack of commercial success" (Shuker 140–41).

7. This account of She's history derives from the CD *She Wants a Piece of You* and the liner notes by Alec Palao and Joey D.

the all-girl garage bands of the period. Suzi Soul and the Pleasure Seekers and Cradle, active collectively for about seven years, released a few singles, one on a major label, but never achieved visibility outside of Detroit. Although such groups provided young women with opportunities to participate in rock and some experienced regional success, they were the exceptions that proved the rule of rock's gender bias: not one of these groups achieved success on a larger scale as recording artists or live performers. Perhaps as a result, the all-girl garage band phenomenon did not provide viable templates for women's ongoing participation in rock, leaving women like Quatro to seek elsewhere for them.

Although Quatro has acknowledged repeatedly in interviews that Janis Joplin innovated the persona of the tough, uncompromising female rocker in which she feels she participates, she did not take the few women rock musicians who were prominent when she came of age musically as role models. Describing herself as always having been "a blue jean leather jacket tomboy" (e-mail, Jan. 24, 2001) who aspired from the first to be "a rocker from the Elvis, Little Richard school" (e-mail, Nov. 6, 2000), Quatro explicitly looked to male musicians as models, finding even Grace Slick (of the Jefferson Airplane), who is not always considered a paragon of traditional femininity, "too female and swooshy" (e-mail, Jan. 24, 2001).[8] Like all rock musicians' performance personae, Quatro's masculine image was carefully constructed and maintained. Many of the songs Chinnichap wrote and produced for her, such as "The Wild One," "Too Big," and "Devil Gate Drive" (all 1974) not only allowed her to exercise her characteristic vocal aggression but also mythologized her past identity as a teenaged bar musician and emphasized the masculine belligerence and braggadocio of her persona.

---

8. Grace Slick is one of those figures that are frequently mentioned as representing important phenomena (e.g., women in rock, psychedelic music) but are seldom actually discussed in detail. This is a shame in Slick's case because she was a very interesting performer who combined a conventionally glamorous feminine appearance and fashion sense with a deep, powerful voice that she often used in unconventional ways and a musical sensibility that leaned toward the experimental. In addition, Jefferson Airplane was a distinctive group in that it had two members who performed primarily as singers, one male (Marty Balin) and one female (Slick). The interaction between these two singers and their respective and collective relationships to the group would make an interesting study in relation to the characterization of "singer" as a feminized position in rock.

Like Bowie, Quatro performed her persona offstage as well as on. In interviews, she frequently portrayed herself as tough and masculine (she once described herself as "a different [kind of] female altogether" [qtd. in Altham]) by drawing attention to the smallness of her breasts, using salty language, and ogling voluptuous women (see Benton, "Suzi" 13). In an incident recounted in the *Rolling Stone* profile, Quatro responded to a female fan's query, "Are you Suzi Quatro?" by pointing to the unshaven male reporter and saying, "That's Suzi Quatro." After the fan dutifully approached the reporter, Quatro's reaction was to say, "'Jesus Christ . . . What sort of image do I have?' 'Butch,' says Len Tuckey," the guitarist in her group and, later, her first husband (Haden-Guest 49). In the same profile, Quatro talks about hanging out with Hell's Angels, makes veiled references to an incident in Detroit in which she extricated herself from a sticky situation by pulling a knife, and suggests that had she not become a musician, she probably "would have ended up some sort of criminal. Because I need excitement" (qtd. in Haden-Guest 52).[9] She also insists that her leather-clad, biker look was her original style, to which she had returned after being forced to dress more femininely as a member of all-girl groups.

Fully recognizing that rock was dominated by men, Quatro saw herself as "kicking down the male door in rock and roll and proving that a female MUSICIAN . . . and this is a point I am extremely concerned about . . . could play as well if not better than the boys" (e-mail, Oct. 23, 2000). Quatro's emphasis on her status as an instrumentalist, not just a singer, is well placed. As Ruth Padel puts it, "You don't change gender stereotypes [in rock]—threatening misogynist defences *en route*—by singing but by playing" (322; see also Clawson 195). Even as commanding a performer as Joplin ultimately cannot be seen as a powerful figure in the context of the rock culture of her time because she did not play guitar on stage. Padel continues: "Performing on guitar, the core act of rock, is whipping out your cock" (323).[10]

9. Although Quatro only occasionally foregrounds her Italian-American heritage, her tough, leather-clad image certainly evoked a female version of the Italian-Americanistic greaser image I discussed in chapter 1. Her playing Leather Tuscadero, a character specifically identified as Italian-American, on *Happy Days,* could have reinforced this connotation.

10. Paradoxically, the artists identified by Frith and McRobbie (374) as archetypal male cock-rockers perform only as singers: Mick Jagger of the

When Simon Frith describes the cock-rocker, perhaps the quintessential image of the male rock musician, he could be describing Suzi Quatro:

> cock-rock performance means an explicit, crude, "masterful" expression of sexuality. . . . Cock-rock performers are aggressive, boastful, constantly drawing audience attention to their prowess and control. Their bodies are on display . . . mikes and guitars are phallic symbols (or else caressed like female bodies), the music is loud, rhythmically insistent, built around techniques of arousal and release. Lyrics are assertive and arrogant, but the exact words are less significant than the vocal styles involved, the shrill shouting and screaming. (*Sound Effects* 227)

To paraphrase the Ramones, Suzi is a cock-rocker. A television performance of Tom Petty's "Breakdown" (ca. 1979) demonstrates Quatro's use of the physical vocabulary of cock-rock. She stood in the typical male guitarist's stance, legs spread wide apart. She emphasized the downbeats by pumping the air with her right fist and gripping the fret board of her bass guitar hard with her left hand. As she screamed the chorus—"Break down / Go ahead and give it to me"—she pulled her right fist down through the air, and pushed her hips against the bass. On the bridge, she moved across the stage in a crouch, faced the audience, lifted her bass, and brought it down between her legs so that it pointed straight out at the crowd in a phallic display employed by male guitarists (including Bolan and Mick Ronson, of course) since the earliest days of the blues (Padel 71). She jerked it up on each downbeat, then held it up in a pose of erotic ecstasy with her head thrown back. When the chorus came around again, she ran back to the vocal mike, stamping and kicking her left leg out as she shouted "Bay-beh!" Because Quatro was the only musician in motion during the guitar solo, she appeared to be the author of that solo—by miming the lead guitarist's solo, she temporarily usurped his position in the band. Quatro thus addressed "rock's sexual ideology of collective male activ-

---

Rolling Stones, Roger Daltrey of the Who, and Robert Plant of Led Zeppelin (Jim Morrison of the Doors also belongs on this list). Arguably, such performers had to compensate for occupying that feminine position by engaging in lewd and lascivious conduct onstage and off, using the microphone as a substitute for the guitar, and—in the case of Morrison—allegedly exposing himself on stage.

Suzi Quatro performing in 1974. © MichaelOchsArchives.com.

ity and female passivity" (Frith and McRobbie 376) by preserving the active role for herself. Whereas the male musicians on stage with her hardly moved and were, in that sense, relatively passive even while playing, she was continuously in motion and was clearly the active center of attention and the group's leader. The assertiveness of her persona was underlined by the titles of her first two albums: *Suzi Quatro* (1973) and *Quatro* (1974).

Despite Quatro's adherence to the performance conventions of cock-rock guitarists, she plays bass guitar, not guitar. Mary Ann Clawson suggests that in the indie rock of the 1980s and 1990s, the bass guitar became feminized as more women became rock bass players. Many of those women explained their choice of instrument by arguing that the musical role of the bass guitarist is congruent with women's "supportive nature" and their intrinsic willingness to subordinate their individual needs to those of the group (204–5; needless to say, Clawson critiques the essentialism of these claims). Quatro, the forerunner of these female indie rock bassists, did not interpret the role of bass player as feminized and supportive; rather, she played bass with the all showy, phallic panache of a lead guitarist.[11] Quatro wore the bass far down on her hips in the fashion of a cock-rock guitarist, a typically masculine position (Bayton 43–45). Whereas some of Clawson's respondents characterized the bass guitar as a sensual instrument by saying, "it's primal . . . more earthy" (206), cock-rocker Quatro said directly, "Yeah, it's phallic" and went on to add that "the guitar is for the head, but the bass 'gets you right between the legs'" (qtd. in Haden-Guest 5, see also Benton, "Suzi Q" 3).

Quatro staked out her territory on her first album, *Suzi Quatro*. The song "Get Back Momma" is a six-minute, largely instrumental piece that Quatro composed and on which she both sings and demonstrates her instrumental skill by playing a well-shaped bass solo. She has often performed in contexts that showcased her bass playing: jamming on television with progressive jazz-rock musicians like drummer Jon Hiseman and saxophonist Barbara Thompson, for instance, or playing blues and rock-and-roll standards on an episode of *GasTank* with keyboardist Rick Wakeman and others.[12] By foregrounding her status as a rock player, not just a singer, Quatro declared symbolic ownership of the rock cock.

11. Quatro's performance as a bass player who fronts a band and has the presence of a lead guitarist is unusual, as the typical rock bassist's performance is that of a taciturn background figure. Kim Gordon, the female bass player for Sonic Youth, interprets the usual recessiveness of bassists in terms of a heterosexual female imaginary related to, yet quite different from, Quatro's: "Before picking up a bass I was just another girl with a fantasy. What would it be like to be right under the pinnacle of energy, beneath two guys crossing their guitars . . . ? For my purposes, being obsessed with boys playing guitars, being as ordinary as possible, being a girl bass player is ideal, because the swirl of Sonic Youth music makes me forget about being a girl. I like being in a weak position and making it strong" (qtd. in Reynolds and Press 246).

12. *GasTank* was a short-run music series produced in 1982 for the UK's Channel Four. It was hosted by two well-known rock keyboard players, Rick Wakeman and Tony Ashton, who also served as the nucleus of the program's "house band" that would jam with the various guest musicians who appeared. Wakeman also conducted informal interviews with the guests.

The difference gender makes in rock is particularly apparent with respect to the question of authenticity. Because rock is culturally understood to be a male form, female rockers are automatically assumed to be inauthentic. Barbara Bradby points, for example, to the ways "'rock' criticism has continually used traditional models of authorship to discredit female performers in the search for male authority figures such as 'the producer'" (33). Since the female rock or pop music performer is often assumed to be nothing more than "a malleable 'body with a voice'" (Gaar xii), it has often been supposed that real creativity lies with her (usually male) producers, managers, songwriters, recording engineers, and so on. Quatro sustained this kind of criticism early in her career, particularly at the hands of rock critics, one of whom declared her to be "the biggest hype of them all, so manufactured you can see the joins" (Watts and Partridge 10). In a somewhat appreciative review of Quatro's second album, *Quatro*, Richard Cromelin nevertheless accuses her of being too much under the influence of her producers in terms that make it clear that female rockers are assumed to be the creations of male producers: "Suzi Quatro appeared to be on the verge of proving that women don't have to become products in order to make it as rock 'n' rollers, and suddenly she's uncomfortably close to being just that" (70). Critics also leveled the same accusations at male musicians, of course—the Monkees are the obvious case in point. But whereas male rockers were presumed to be authentic until proven otherwise, the opposite assumption applied to female musicians. Whereas male glam rockers could use their presumed authenticity as a platform from which to question the whole concept of authenticity, Quatro, as a female rocker, was presumed at the outset to be an inauthentic construct created by her male handlers; she therefore had to establish her authenticity through her performances in order to have any credibility. Aside from songs by Chinnichap or Quatro herself, much of Quatro's repertoire was taken from the work of well-known male singers and songwriters, including such iconic male rockers and rhythm and blues artists as Chuck Berry, Elvis Presley, Little Richard, Ray Charles, the Beatles, and Bruce Springsteen. She performed such classic rock songs as "All Shook Up," "Keep A-Knockin," and "Born to Run." This material did not just a reflect Quatro's musical taste: performing it was part of her bid to be seen as a legitimate rocker by demonstrating her mastery of the genre's canonical literature and performance idioms.

Quatro's recordings of classic rock songs belong in the category of cover songs, a well-established trope in rock music. As Deena Weinstein points out, cover songs are unique to rock as a popular music genre in that they iterate "a prior recorded performance of a song by a particular artist, rather than simply the song itself as an entity separate from any performer or performance" (138). Covers are therefore intrinsically intertextual and invoke the previous recording's historical presence. They may serve various ideological purposes—historical precedent may be re-created or rejected, revered or reviled, but functions in all cases as the cover's point of reference. One ideological use rock musicians make of covers is to "validate their own authenticity as musicians" (Weinstein 141) by referring to artists, songs, and recordings considered as authentic within a particular rock subgenre. (Weinstein's example is of British Invasion groups of the early 1960s who recorded American blues and rhythm and blues songs to establish their own musical and cultural credentials.)

By performing songs closely associated with archetypal male rockers, Quatro did much the same ideological work, though the line she crossed was different, having to do with establishing credibility as a female rocker rather than a non-American one. (The fact that Quatro is an American who worked primarily in the UK and Europe makes it somewhat ironic that her desire to transgress gender boundaries in rock caused her to recapitulate the authenticating process undertaken by British rockers seeking the cachet of Americanness.) Thus, when Quatro recorded the song "Trouble," originally performed by Elvis in the film *King Creole* (1958), for her second album, she not only played out the exaggerated, masculine swagger of the lyric but also aligned herself with a performance tradition of male boastfulness that includes Elvis but reaches deep into the history of rock and roll and rhythm and blues. "Trouble," written by Jerry Lieber and Mike Stoller, is one member of a song family that includes at least three other songs that are musically almost identical, but have different lyrics. These include the hard-bitten prison saga "Riot in Cell Block #9," also by Lieber and Stoller, recorded by the Robbins in 1954; and one of the ur-texts of blues machismo, "Hoochie Coochie Man," written by Willie Dixon and recorded famously by Muddy Waters, also in 1954.[13] Another mem-

13. For a discussion of the concept of song families, see Shuker (75). It is tempting to assert that Quatro aligns herself not just with masculinity through

ber of this song family is the well-known Lieber-Stoller composition "I'm a Woman," recorded by Peggy Lee in 1962. Although this latter song is assertive in its own way, it requires the female singer to present herself as a male fantasy of womanhood, simultaneously breathtakingly seductive and completely domestic. The American folk-blues singer Maria Muldaur covered "I'm a Woman" in 1974, close in time to when Quatro's version of "Trouble" was released. One need only imagine hearing Quatro's and Muldaur's respective recordings one after the other on the radio to understand how each artist aligned herself with a different strand of gender representation in popular music by choosing one musically similar Lieber and Stoller song rather than the other.

From the perspective of the ongoing cultural critique of gender in rock, Quatro is a troubling figure who is usually ignored, maligned, or marginalized in historical accounts. In this critique, rock is characterized as a fundamentally male enterprise: the music, created primarily by men, reflects masculine concerns and sexuality, tends toward misogyny, and excludes women as significant artistic voices. "As a result," writes rock critic Dave Marsh, "rock's sexual dialogue became stunted. In soul, Otis Redding had to answer to Carla Thomas; in country, Conway Twitty's roving eye was matched by Loretta Lynn's sass and suss. But in rock . . . sexual expression is characterized by a startling, matter-of-fact adolescent chauvinism" (*The First* 160).[14] For a woman to participate in such an overtly masculinist enterprise is often seen as embarrassing from a gender-political standpoint.

Although they do not address this issue (or Quatro) directly, Lori Burns and Mélisse Lafrance's valorization of the concept of disruption in *Disruptive Divas: Feminism, Identity & Popular Music* illuminates the imperatives to which female rock artists must respond

---

her choice of repertoire, but also with blackness (African-American masculinity, to be precise). To the extent that the rhythm and blues tradition she invokes is primarily associated with African-American performers, that is true. But the issue is made immeasurably more complex by the fact that many "black" rhythm and blues songs were written by such white (and frequently Jewish) songwriters as Lieber and Stoller. In certain respects, the gender line in rock is historically a much simpler phenomenon than the color line.

14. Frith and McRobbie make much the same point but present the situation in somewhat more complex terms: "In general, it seems that soul and country musics, blatantly sexist in their organization and presentation, in the themes and concerns of their lyrics, allow their female performers an autonomous musical power that is rarely achieved by women in rock" (384).

if their work is to be considered valuable from the point of view of gender critique. Lafrance outlines the four conditions that have to be met for an artist to be considered a disruptive diva: she must engage in "the creative interrogation of dominant normative systems"; create music that has an unsettling or disquieting effect on the listener; produce "manipulations of conventions and styles [such as] unexpected instrumental and/or vocal strategies"; and participate extensively in "the technical and creative operations of music making" (2–3). Without disputing the value of these four facets for socially progressive music-making by women, I find it troubling that an artist as provocative in her time as Quatro was cannot qualify as a disruptive diva under these terms. Quatro's composing and musical styles were not unsettling or disquieting precisely because she worked for the most part within the normative conventions of rock, and she did not participate any more or less actively in the production and promotion of her work than most rock artists. The only condition under which Quatro qualifies as disruptive is the first one, which I intend to explore here.[15]

Many contributors to the gender critique of rock warily navigate the shoals of essentialism, taking care to avoid making claims that either the music itself or the ways it is performed are intrinsically male. But many such arguments, while technically avoiding essentialism, ultimately inscribe heterosexual masculinity in rock so firmly as to leave little room for other formulations. For instance, Padel begins her engaging book *I'm a Man: Sex, Gods, and Rock 'N' Roll* by arguing that music is not a "natural" expression of anything, but is culturally defined and produced. In a subsequent chapter, she skillfully teases out how first the acoustic guitar, then the electric guitar came to be culturally constructed as male instruments in the discourses of blues, country music, and rock and roll, all musical genres that contributed to the development of rock. But the final step of Padel's argument is to suggest that when the electric guitar was taken up as the central instrument of rock, it was put into the service of a music that "was the sound of the male teenage body, and the symbolism of its music—swollen volume plus 'dex-

15. Quatro's relationship to Lafrance's third condition is ambiguous. One certainly could argue that her screaming vocal style on songs such as "Can the Can" constitutes an unexpected vocal strategy if one assumes that female singers are expected to sound sweet rather than aggressive. But Quatro is a rock singer, and aggressive vocalizing is expected and conventional within that genre.

terity'—is deeply male" (81). Because this conclusion seems to root musical expression in physical properties attributed to a specific kind of body and sexuality, it becomes necessary to remind oneself that Padel previously posited this musical gendering as an historical and cultural process, not a biological one. As a consequence of such arguments, the assertion that "rock is a male form" (Frith and McRobbie 373) has become so powerful a critical dictum that it functions as an essence even when the argument supporting the assertion manages to skirt essentialism.

I trust it is clear that I do not at all discount the importance of showing how powerfully and completely rock and rock culture have been "sexed" as male and how difficult that has made it for women to participate meaningfully in rock.[16] But the gender critique of rock severely forecloses the critical options for thinking about a performer such as Quatro as anything other than a gender traitor. As Frith sees it, the basic problem for the female rock performer was "not whether rock stars are sexist, but whether women could enter their discourse, appropriate their music, without having to become 'one of the boys'" (*Sound Effects* 239). Simon Reynolds and Joy Press identify being "one of the boys," which they call "female machisma," as one of four strategies women musicians may adopt to enter rock discourse, describing it as a "tradition [of] . . . hard-rock, punky attitude, women impersonating the toughness, independence, and irreverence of the male rebel posture" (233).[17] Such accounts frequently represent the woman rocker who chooses the path of female machisma as misguided at best and a tragic figure at worst. The sad end to which Joplin came is often said to exemplify the consequences of trying to be one of the boys (e.g., Frith and McRobbie 377). Joanne Gottlieb and Gayle Wald, responding to Frith, have criticized this approach, rightly saying that it "reifies the roles available to women, closes off the resistive possibilities of rock for women, and ultimately begs the question of rock's masculine hegemony" (260).

16. I am thinking here of Keith Negus's useful statement that "rock is a genre that has been sexed in a very particular way, and as such its generic codes and conventions can present a formidable barrier to musicians who want to challenge and change them" (127–28).

17. The other three strategies are "the affirmation of 'feminine' qualities" in rock, the postmodernist celebration of "female imagery and iconography" as "a wardrobe of masks and poses to be assumed," and "an aesthetic that concerns itself . . . with the trauma of identity formation" (Reynolds and Press 233–34).

Women rockers, especially those of the first generation,[18] are forced by this critique into a position between rock and a hard place. The assumption is that rock is so fundamentally sexist and misogynist that for a woman to base her performance of rock on the most readily available models—those provided by male performers—cannot be considered a respectable option. For their part, Reynolds and Press provide assessments of each of the four strategies they identify, noting the value and limitations of each one. Their treatment is evenhanded, except when it comes to female machisma, which they dismiss out of hand as "unsatisfactory [because] it simply emulates male rebellion, including its significant component of misogyny" (233). Taken as a whole, the gender critique of rock holds female rockers hostage to an historical imperative underwritten by a master narrative of progress: it is not enough for women to make rock music; they must also remake rock by transcending its masculinist origins and gendering it specifically female. Although Gottlieb and Wald point out the flaws of such a narrow position, their own analysis imposes other limitations. In assessing the riot grrrls phenomenon of the early 1990s, Gottlieb and Wald suggest that it is acceptable for women to be loud, aggressive, hard-rockers as long as their performance constitutes an overtly critical inversion of cock-rock performance style clearly intended to expose rock's male dominance and make political points.

In a book on heavy metal rock, a musical genre regarded with great suspicion by proponents of the gender critique I have been discussing here, Robert Walser puts forth an alternative to that critique's demand for a music that is both identifiably rock and certifiably nonmasculinist, suggesting that

> we can spot many extant examples of rock music that use the powerful codings of gender available in order to engage with, challenge, disrupt, or transform . . . rock's representations of gender. . . . The point of criticism should not be to decide whether rock music is oppositional or co-optive with respect to gender, class, or any other social category, but rather to analyze how it arbitrates tensions between opposition and co-optation at particular historical moments. (136)

18. Even though Quatro is younger than many first-generation rockers, I place her in that category because she started her professional career in 1964, close to the beginning of the rock era.

In this spirit, I propose to take a close look at Suzi Quatro's performance practices. I hope to show that Quatro did not simply embody "female machisma," that her performances of gender and sexual identity were layered and complex in ways that belie such a simple characterization. By capitalizing on the productive tensions within the role of female cock-rocker and interweaving it with other gender performances, Quatro successfully used that role as a position from which to destabilize not only the gender codings from which it is constructed but the very notion of a reified gender identity. Quatro describes her relationship to gender performance by saying: "I am able to be a chameleon quite easily switching genders in every sense . . . I still haven't perfected peeing in a urinal yet but give me time" (e-mail, Nov. 6, 2000). I intend to take Quatro's self-description as a gender chameleon seriously, as I see her ability to move through and across differently gendered musical identities as her central performance strategy.

Quatro's engagement with gender-play is apparent in all of her performance strategies, from her masculine persona and cock-rocker gestures on stage to the songs she chose and the ways she performed them.[19] Some of the songs she has recorded are clever gender-reversals of earlier songs identified with male artists. Chinnichap's "Daytona Demon" (1973), for instance, is clearly a revision of "Tallahassee Lassie," recorded in 1959 by Freddy Cannon, in that both songs are paeans to love objects that equate the lover (female for Cannon, male for Quatro) with a fast car by reference to a city in Florida. I am also convinced that Quatro's first big UK hit of Chinnichap authorship, "Can the Can," is a response to Bolan's "One Inch Rock." Bolan's fanciful lyric describes his protagonist as being reduced magically to a height of one inch by a

---

19. It is noteworthy that Quatro has twice performed onstage in the roles of historical women famous for exemplifying "gender trouble." Quatro played Annie Oakley in the 1986 London production of Irving Berlin's 1946 musical *Annie Get Your Gun*. Oakley, a sharpshooter in Buffalo Bill's Wild West Show, was, much like Quatro herself, a female entertainer performing a masculine role in a male-dominated cultural arena. Quatro emphasized these parallels in print and television interviews. In 1991, Quatro portrayed American actress Tallulah Bankhead—famous for her deep, masculine voice, preference for male attire, and bisexuality—in *Tallulah Who?*, a musical theater treatment of Bankhead's life written by Quatro herself with Shirlie Roden.

sorceress who then places him in a can. (Bolan's protagonist does not find this situation to be altogether unpleasant, especially since he's immediately joined in the can by a woman of equivalent stature.) Inasmuch as the chorus of "Can the Can" includes the lines "Put your man in the can, honey / Get him while you can," the song seems to examine the situation of Bolan's protagonist from the point of view of the female warden rather than that of the male prisoner.

Some of the songs Quatro coauthored for her first two albums go beyond gender reversal to offer new representations of female subjects. The songs "Rockin' Moonbeam" (from *Suzi Quatro*) and "Friday" (from *Quatro*), for example, are celebratory portraits of sexually aggressive, if not to say promiscuous, women presented in direct, even crude, terms (the chorus for "Friday" begins "What's she doing / Who's she screwing?"). At one level, the protagonists of these songs are female equivalents for Ricky Nelson's "Travellin' Man" (who literally has a girl in every port), Dion's "The Wanderer" (both 1961), and all their male progeny in later rock. But these songs also make room for the expression of a celebratory attitude toward female sexual potency not generally found in rock, especially not in the early 1970s. As Frith and McRobbie point out, male rock musicians conventionally portray sexually aggressive women as either "doomed and unhappy, or else sexually repressed and therefore in need of male servicing" (374); these portrayals, they conclude, "express a deep fear of women" (382). Quatro's sexually aggressive female characters, by contrast, are neither doomed nor unhappy: every aspect of these upbeat songs and Quatro's energetic performances of them suggests that the women they depict enjoy their lives and seek sexual pleasure on their own terms. Their lustiness is important not for how men perceive it but as an exemplary expression of female sexuality. As a songwriter, Quatro participates in cock-rock's emphasis on crude heterosexual expression but not, I argue, in cock-rock's misogyny. Because these songs celebrate female sexual aggression, they challenge rather than reify the cock-rocker attitude toward women. And Quatro brought other new things to the table as well. In "Rockin' Moonbeam," for instance, Quatro honors an enthusiastically sexual middle-aged woman ("twenty years past [her] teens") in an infectious, 1950s-inflected boogie that calls into question pop music's leering sexual objectification of teenaged girls (think of The Lovin' Spoonful's

"Younger Girl" [1967], The Union Gap's "Young Girl" [1968], Donovan's "Superlungs My Supergirl" [1969], and countless other songs).

Quatro's performances of songs strongly identified with male artists raise questions other than those concerned with establishing her authenticity as a rocker. In the remainder of this chapter, I shall focus on this aspect of Quatro's work—not to deemphasize her status as a composer in her own right, but to focus on her performance strategies. As Nicholas Cook suggests, "it might be argued that music is projected most strongly as an art of performance precisely when the work itself is so familiar . . . that the individual performance becomes the principal focus of the listener's attention" (par. 11). By listening to Quatro's performances of well-known songs written by men for male voices, we can address the question inherent in all her work: What does it mean for a woman to perform "masculine" music primarily as a way of participating in rock discourse, not of critiquing it or ironizing it?

To indicate that a performer like Quatro disappears behind her material to become only a replication of a male image and attitude is to seriously misjudge the effect of her performances. Quatro herself summarizes her position by saying: "I was enjoying the delights of beating the men at their own game *and still being a woman*" (e-mail, Jan. 24, 2001; emphasis added). These last few words are critically important—watching Quatro perform or listening to her recordings, we do not somehow forget that she is a woman. She no more becomes a man (or an imitation of a man) by wearing leather and rocking out than Bowie became a woman by wearing a dress or mincing around the stage. Quatro's gender performance is best understood as an instance of what Judith Halberstam calls "female masculinity," which she defines not as the imitation of men by women but, rather, as a refusal on the part of masculine women to repress that aspect of themselves in favor of the masquerade of normative femininity. Halberstam argues that female masculinity can represent "the healthful alternative to what are considered the histrionics of conventional femininities" (*Female Masculinity* 9), and this, I suggest, is what Quatro represented in the rock culture of the early 1970s. By refusing to suppress her "tomboy instincts" (Halberstam, *Female Masculinity* 6), Quatro created something new: a dynamic, masculine female rocker who was not fully understandable either in terms of conventional femininity or as "one of the boys." The threat this persona posed to normative gender definitions is measurable, perhaps, by the consistency with which critics attempted to reduce Quatro to a sex object or to deny her rock authenticity. In addition, Quatro was periodically characterized in ways that explicitly assigned her to the conventional feminine roles of wife and mother. She was described in a 1975 *Melody Maker* article that sought to debunk her tough image as "a girl no anxious parent would be sad to see her son taking up the aisle" (qtd. in Gaar 219). In 1982, after the birth of Quatro's daughter, television interviewers repeatedly asked her whether motherhood meant that she would retire from rock performance or, at least, soften her image. Clearly anticipating these questions, Quatro insisted repeatedly that, much as she loved her baby, she would do neither. (Suffice it to say that Bowie was not asked comparable questions following the birth of his son.)

In Quatro's musical performances, her body and voice, socially encoded as feminine, convey songs and gestures culturally encoded as masculine. Neither signification absorbs or negates the other; rather, they form an unstable compound—the female cock-rocker—whose internal tensions open up other possibilities for signification. The dynamic of gendered signification within Quatro's performances thus embodies the complex interplay of masculinity and femininity Judith Butler sees in lesbian butch-femme identities.[20] Quatro has acknowledged the butchness of her perfor-

---

20. Sue-Ellen Case argues in "Toward a Butch-Femme Aesthetic" that these two lesbian identities exist only in a dialectical relationship to one another and are inseparable (283). Halberstam, by contrast, argues that butch and femme "are separate constructions with different trajectories" ("Between Butches" 61). Butler does not address this question directly in *Gender Trouble* but does discuss the butch solely from the perspective of femme desire. On the other hand, she discusses lesbian butch-femme identities as the products of a system of figure-ground relations in which desire results from the "sexual tension" generated by gender transgression, a possibility she does not restrict to the lesbian context (123). Likewise, Halberstam's more general notion of female masculinity is not specifically lesbian—Halberstam states directly that there are heterosexual female masculinities as well as homosexual ones (*Female Masculinity* 28). My own approach has greater affinities with Butler and Halberstam than with Case in the sense that I am postulating Quatro's performance persona as a butch identity that is not specifically accompanied by a complementary femme presence the way Ronson's butch male cock-rocker had Bowie's femme male singer as its complement. Like Bolan, Quatro did not share the spotlight. At the end of this chapter, I suggest that Quatro's audience becomes the femme presence that desires her butch persona. For other uses of the butch-femme matrix in analyses of popular music, see Martha Mockus, who draws on Case, and Stella Bruzzi, who draws on Butler. Mockus and Bruzzi both employ the concept of butchness in discussions of k. d. lang.

mance persona. Asked by an interviewer from *Creem* magazine about her appeal to a lesbian audience, Quatro replied, "It's only natural if you're gay, I'm a girl up there doing a butch thing, and you're attracted" (qtd. in Uhelszki 50). Butler defines the butch identity as one in which "masculinity . . . is always brought into relief against a culturally intelligible 'female body.' It is precisely this dissonant juxtaposition and the sexual tension that its transgression generates that constitute the object of desire" (123). Butler goes on to describe butch-femme identities in terms of figure-ground relationships in which masculinity and femininity can serve as figure or ground to one another in alterable configurations. In Quatro's performance as a female cock-rocker, her masculine appearance and aggressive demeanor constitute the masculine figure that sometimes appears against the ground of her female body. But this configuration does not remain fixed: at other times (as on the bluesy ballad "Cat Size" [from *Quatro*] when she sings more sweetly in her upper register) Quatro's voice can become the feminine figure against the ground of her masculine appearance.

Quatro explores the potential of unstably gendered figure-ground relationships throughout her work. In her recording of the Little Richard song "Keep A-Knockin'" (1957), from her second album, Quatro imposes her own narrative on the song, turning what originally may have been a depiction of a prostitute speaking to a prospective customer (Lhamon 87) into a cautionary coming-of-age tale for "all you sixteen-year-old girls out there," to whom she dedicates her rendition in a spoken introduction (the recording is not live but simulates liveness with audience sounds to make it seem that Quatro is addressing a crowd). Quatro makes the song into a lesson in female coquetry, advising teenage girls to tell their male suitors, on the one hand, "You keep a-knockin' but you can't come in" and, on the other, "Come back tomorrow night / And try it again." Quatro thus turns Little Richard's bawdy lyric into a comedy of heterosexual female virtue under siege.

In the latter part of the recording, Quatro again addresses her audience, this time to ask that they sing along with her. She divides the audience into boys and girls, asking that the boys sing the line "Keep a-knockin'" and that the girls respond with "But you can't come in." Quatro sings along with the boys, assigning herself to the masculine position even though her overall posture is that of an older confidante dispensing sexual advice to younger women. A close listening reveals, however, that the voices of the "girls" who demurely sing, "But you can't come in" in response to the boys' overture all belong to Quatro, her voice multitracked to sound like a throng of girls, much as Roy Wood simulated the Andrews Sisters. Like Wood, Quatro used recording technology to play several roles of different genders simultaneously, identifying herself alternately with the male assault on female virtue and a flirtatious feminine defense of that virtue.[21] She thus creates a field of shifting figure-ground relationships in which her masculine identity as rock and roller is sometimes the figure set against the ground of her woman's voice, while at other times Quatro's masculine identity becomes the ground against which we hear her feminine voice as figure. Through these shifting juxtapositions of differently gendered performances, the terms *masculine* and *feminine* "lose their internal stability and distinctness from each other," as Butler suggests (123).

Although Quatro's rendition of "Keep A-Knockin'" creates gender trouble for a rock-and-roll classic, it does not disturb the overwhelmingly heterosexual frame of reference from which the meanings of rock music normally derive. As Halberstam indicates, female masculinity always "menaces gender conformity" but is relatively nonthreatening when presented in a heterosexual context. But "when and where female masculinity conjoins with possible queer identities, it is far less likely to meet with approval" (*Female Masculinity* 28). One performance strategy Quatro uses quite frequently points in precisely that direction. Quatro is not, of course, the first artist in the history of rock to perform songs written for a singer of the opposite sex, actually a fairly common practice.[22] One aspect of her approach is unusual, however—when she performs

21. As Patricia Juliana Smith points out, Dusty Springfield used the same strategy much earlier. On her 1964 recording of "Mocking Bird," a song that, like "Keep A Knockin'," was originally recorded by African-American artists (Charles and Inez Foxx), Springfield sings both the male and female parts. Reading this recording through Springfield's lesbian identity, Smith concludes that her singing the male part is Springfield's way of implying that she "can do without" men (108). Whereas Smith treats Springfield's lesbianism as a stable identity that was allowed only coded expression in her music, I am interested in performance practices that emphasize the malleability and uncertainty of gender and sexual identities.

22. Theodore Gracyk provides a list of performances by female artists of songs originated by male performers. He argues that "take-overs of male-identified songs are an important tool for demanding [gender] parity" in rock (209–10).

songs associated with male artists and masculine subjectivity, she does not change the lyrics. Thus, when Quatro recorded the John Lennon–Paul McCartney composition "I Wanna Be Your Man" (recorded first by the Rolling Stones in 1963, then the Beatles) on her first album, she left the lyrics intact and sang "I wanna be your man," not "I wanna be your girl," which would have been the conventional way of altering the song for a female singer. Before discussing Quatro's particular performances further, I shall consider this strategy in general terms.

When the Paris Sisters, a girl-group, recorded Bobby Darin's song "Dream Lover" in 1964, they followed the conventional practice of giving the lyrics a sex-change operation, substituting, for instance, the word *boy* for the word *girl* when the singer expresses the desire for a lover. Such a change can be read as underlining differences between male and female desire. Men and women want different things; therefore, the words to the song have to be altered to reflect those differences. I will argue that such alterations actually imply the opposite: that male and female desire are not fundamentally different but analogous. The implication is that the song worked as an expression of male desire and, with some cosmetic surgery, works equally well as an expression of female desire. The song is thus posited as a non-gender-specific expression of romantic longing that can alternate unproblematically between expressing male and female subjectivity.

The ease with which pop and rock songs can be resexed is a function of the normative gender identities and heterosexual imperative deeply engrained in the cultural context of popular music. In that context, male and female desire are interchangeable because they are symmetrical: each desires the other and only the other. Bobby Darin's desire for a girl to call his own is structurally identical to the Paris Sisters' need for a boy to call their own. If the lyrics were not altered, if the Paris Sisters were to sing of wanting a girl, the heterosexual matrix of popular music would be called into question, as the song would seem to be expressing a kind of desire for which there are no coordinates in that matrix. This is why, as Frith points out, "gay and lesbian singers can subvert pop standards by *not* changing the words" (*Performing Rites* 195). Although Frith makes an important observation, I think his claim that the *song* is subverted by this strategy is open to question. One of his examples is Ian Matthews's 1971 recording of "Da Doo Ron Ron," a song celebrating a new lover that was written for female voices and recorded originally by a girl-group, the Crystals, in 1963. It is perfectly possible to hear Matthews's performance not as subverting the song but as validating it by showing its expansiveness, demonstrating that it can be used to celebrate homosexual love as well as heterosexual love. In this reading, Matthews's performance does not subvert the song but, rather, the ideology of popular music that makes heterosexuality normative within its discourses. Frith's statement also borders unnecessarily on essentialism. The singer does not have to be gay or lesbian for a performance to have the impact I just described. All that is necessary is that the singer's voice be heard as belonging to the gender other than the one implied by the lyrics. (For example, Bryan Ferry's recording of "It's My Party" with the original lyrics has much the same impact with respect to sexuality as Matthews's recording of "Da Doo Ron Ron" even though Matthews identifies himself as gay and Ferry does not.) The Paris Sisters' hypothetical recording of "Dream Lover" with unmodified lyrics would imply nonheterosexual desire regardless of their actual sexual preference—not even because they are women, but simply because their voices are coded as feminine.

I have used Butler's model of butch-femme identities to characterize Quatro's performance of the female cock-rocker as one based in a productive tension: when a masculinely coded performance style is juxtaposed with a femininely coded body, both sets of significations are present, and figure-ground reversals that subvert reified masculine and feminine identities become possible. Something similar happens when Quatro performs songs identified with male performers. Because she is using those songs to establish her own legitimacy as a rocker, she leaves them intact and performs them unironically—straight, so to speak. But the mere fact that her voice is coded as feminine inevitably puts an unconventional spin on her chosen material. When Quatro performs Elvis Presley's "All Shook Up" on her first album and we hear her sing: "She touches my hand / What a thrill I've got / Her lips are like a volcano that's hot," it is very easy to hear the lyric as describing same-sex eros. Indeed, almost every line in the song is opened to possible new meanings when sung by a female voice, including "My friends say I'm acting queer as a bug." "All Shook Up" (1957) starts to sound like a coming-out song—the female protagonist declares her love for another woman while acknowledging that the whole prospect of falling in love in this (perhaps unexpected) way makes her a bit nervous.

The point I wish to emphasize here is that this queer reading of Quatro's performance does not supplant the straight reading she is giving of the song but complements it. It is equally possible that in "All Shook Up," Quatro is singing from the point of view of a man exulting in new love as it is that she is playing a woman who has discovered a kind of eros that is new to her. The recording supports both interpretations equally; neither is more legitimate than the other. This dual signification is underlined by the use of backing vocals on the recording. In the second part of the song, Quatro provides her own backing vocals through multitracking; in the last part, there are male backing vocals. Both choices position Quatro as a "male" singer. In rock, it is conventional for a male lead singer to be backed by female voices (see Frith, *Performing Rites* 187); Quatro's serving as her own backup group reflects this convention. Elvis, however, used a male backup group, the Jordanaires, on his early recordings. The male backup vocals in the latter portion of Quatro's recording refer to Elvis's version and, thus, implicitly equate Quatro with Presley. But the establishment of that equation also undermines it. The presence of masculinely coded voices both positions Quatro as a male lead singer and reasserts, by contrast and because they sing a repeated refrain of "She's all shook up," the feminine coding of Quatro's own voice. Again, the performance's strength resides in the way that masculinity and femininity continually trade places as figure and ground.

This shifting is particularly evident in Quatro's rendition of "I Wanna Be Your Man," also on her first album. As Quatro sings, "I wanna be your lover, baby / I wanna be your man," it is uncertain whom she is representing through those words, and to whom that character is addressing them. Within the convention of the song's narrative, she could be playing a man declaring love to a woman. If the character is a woman, however, as the timbre of Quatro's voice suggests, to whom is she speaking? The song, as written, is presumably addressed to a woman, but it could be addressed to a man. Butler describes various configurations of desire by referring to a lesbian femme who "likes her boys to be girls" while also hypothesizing a straight woman who "likes her girls to be boys" (123). (The same categories clearly apply to men, both straight and gay, who may also like their boys to be girls or girls to be boys.) By singing, "I Wanna Be Your Man" without changing the lyrics, Quatro makes the song express all of these erotic possibilities. When Quatro repeats the opening line of the song, she pauses significantly before the word *man*—"I wanna be your—man"—and moans that word sensually. This pause has the effect of bracketing the word *man,* of making it stand apart from the flow of the lyrics. This bracketing can be heard as implying that, for Quatro, the word signifies a pose, an erotic identity she can assume in order to have a particular relationship with her partner, whether male or female.[23] The song's subsequent lyrics seem to ask the object of Quatro's erotic attention to embrace these polymorphous possibilities: "Tell me that you love me, baby / Tell me that you understand."

Male backing vocals work much the same way on this recording as on "All Shook Up." Rather than indexing the Jordanaires, the male vocals on "I Wanna Be Your Man" refer to the way the Beatles, like the members of most male rock groups, often served as each other's backup singers. This reference again positions Quatro as a male lead singer. But the voices themselves contrast masculine coding with the feminine coding of Quatro's voice, marking her simultaneously as a woman. This effect is all the more pronounced when, in the second half of the song, the male vocalists sing the line "I wanna be your man" in unison with Quatro, directly juxtaposing a conventional, masculine rendition of the lyric with Quatro's own voice. This doubling provides Quatro with a dual gender identity: insofar as she sings a "male" song from a masculine point of view and occupies a masculine position in her group, she embodies masculine subjectivity. Insofar as the presence of masculinely coded voices contrasts with her femininely coded voice, she occupies a feminine subjectivity. This duality is unresolved, as is the question of the singer's sexual identity, since Quatro's dual gender position makes it impossible to determine to whom the song is addressed and what kind of love relationship is implied.

It is noteworthy that in the one instance in which Quatro did change the lyrics to a well-known song, the change pushes the song in the direction of greater gender subversion. The song, "Glad All Over," first recorded by the Dave Clark Five, a British Invasion

23. Quatro's own comment to me concerning her version of "I Wanna Be Your Man" is, "Men were thought to be strong . . therefore, I was strong and didn't need to change the gender . . . I was saying, I WANT TO BE YOUR MAN, in other words, I am the strength . . . the giver of life, the provider, everything men are supposed to be" (e-mail, Jan. 24, 2001). What Quatro suggests is a bit more mystical than what I am proposing here, but it shows that she thinks of masculinity, however one understands it, as a role that can be performed by either men or women, not a biological essence.

group, in 1964 and by Quatro in 1980 on her album *Rock Hard,*
expresses the joy attendant on the forging of a new love relationship ("I'm feeling glad all over / Now that you're mine"). In the
song's bridge, the singer expresses his loyalty by saying: "Other
girls may try to take me away / But you know it's by your side I will
stay." When performing "Glad All Over," Quatro alters that lyric
to, "Other boys may try to take you away." This revised lyric is
syntactically ambiguous: boys other than whom—the singer or the
addressee of the song?[24] The exact distribution of gender and sexual identities implied by this lyric, let alone the figure-ground relations among them, cannot be fully specified.

Shifting figure-ground relationships appear not only within Quatro's individual performances but from song to song on her albums
as well. "I Wanna Be Your Man," in which Quatro's masculinity is
in the foreground, is followed on her first album by "Primitive
Love," an entertainingly kitschy number replete with jungle sound
effects and "tribal" drums. Most of the singing on this track is by
male voices extolling "primitive love"; Quatro speaks her part as
the caveman's female love interest who does not at all mind being
dragged around by the hair. But her performance is a highly mannered parody of normative femininity: she delivers her lines in a
barely audible, breathy, whispery, sighing voice and uses a vaguely
British accent. It is clear from the self-conscious artificiality of this
performance of passive, heterosexual femininity that we are not to
take it as Quatro's "real" female identity to which she has returned
from the butch masquerade of the previous track (and the next one,
since "Primitive Love" is followed on the album by "All Shook
Up"). In an oft-quoted passage, Sue-Ellen Case has said of butch-
femme identities that "these roles are played in signs themselves,
not in ontologies" (297); Butler makes a closely related point when
she says that "in both butch and femme identities, the very notion
of an original or natural identity is put into question" (123). It is
precisely in this spirit that Quatro performs gender: as she moves
among differently gendered roles in her performances, the figures of

---

24. This syntactic ambiguity parallels one of the best-known cases of textual gender ambiguity in rock, the Kinks' song "Lola" (1970). When this song
became a hit, much discussion surrounded the question of whether the lyric
"I'm glad I'm a man / And so is Lola" means that Lola is also glad the singer
is a man or that "she's" also a man. It is perhaps not surprising, then, to find
that Quatro covered one of the Kinks' best-known songs (see note 25).

masculinity and femininity shift position continuously such that no configuration can be supposed to be ontologically grounded.

I have discussed one performance in which Quatro performs both masculine and feminine roles in a heterosexual context and several in which Quatro's performances open a space within the discourses of rock for a queer imaginary. I will conclude by discussing one performance that shifted from one frame of reference to the other as it moved from one medium to another. Quatro's one major American hit, "Stumblin' In," is a Chinnichap romantic duet about the start of a relationship.[25] Chris Norman and Suzi Quatro adopt entirely normative pop music gender roles by seemingly emulating Sonny and Cher. Norman's gravelly voice, though more conventionally musical than Sonny Bono's, has a similar informality. Quatro, for her part, sings in her lower register and uses a vibrato reminiscent of Cher's characteristic vocal style. The lyric places the female character in a position subordinate to the male by suggesting that she's somewhat younger than he and that he is her guide in things romantic.

But even this very conventional musical performance takes on other meanings when presented through Quatro's preferred performance image. Quatro appeared with Norman in a television performance of "Stumblin' In" wearing a decidedly masculine vested suit. Because both she and Norman had very similar shoulder-length shag haircuts and the whole scene was shot in soft focus and

25. The narrative of a failed relationship threads through the songs on the U.S. edition of *If You Knew Suzi. . . ,* the album on which "Stumblin' In" appears. The first song, "If You Can't Give Me Love," describes a couple's meeting in a discotheque; the woman declares that she is interested in love, not just a one-night stand. By the next song, "Stumblin' In," the couple is in love. The fourth song on the first side of the album, a cover of the Kinks' "Tired of Waiting for You," indicates that already there is trouble in paradise, as the song has to do with one lover's waiting for the other to make a commitment. The last song on that side, entitled "The Race is On," depicts a scenario very much like Edward Albee's *Who's Afraid of Virginia Woolf:* the couple, still together but embittered, are described as subjecting their friends to their own psychological warfare. The second side begins with "Don't Change My Luck," in which the woman and man meet in a restaurant (in contrast to the disco in which the album begins) so that she can tell him she has found someone else. And the album ends with "Wiser Than You," in which the woman looks back on the whole relationship, judges that she is well out of it, and assesses the wisdom she has gained from the experience.

as if lit by candles, the two singers looked very similar—they could have been mistaken for two men, one somewhat more boyish than the other, especially when seen from behind. This image further complicates the issues implicit in Quatro's performances of gender and sexuality by suggesting that a performance of female masculinity can also be read, in this instance, as a performance of masculine femininity. In the context of a male homosexual romance, the status of one lover as older than the other and lyrics like "Baby, you've shown me so many things that I never knew" take on very different meanings than those most likely to be apprehended from just listening to the record. Quatro's video performance destabilizes the gendered sexual implications of her own recorded song in much the same way that Quatro's performances of rock songs associated with male performers create shifting figure-ground relationships.

I return one last time to Butler's observation that the reasons why the butch is an object of desire for the femme reside neither in the butch's masculinity nor her female body but in "the dissonant juxtaposition" between them that leads to "the destabilization of both terms." The subversiveness of Quatro's performances—the reason she should be considered a disruptive diva—stemmed not solely from her having assumed a masculine musical role as a woman but also from her use of her performance as female cock-rocker as a position from which to create tensions among discourses of masculinity and femininity. If Quatro's performance persona was butch in that it was an example of "masculinity brought into relief against a culturally intelligible 'female body,'" she offered her audiences, whether female or male, straight or gay, the opportunity to take on the role of the desiring femme attracted to the "sexual tension that [her] transgression [of gender categories] generates" (Butler 123). With respect to gender and sexuality, Quatro played multiple roles in her musical performances. To the extent that her performances constituted a kaleidoscope of shifting relationships between masculinity and femininity (and heterosexuality and homosexuality) as figure and ground, she enacted the polymorphousness and performativity of gender identities and the pleasures of the "erotic havoc" created by pulling the rug out from under them.

Although Suzi Quatro is the only female musician to be considered a canonical glam rocker, other female voices are heard on glam rock anthologies. The frequent inclusion of items such as Lulu's 1973 recording of the Bowie song "The Man Who Sold the World" (one of several Bowie songs she recorded with Bowie as producer) is somewhat deceptive.[26] Though the presence of more than one female voice on the anthologies is certainly welcome, Lulu cannot be considered a glam rock artist. Although she seems to have gotten into the glam spirit by performing Bowie's song on television while wearing a man's suit with her red hair cut in a style similar to Bowie's (Joshua Sims notes the irony of her doing this in light of the fact that Bowie appeared on the cover of the album containing his version wearing a dress [129]), her inclusion on glam anthologies may simply be a function of the cost of licensing her recording as opposed to Bowie's own recordings. But the appearance of the Runaways on *The Best Glam Rock Album in the World . . . Ever!* is more thought-provoking, for there is a credible argument to be made that the Runaways carried on the part of the glam legacy represented by Quatro.

In 1974, Quatro offered herself to aspiring female rockers as a role model of the sort she never had: "I want chicks to say, if she can do it, so can I. I'll bet anything there'll be three or four girls imitating me by the end of next year" (qtd. in Uhelszki 48). The Runaways, a Los Angeles based group made up of five teenaged women, could have been the musicians to whom Quatro was referring. Although there is some dispute between guitarist and singer Joan Jett and Kim Fowley, the group's male producer and impresario, as to exactly how the group was formed, it is generally conceded that both Jett and Fowley took Quatro's success in Great Britain to mean that there could be room for a group made up of female rock musicians. Jett, who is reputed to have stolen a poster of Quatro from the wall of Rodney Bingenheimer's English Disco

26. The inclusion of Bonnie St. Clair's "Clap Your Hands and Stamp Your Feet" (1972) on *Dynamite: The Best of Glam Rock* is an example. St. Clair is a Dutch pop singer whose connection to glam is not attested to anywhere but on this collection. That said, the track itself has considerable charm—St. Clair sounds like the bastard child of Suzi Quatro and the women from Abba. A collection with a slightly different scope, entitled *Wham Bam, Thank You Glam!*, includes Patti Smith and Blondie alongside of such certified glam rockers as Mott The Hoople, Gary Glitter, and Kiss. The liner notes (by Scott Schinder) argue that Smith "drew verbal inspiration from glam's anything goes spirit." While this assertion is questionable, especially given the stronger affinities between Smith and the Doors' Jim Morrison, both self-styled rock poets, the inclusion of Blondie as a New Wave group that continued the glam aesthetic is more obviously defensible, especially since Mike Chapman frequently produced their records.

in Los Angeles, followed her idol around during a visit by Quatro to Hollywood in 1974 (when Jett was fourteen years old, the same age at which Quatro first performed professionally), and started an all-female rock group the next year (Epand).

The Runaways' music reflects Quatro's influence in a number of ways. The group's best-known song, "Cherry Bomb," coauthored by Jett and Fowley, is an exaltation of female independence and sexual aggression of the sort that Quatro herself wrote and performed. I take "Blackmail" (which appears, like "Cherry Bomb," on the group's first album, *The Runaways* [1976]) to be a direct musical tribute to Quatro. The song is a rock-and-roll boogie based on a straightforward blues progression of the kind Quatro frequently employed; it opens with a Quatroesque, nonverbal scream, followed by a brief bass guitar solo. The title "Born to Be Bad" (from the Runaways' second album, *Queens of Noise* [1977]), which could be a biker's tattoo, conjures up the same associations as Quatro's "The Wild One" *(Quatro)*, a title that evokes the 1954 movie of that name in which Marlon Brando famously played a biker. The spoken narration on the Runaways' "Born to Be Bad," in which the protagonist calls her parents late one night to tell them that she's left home to join a rock band, actually retells a story that Quatro had shared with many interviewers concerning her decision to leave school at the age of fifteen to pursue a musical career. Quatro called her parents while on tour in Europe to report her decision and was greeted with the same parental anger and resignation as the character in the Runaways' song. While this story is surely archetypal in its association of a career in rock with a youthful declaration of independence, the similarity between the Runaways' narration and the story Quatro had circulated is remarkable in light of the other connections between them.

Like Quatro, the Runaways were not very successful in their own country, where they were subjected to some critical praise and much undeserved scorn, but were better received abroad, particularly in Japan. After the group dissolved in 1979 (following a year of being overseen by Quatro's manager), two of its members went on to highly visible solo careers: Lita Ford as a heavy metal guitarist and Joan Jett as a hard rock guitarist and singer. Jett has acknowledged her debt to glam rock through her choices of songs to cover: her biggest hit, "I Love Rock and Roll" (1982), was originally recorded by a minor British glam group, the Arrows in 1974, and she also included two Gary Glitter songs on her first album, *Bad*

Reputation (1981). Like Quatro, Jett adopted a tough, leather-clad look—she even posed on a motorcycle for *Outlaw Biker* magazine in 1988—allied herself with a production team consisting of two men (Kenny Laguna and Ritchie Cordell) with reputations for producing commercially successful pop music, and surrounded herself with a band, the Blackhearts, made up of male musicians. Also like Quatro, Jett has frequently depicted sexually aggressive women in her music. Additionally, Jett has employed many of the same strategies for endowing her persona with ambiguous gender and sexuality as Quatro: she uses both a raucous masculine scream and a quieter, more feminine style of singing and sings songs originally written for male voices, sometimes feminizing the lyrics and sometimes not. In "I Love Rock and Roll" and Glitter's "Do You Want to Touch Me," for example, she reverses the gender of the lyrics but retains the posture of masculine sexual aggression they imply. As Kathleen Kennedy suggests, Jett's conversion of the word "man" into "ma'am" in "Do You Want to Touch Me" creates the same kind of syntactic ambiguity and identity confusion in which Quatro specializes (98). In Jett's version of "Crimson and Clover," recorded by Tommy James and the Shondells in 1968, on the other hand, she leaves the lyrics intact but undermines the song's normative sexuality by singing of the desire to seduce a woman in a sweet, feminine voice (Kennedy 99–100).

Rick Gershon, an observer of the Los Angeles music scene in the mid-1970s, indicates that the Runaways and other groups of that moment were "on the fringe of the glam thing and simultaneously on the fringe of punk" (qtd. in Hoskyns, *Waiting for the Sun* 292). Although I shall save further discussion of the continuities between glam and punk for the conclusion, I will point here to the ways that Quatro anticipated punk both in her desire to return to a stripped-down, basic rock style and in her sartorial choices. As much as her leather catsuit refers to the biker woman image and to Elvis, it also has overtones of sadomasochism, especially when accessorized with studded bracelets and a dog collar. In some publicity shots, Quatro is represented as a camp dominatrix, standing in a triumphant posture over the prone members of her band or controlling them with chain leashes. Although this aspect of Quatro's persona was mostly implicit, it anticipated the way leather and bondage gear became fashionable in the context of British punk, particularly through the agency of Malcolm McLaren and Vivien Westwood's clothing store, Sex, which featured the S-M look and became the staging ground for the Sex Pistols (Gorman 118–21). In addition to anticipating an aspect of punk fashion, the leather look Quatro pioneered for female rockers was taken up by female musicians in other subgenres: not only hard rockers like Jett, but also the members of British all-women heavy metal groups that emerged in the 1980s, such as Girlschool and Rock Goddess.

Although Reynolds and Press are dismissive of "female machisma" as a performance strategy for women rockers, they outline its genealogy: "this tradition runs from Suzi Quatro through Joan Jett to L7" (233) and includes Patti Smith, Chrissie Hynde (of the Pretenders), Kate Bush, P. J. Harvey, Ann and Nancy Wilson (of Heart), Lita Ford, and Kim Gordon (of Sonic Youth) (236–48). It continues, presumably, with the Donnas, a more recent group of young, postpunk female hard rockers on the model of the Runaways. Greg Shaw, writing in 1974, subsumes the tradition of female machisma to one of two larger traditions of rock music: the "wild, rebellious, violent stuff" and the "safe, acceptable, cleancut . . . stuff." He suggests, correctly, that although female performers have participated in both traditions, "women have almost always ended up on the latter side." He goes on to suggest that Quatro represented a revivification of the wilder tradition: "She is the first female singer to return to hard basic rock & roll, after nearly seven years in which women have had very little to do with the form." Quatro took advantage of the opportunity created by glam's destabilization of gender norms in rock to fulfill her ambition of "kicking down the male door in rock and roll" and opening it for other women. In the end, it makes perfect sense that glam, a rock subgenre focused on proposing alternative images of masculinity, provided a space within which female masculinity could be enacted in rock and thus helped to broaden the opportunities available to hard-rocking women.

glamology

Glam Rock and the Politics of Identity

> Being homosexual, or at least seeming homosexual, was the new
> way to be black in rock 'n' roll. To seem homosexual was the
> new way to be different, cool, special, a romantic outlaw
> (and in this case, truly a *romantic* outlaw).
> —Robert Duncan (93)

At one level, Robert Duncan is right: glam rockers unquestionably
used their performances of queer identities to provoke and rebel
against the status quo in a way that roughly parallels earlier rockers' use of black music and identities. But there is also a crucial difference: whereas black music has always been central to the rock
imaginary, queer identities were relegated to its periphery until
glam came along. Rock culture sees the music's roots and, therefore, its authenticity as residing in a historical relationship to the
blues and other African-American forms.[1] Even though it is
arguable that rock is equally steeped in a long tradition of masculine display that was often effeminate and implicitly queer, evoca-
tions of that tradition are not generally seen within rock culture as
celebrations of rock authenticity.

Iain Chambers indicates the historical importance of glam rock's
engagement with questions of sexuality by placing it against the

---

1. Hoskyns sees the legacy of glam in the work of flamboyant African-
American artists ranging from Labelle and Parliament-Funkadelic to Prince
and Michael Jackson (*Glam!* 108–9). Although there are surface similarities, it
is not at all clear that any of these artists was directly influenced by glam rock
(with the obvious exception of Prince). There are traditions of glamour and
spectacle within African-American music itself that would need to be taken
into consideration in assessing the relationship of these performers to glam
rock. Here, I will simply suggest that their penchant for spectacle be seen as a
phenomenon that is parallel to glam rock rather than derivative of it.

backdrop of British society's "mounting resistance" in the 1970s to the personal freedoms gained in the 1960s: "the spaces for social experiments began closing down, earlier boundaries were pulled back and prospects retracted as the solid values of 'tradition' closed ranks." In Chambers's view, glam rock turned "public attention to the details of sexuality . . . when precisely at that time a new, authoritarian morality was spreading over Britain's cultural landscape." In so doing, glam offered "new possibilities, particularly involving the public construction of sexual roles in youth culture" (134–35). Glam rock, in other words, created opportunities for both performers and their fans to defy the increased conservatism that followed the 1960s by engaging publicly in nonnormative performances of gender and sexuality.

There is ample testimony that glam rock was important in this way, especially to young people who were uncertain of their own sexual identities and in search of role models. Todd Haynes's film *Velvet Goldmine* (1998), a fictionalized account of the rise of glam rock, eloquently depicts how glam provided such models by placing queer images in the public sphere. The teenaged Arthur Stuart, who later becomes a journalist sent to track down the reclusive former glam rock star Brian Slade (a Bowie-like figure who also incorporates aspects of Marc Bolan, Brian Eno, and others) sees Slade being interviewed in 1972 while watching television at his parents' home in suburban Manchester. As Slade acknowledges his homosexuality, "Arthur leaps in front of the set, shrieking at the top of his lungs like a lunatic. 'That is me! That is me! That that that is *me*!" (Haynes, *Velvet* 63). In another scene that appears earlier in the film but may take place later in the story, Arthur is seen sneaking out of the house in a trench coat. He drops the coat in the bushes, revealing a glam outfit underneath (13–14). Haynes thus suggests that Slade's public performance of a queer identity catalyzes Arthur's own exploration of his sexual identity, which begins with his identifying with the rock star and becoming a secret glitter kid.

Glam rock's central social innovation was to open a safe cultural space in which to experiment with versions of masculinity that clearly flouted social norms. It was in this respect a liminal phenomenon in Victor Turner's sense of that term, a performance practice through which alternative realities could be enacted and tested (85). Jim Farber, in a moving account of the role glam rock played in his own life as a gay man, observes that this liminal space was open to anyone of any sexuality interested in exploring gender and sexual identities. He describes a subway trip he undertook with a straight friend, both dressed in full Bowie drag:

> At perhaps no other time in history could two sixteen-year-old boys have made such a trip and not been slandered, beaten or worse. Yet here we were, graced by a time (the mid-Seventies) and buoyed by a trend (glitter rock) that turned out to be golden—a time when the relationship between flouncy affectation and sexual orientation seemed tenuous at best. . . . In such a topsy-turvy sliver of time, no one had to know that I was precisely as gay as my clothes might inform anyone from a later—or earlier—generation. . . . Pledging allegiance to glitter rock awarded me a safety zone in which I could both sidestep old definitions of what it meant to be a boy and stave off a commitment to what it would eventually mean for me to be a gay man. (142)

Since glam rock's queer identities were equally accessible to people of any sexual orientation, glam flourished briefly as a context in which those differences did not matter because they were rendered invisible.

It would be unwise to overstate this case, of course. Popular music is not entirely constrained by dominant ideologies, but neither is it entirely free of their influence. Glam rock was almost completely dominated by men and took the performance of masculinity as its terrain. Even though that terrain included Suzi Quatro's performances of female masculinity, glam offered no substantial challenge to the conventions of rock as a traditionally male-dominated cultural form that evolved from male-dominated social contexts.

And while glam rock created a space in which both performers and audiences could explore queer identities in relative safety, it did not protect either group fully from the real-life consequences of doing so. Haynes dramatizes the social risks involved in Arthur's attraction to glam: the furtiveness with which he hides his identity as a glitter kid under the trench coat; the rebukes he suffers at the hands of his brother and his brother's friends for liking "pansy" music; and his father's emotionally violent response to his discovery of his son masturbating while looking at a photo of two glam rockers. Although Arthur is a fictional character, the risks to which Haynes alludes were very real.

Taking the concept of space quite literally, the safe spaces initiated by glam rock included concert halls and the living rooms and bedrooms where glam rock fans might see the performers on television, listen to their recordings, and gaze at their images. But carrying the identities forged in these spaces into more public places carried a risk for both performers and audience members. Chambers assesses the situation from the fan's perspective:

> In everyday life, the cultural map of glam rock was destined to remain largely restricted to pop music's internal geography. Attempts to translate its imaginative gestures into the more rigid performances of daily cultures often encountered vindictive male outrage. . . . To play with "masculinity" was still condemned to remain more an imaginary than a practical option for the majority of boys. (135–36)

Although glam rock made it more possible to enact queer identities in public, it could not completely shield its adherents from the real-world consequences of their experiments.

While touring the United States early in 1971, Bowie was threatened with physical harm for wearing one of his Mr. Fish dresses in Texas (Cann 72). A few years later, Joey Ramone, then still known as Jeffrey Hyman, had a similar experience in New York. Before joining the group that would become the Ramones, Hyman was the singer for a glam rock band called Sniper. He describes his outfit: "I used to wear this custom-made black jumpsuit, these like pink, knee-high platform boots—all kinds of rhinestones—lots of dangling belts and gloves." His brother, Mickey Leigh, recalls that he would hitchhike dressed this way: "At that time, you really couldn't be doing that safely. You were taking a chance hitchhiking down Queens Boulevard like that. . . . He eventually got beat up. He got his nose bashed in. We had to pick him up and bring him to the Elmhurst hospital. I felt bad" (qtd. in McNeil and McCain 181).

The importance of glam rock resides not only in its social effects but also in its lasting influence on later music (though these two aspects of its legacy are intertwined). Glam pointed the way for several rock and pop genres of the 1970s and 1980s. Most immediately, glam's emphasis on constructed personae paved the way for punk rock, as Dave Laing suggests in his discussion of stage names (it is worth remembering here that neither David Bowie nor Marc Bolan was a birth name):

In 1972, former singer Paul Raven re-emerged as Gary Glitter, followed a year later by Alvin Stardust (former stage name Shane
Fenton, original name Bernard Jewry). These names clearly could
not be easily "domesticated." They announced themselves as
artifice, even in their show business referents. "Glitter" could not
easily be seen as a character trait of the singer as "real person."
. . . It was more like a description of his *persona,* his adopted pose
in his work.

    Enter Johnny Rotten, Sid Vicious, Rat Scabies, Joe Strummer,
Ari Upp, Poly Styrene *et al.* As chosen names these were clearly
ranged on the side of explicitly artificial (in the manner of Glitter
and Stardust). (50–51)

There are, of course, important differences between the ways that
glam rockers and punk rockers created and named their respective
personae, but it is clear that glam innovated the idea of the rock
performance persona as a self-declared construct that was also fundamental to punk. Performers like Roy Wood, for whom experimentation with gender identity was much less important than
experimentation with musical identity, participated fully in this
aspect of glam, which remained influential beyond punk to the
New Romantics. Billy Idol and Adam Ant were heavily and directly
influenced by Bolan, especially in their sartorial choices. Beyond
them, the New Wave glitter of Blondie (whose frequent producer,
Mike Chapman, had co-produced many of the most commercial
British glam acts with Nicky Chinn) and the overt theatricality of
Talking Heads also owed debts to glam rock.

    The strongest evidence of glam's long-term importance as a
musical style may reside in the way the term *glam* has transcended
its particular historical moment.[2] Consider, for example, the following passage from a record review of 2003: "The Spiders are a
metalglam band as opposed to a glammetal band—the difference

    2. Robert Palmer argues that one can see "punk" as a recurrent sensibility
in rock rather than a style confined to a specific moment in the 1970s. Palmer
nominates "rockabilly wild men" as the punks of 1950s rock and roll and Iggy
Pop and the Stooges, the MC5, the Velvet Underground, and others, as the
punks of the 1960s (261). A similar claim could be made for glam as a recurrent
sensibility. Fifties glam would include Little Richard, Esquerita, Jerry Lee
Lewis, and others, while sixties glam could include a range of performers from
the Beatles, whose boyishness was often perceived as androgynous, to underground dandies such as Syd Barrett of Pink Floyd and even Jimi Hendrix.

being that glammetal bands are hairmetal bands that dress in spandex and incorporate the vocal extravagances of the '70s, while metalglam bands are glam bands that insert the dark chords of modern metal" (Kogan). This analysis not only suggests that glam rock remains an explicit reference point for contemporary musicians (the Spiders may be well be descended from Ziggy's Martian variety) but also that *glam* has become a stylistic descriptor used to denote a certain set of tendencies in a musician's musical and performance styles that can be combined (as prefix or suffix) with other stylistic terms to describe and distinguish complex musical hybrids.

The aspects of glam that alluded to androgyny and queer identity, most especially Bowie's performance as Ziggy Stardust, created a broad ripple effect as well. Boy George, for example, was directly inspired by Bowie: "For me, Bowie was a life-changer. . . . If you're a kid living in an environment where you feel alien most of the time, and you suddenly see this guy on telly in a catsuit with no eyebrows putting his arm around another man, it's incredible" (qtd. in Sweeting). Arguably, glam was a significant factor in opening the door for such overtly gay pop music acts of the 1980s as Frankie Goes to Hollywood, Culture Club, Flock of Seagulls, Bronski Beat, and others. In addition to extending itself into Brit Pop and dance music, glam formed alliances with hard rock, producing the so-called glam metal bands of the 1980s, including Motley Crüe, Twisted Sister, and Poison (Walser 24–36). Through Suzi Quatro, glam also inspired a generation of young women to think of themselves as potential rockers.

Some commentators suggest, in fact, that the chief historical value of glam resides in the way it opened the door for gay musicians. Jim Farber, for instance, inserts glam rock into a teleological narrative, characterizing it as a step in the right direction that ultimately led to the appearance of such "really" gay performers as Boy George and the Pet Shop Boys. Farber contends that although these subsequent performers "didn't literally 'come out' at first, any gay kid could tell they weren't just pretending like the earlier crew." This generation of performers was followed, in turn, by still later "pop stars [who] can speak their love's name and suffer no material consequences, from Elton John to k.d. lang" (145).

I certainly agree with Farber that glam rock helped to open the door to gay performers in popular music, and I am sympathetic to his idea that young people struggling with sexual identity benefit from having visible role models in the mass media. I also fully understand what Thomas Geyrhalter means when he points to the "constant disappointment to be experienced from a gay perspective as these so called radicals 'come out' as normal heterosexuals, revealing that their act, that promised more, was just an act, therefore commodifying the flirt with the sexually diverse" (223). Nevertheless, I find a position such as Farber's highly problematic, as I would any argument that insists that performers must belong unequivocally to a particular identity category in order to be useful exemplars to people grappling with what it means to belong to that category. Ultimately, such an argument recuperates glam rock for the very discourses of essentialism and authenticity it sought to resist and positions sexual identity as ontological rather than performative.

Theodore Gracyk, writing on rock music and the politics of identity, recognizes that what is finally at stake in the interaction between musical performers and their audiences is the audience's identity, not the performer's:

> an artist's performance of eccentric identity is only a means to an end. That end is an atmosphere of freedom in which the audience will feel free to explore eccentric identities. . . . The real contribution of popular music may be its power to expose listeners to a vast arsenal of possible identities. . . . In allowing a listener to "inhabit" new positions . . . mass art can suggest life options that were previously unthinkable. (215)

The way that audiences participate in this process is not limited to simple identification with a performer with whom they share some crucial identity trait. Rather, an audience actively *constructs* the performer's identity in ways that speak to what it wants and needs that performer to be. Barbara Bradby shows in an ethnographic study of a community of Irish lesbians that her subjects employ a combination of "myth-making, fantasizing and rumor circulation" to construct the musical performers that interest them as lesbian. In many instances, "the actual identity of the performer is not what is important but the ability to create fantasies around that identity" (41). Performers, then, are valuable to a particular audience not because they can demonstrate definitively that they belong to the same identity category as the members of that audience but because they give those audience members material from which to construct the performers' identities in terms of their own identities and desires.

Haynes suggests something like this in *Velvet Goldmine*. In the recognition scene where Arthur howls, "That's me!" at the television set, Brian Slade does not make an unambiguous declaration of his sexuality. Instead, like Bowie talking with Michael Watts, Slade at first seems to aver that he is indeed homosexual, then implies that he is bisexual and goes on to talk about his relationship with his son and bisexual wife. But the precise nature of Slade's sexual identity does not seem to matter to Arthur—what matters is the pleasurable shock of seeing someone who displays externally what he suspects himself to be internally. Arthur constructs Brian Slade's identity in a way that helps him clarify his own. In a later scene, we see Arthur in the privacy of his own room as he listens to a Brian Slade record and looks at a photo of Slade "going down" on another musician's guitar (modeled on Bowie's stage routine with Mick Ronson). We see "Arthur's face, breath CLOSE"; then, the camera moves in "VERY CLOSE on his open hand, circling slowly over stretching underwear" (Haynes, *Velvet* 85–86). Again, what matters is not what actually happened on stage and whether or not Slade and Curt Wild, the other musician, are actually gay or bisexual or what. What does matter is the way Arthur constructs the identities and actions represented in the photograph and the way that construction serves his own developing sense of sexual identity.

Glam provided very public images of alternative ways of imagining gender and sexuality, images that audiences seized upon and from which they constructed the musicians' identities and articulated those identities to their own. The demand for the freedom to explore and construct one's identity, in terms of gender, sexuality, or any other terms, is glam rock's most important legacy.

works cited

Alice Cooper. *Love It to Death*. LP. Warner Bros., 1971.

Alterman, Loraine. "How Winter Went Glam and Created a Frankenstein Monster." *Melody Maker,* June 30, 1973: 3.

Altham, Keith. "Suzi Quatro: A Nice Pair—Pop's Top." *Music Scene,* September 1974. *Rock's Back Pages.* April 11, 2003. http://www.rocksback pages.com/print.html?ArticleID=29.

Altz, Heather. "Greaser." *The Interactive Dictionary of Racial Language.* Ed. Kim Pearson. February 28, 2002. College of New Jersey. August 5, 2003. http://kpearson.faculty.tcnj.edu/dictionary/greaser.htm.

Amram, David. *No More Walls,* LP. RCA, 1971.

"Androgyny in Rock." *Creem,* August 1973: 29–33.

Antonia, Nina. *The New York Dolls: Too Much Too Soon.* London: Omnibus Press, 1998.

Auslander, Philip. "Fluxus Art-Amusement: The Music of the Future?" *Contours of the Theatrical Avant-Garde: Performance and Textuality.* Ed. James M. Harding. Ann Arbor: University of Michigan Press, 2000. 110–29.

———. *From Acting to Performance: Essays in Modernism and Postmodernism.* London: Routledge, 1997.

———. General introduction. *Performance: Critical Concepts in Literary and Cultural Studies.* 4 vols. Ed. Auslander. London: Routledge, 2003. 1–24.

———. "Good Old Rock and Roll: Performing the 1950s in the 1970s." *Journal of Popular Music Studies* 15.2 (2003): 166–93.

———. *Liveness: Performance in a Mediatized Culture.* London: Routledge, 1999.

———. *Presence and Resistance: Postmodernism and Cultural Politics in Contemporary American Performance.* Ann Arbor: University of Michigan Press, 1992.

Bailey, Beth. "Sex as a Weapon: Underground Comix and the Paradox of Liberation." *Imagine Nation: The American Counterculture of the 1960s and '70s.* Ed. Peter Braunstein and Michael William Doyle. New York: Routledge, 2002. 305–24.

———. "Sexual Revolution(s)." *The Sixties: From Memory to History.* Ed. David Farber. Chapel Hill: University of North Carolina Press, 1994. 235–62.

235

Bailey, Steve. "Faithful or Foolish: The Emergence of the 'Ironic Cover Album' and Rock Culture." *Popular Music and Society* 26.2 (2003): 141–59.

The Bangles. "The Glitter Years." *Everything*. Columbia, 1988.

Bangs, Lester. "Chicken Head Comes Home to Roost." *The Bowie Companion*. Ed. Elizabeth Thomson and David Gutman. New York: Da Capo Press, 1996. 130–33.

———. "Swan Dive into the Mung." *The Bowie Companion*. Ed. Elizabeth Thomson and David Gutman. New York: Da Capo Press, 1996. 117–19.

Barthes, Roland. "The Rhetoric of the Image." Trans. Stephen Heath. *Studying Culture*. Ed. Ann Gray and Jim McGuigan. London: Edward Arnold, 1993. 15–27.

Baxandall, Lee. "Spectacles and Scenarios: A Dramaturgy of Radical Activity." *Performance: Critical Concepts in Literary and Cultural Studies*. Ed. Philip Auslander. London: Routledge, 2003. 3:253–65.

Bayles, Martha. *Hole in our Soul: The Loss of Beauty and Meaning in American Popular Music*. Chicago: University of Chicago Press, 1996.

Bayton, Mavis. "Women and the Electric Guitar." *Sexing the Groove: Popular Music and Gender*. Ed. Sheila Whiteley. London: Routledge, 1997. 37–49.

The Beatles. "Octopus's Garden." *Abbey Road*. LP. Apple, 1969.

———. *Sgt. Pepper's Lonely Hearts Club Band*. LP. Capitol, 1967.

———. "Yellow Submarine." *Revolver*. LP. Capitol, 1966.

Benarde, Scott R. *Stars of David: Rock 'n' Roll's Jewish Stories*. Hanover, N.H.: Brandeis University Press, University Press of New England, 2003.

Benshoff, Harry M. *Monsters in the Closet: Homosexuality and the Horror Film*. Manchester: Manchester University Press, 1997.

Benton, Michael. "Suzi." *Melody Maker*, June 16, 1973: 13+.

———. "Suzi Q!" *Melody Maker*, June 2, 1973: 3.

———. "Wizzard." *Melody Maker*, June 30, 1973: 42–43.

Bering, Rüdiger. *Musicals: An Illustrated Historical Overview*. Hauppauge, N.Y.: Barron's, 1998.

The Best Glam Rock Album in the World . . . Ever! CD. Virgin, 1998.

The Best of Musik Laden: Roxy Music & T. Rex. DVD. Pioneer Entertainment, 2002.

Blau, Herbert. *The Audience*. Baltimore: Johns Hopkins University Press, 1990.

Bockris, Victor. *Transformer: The Lou Reed Story*. New York: Simon and Schuster, 1994.

Bolan, Marc. *The Best & the Rest of Marc Bolan*. CD. Action Replay Records, 1992.

———. "Music Hall Humorist." *The Bowie Companion*. Ed. Elizabeth Thomson and David Gutman. New York: Da Capo Press, 1996. 14–15.

The Bonzo Dog Band. *Four Bonzo Dog Originals*. 1967–69. CD. EMI, 1996.

Born to Boogie. Dir. Ringo Starr. Perf. Marc Bolan and T. Rex. Videotape. MPI Home Video, 1992.

Bowie, David. *Aladdin Sane*. LP. RCA, 1973.

———. *David Bowie*. LP. Deram, 1967.

———. *Diamond Dogs*. LP. RCA, 1974.

———. *Dollars in Drag*. LP. The Amazing Kornyfone Record Label, 1974.

———. Foreword. *Blood and Glitter.* By Mick Rock. London: Vision On, 2001. N.p.

———. *Hunky Dory.* LP. RCA, 1971.

———. "Life on Mars." Dir. Mick Rock. *Best of Bowie.* DVD. Virgin/EMI, 2002.

———. "The London Boys." 1967. *David Bowie.* LP. Armando Curcio Editore, n.d.

———. *The Man Who Sold the World.* LP. Mercury, 1971.

———. "The 1980 Floor Show." *The Midnight Special.* NBC, 1973.

———. *Pin-ups.* LP. RCA, 1973.

———. "Queen Bitch." *Best of Bowie.* DVD. Virgin/EMI, 2002.

———. *Space Oddity.* 1969. LP. RCA, 1972.

———. "Space Oddity." Dir. Mick Rock. *Best of Bowie.* DVD. Virgin/EMI, 2002.

———. "Starman." *Best of Bowie.* DVD. Virgin/EMI, 2002.

———. "Young Americans." *Best of Bowie.* DVD. Virgin/EMI, 2002.

———. *Young Americans.* 1975. CD. Rykodisc, 1991.

———. *Ziggy Stardust and the Spiders from Mars.* 1972. CD. Rykodisc, 1990.

Bradby, Barbara. "Lesbians and Popular Music: Does It Matter Who's Singing?" *Popular Music: Style and Identity.* Ed. Will Straw, Stacey Johnson, Rebecca Sullivan, and Paul Friedlander. Montreal: Center for Research on Canadian Cultural Industries and Institutions, 1995. 33–43.

Bramley, Jan, and Shan Bramley. *Marc Bolan: The Legendary Years.* London: Smyth Gryphon, 1992.

Braun, Hans-Joachim. "'Movin' On': Trains and Planes as a Theme in Music." *Music and Technology in the Twentieth Century.* Ed. Hans-Joachim Braun. Baltimore: Johns Hopkins University Press, 2002. 106–20.

Braunstein, Peter. "Forever Young: Insurgent Youth and the Sixties Culture of Rejuvenation." *Imagine Nation: The American Counterculture of the 1960s and '70s.* Ed. Peter Braunstein and Michael William Doyle. New York: Routledge, 2002. 243–73.

Braunstein, Peter, and Michael William Doyle, eds. *Imagine Nation: The American Counterculture of the 1960s and '70s.* New York: Routledge, 2002.

Bruzzi, Stella. "Mannish Girl: k. d. lang—from Cowpunk to Androgyny." *Sexing the Groove: Popular Music and Gender.* Ed. Sheila Whiteley. London: Routledge, 1997. 191–206.

Buckley, David. "Political Animal." *The Bowie Companion.* Ed. Elizabeth Thomson and David Gutman. New York: Da Capo Press, 1996. 207–13.

Burdon, Eric, and the Animals. *Eric Burdon and the Animals.* Historia de la Musica Rock. Vol. 14. LP. Polydor, 1982.

Burns, Lori, and Mélisse Lafrance. *Disruptive Divas: Feminism, Identity & Popular Music.* New York: Routledge, 2002.

Butler, Judith. *Gender Trouble: Feminism and the Subversion of Identity.* New York: Routledge, 1990.

The Byrds. "Mr. Spaceman." 1966. *The Byrds' Greatest Hits.* LP. Columbia, 1967.

———. "So You Wanna Be a Rock and Roll Star." 1967. *The Byrds' Greatest Hits.* LP. Columbia, 1967.

Cagle, Van. *Reconstructing Pop/Subculture: Art, Rock, and Andy Warhol.* Thousand Oaks, Calif.: Sage, 1995.

Cann, Kevin. *David Bowie: A Chronology.* New York: Simon and Schuster, 1983.

Canned Heat. *Future Blues.* LP. Liberty, 1970.

Carr, Roy. Rev. of *Introducing Eddy and the Falcons.* By Wizzard. *New Musical Express,* August 3, 1974: 14.

———. "Who's a Knackered Rock Star, Then?" *New Musical Express,* March 2, 1974: 21–22.

Case, Sue-Ellen. "Toward a Butch-Femme Aesthetic." *Making a Spectacle: Feminist Essays on Contemporary Women's Theatre.* Ed. Lynda Hart. Ann Arbor: University of Michigan Press, 1989. 282–99.

Cato, Philip. *Crash Course for the Ravers: A Glam Odyssey.* Lockerbie: S. T. Publishing, 1997.

Chambers, Iain. *Urban Rhythms: Pop Music and Popular Culture.* Houndmills: Macmillan, 1985.

Chapman, Rob. "Marc Bolan: The Jurassic Years." *Mojo,* September 2002. *Rock's Back Pages.* April 14, 2003. http://www.rocksbackpages.com/print.html?ArticleID=3587.

———. "Roxy Music: They Came from Planet Bacofoil." *Mojo,* December 1995. *Rock's Back Pages.* February 10, 2004. http://www.rocksbackpages.com/print/html?ArticleID=2539.

Charlesworth, Chris. "Bowie: Birth of the New Rock Theatre." *Melody Maker,* June 22, 1974: 3.

Charlton, Katherine. *Rock Music Styles: A History.* 4th ed. Boston: McGraw Hill, 2003.

Cixous, Hélène. Excerpt from "Sorties." *Performance Analysis: An Introductory Coursebook.* Ed. Colin Counsell and Laurie Wolf. London: Routledge, 2001. 66–71.

Clawson, Mary Ann. "When Women Play the Bass: Instrument Specialization and Gender Interpretation in Alternative Rock Music." *Gender and Society* 13.2 (1999): 193–210.

Coates, Norma. "(R)evolution Now? Rock and the Political Potential of Gender." *Sexing the Groove: Popular Music and Gender.* Ed. Sheila Whiteley. London: Routledge, 1997. 50–64.

Cohen, Stanley. *Folk Devils and Moral Panics.* 3rd ed. London: Routledge, 2002.

Cook, Nicholas. "Between Process and Product: Music and/as Performance." *Music Theory Online* 7.2 (2001). March 16, 2004. http://societymusictheory.org/mto/issues/mto.01.7.2/mto.01.7.2.cook.html#FN16REF.

Coon, Caroline. "Bryan Ferry: Putting on the Style." *Melody Maker,* July 12, 1975. *Rock's Back Pages.* December 9, 2003. http://www.rocksbackpages.com/print/html?ArticleID=170.

Copetas, Craig. "Beat Godfather Meets Glitter Mainman." *Rolling Stone,* February 28, 1974. Reprinted in *The Bowie Companion.* Ed. Elizabeth Thomson and David Gutman. New York: Da Capo Press, 1996. 105–17.

Counsell, Colin, and Laurie Wolf, eds. *Performance Analysis: An Introductory Coursebook.* London: Routledge, 2001.

Cream. "Rollin' and Tumblin'." *Fresh Cream*. LP. Atco, 1967.

Cromelin, Richard. Rev. of *Quatro*. By Suzi Quatro. *Creem*, December 1974: 70.

Crowe, Cameron. "T. Rex: What They Tried to Do with David Bowie Was Create Another Marc Bolan." *Creem*, July 1973: 38–40.

Cuscuna, Michael. Interview with Marc Bolan. 1971. The *Electric Warrior* Sessions. By T. Rex. CD. Pilot, 1996.

Dalton, David. "The Kinks: Remembrance of Kinks Past." *Gadfly*, March 1999. *Rock's Back Pages*. February 10, 2004. http://www.rocksbackpages .com/print.html?ArticleID=221.

Davis, Arthur. Liner notes. *Suzi Quatro/Quatro*. By Suzi Quatro. CD. BGO Records, 2000.

Debord, Guy. *The Society of the Spectacle*. Trans. Donald Nicholson-Smith. New York: Zone Books, 1995.

DeRogatis, Jim. *Kaleidoscope Eyes: Psychedelic Rock from the '60s to the '90s*. Secaucus, N.J.: Citadel Press, 1996.

Dister, Alain. *L'age du rock*. Paris: Gallimard, 1992.

Donovan. *Troubadour: The Definitive Collection, 1964–1976*. CD. Epic/Legacy, 1992.

Doyle, Michael William. "Staging the Revolution: Guerilla Theater as a Countercultural Practice, 1965–68." *Imagine Nation: The American Counterculture of the 1960s and '70s*. Ed. Peter Braunstein and Michael William Doyle. New York: Routledge, 2002. 71–97.

Du Noyer, Paul. *Marc Bolan*. London: Virgin, 1997.

Duncan, Robert. *The Noise: Notes from a Rock 'N' Roll Era*. New York: Ticknor and Fields, 1984.

Dynamite: The Best of Glam Rock. CD. Repertoire, 1998.

Edmonds, Ben. "Bowie—Station to Station—'It's not a Musical Album as much as an Emotional One.'" *Phonograph Record*, January 1976. *Rock's Back Pages*. April 16, 2003. http://www.rocksbackpages.com/print .html?ArticleID=309.

———. "The New York Dolls Greatest Hits Volume 1." *Creem*, October 1973: 39–42.

———. "Time Capsule: The Move." *Creem*, December 1972. Reprinted as liner notes. *Split Ends*. By the Move. LP. United Artists, 1972.

Ennis, Philip. H. *The Seventh Stream: The Emergence of Rocknroll in American Popular Music*. Hanover, N.H.: Wesleyan University Press, 1992.

Epand, Len. Liner notes. *The Best of the Runaways*. By The Runaways. CD. Mercury, 1987.

Farber, David. "The Intoxicated State/Illegal Nation: Psychedelic Drugs in the Sixties Counter-Culture." *Imagine Nation: The American Counterculture of the 1960s and '70s*. Ed. Peter Braunstein and Michael William Doyle. New York: Routledge, 2002. 17–40.

Farber, Jim. "The Androgynous Mirror: Glam, Glitter and Sexual Identity." *Rolling Stone: The Seventies*. Ed. Ashlye Kahn, Holly George-Warren, and Shawn Dahl. Boston: Little, Brown, 1998. 142–45.

Farren, Mick. "Surface Noise: The Trouble with Bowie." *The Bowie Com-*

panion. Ed. Elizabeth Thomson and David Gutman. New York: Da Capo Press, 1996. 192–95.

Fast, Susan. *In the Houses of the Holy: Led Zeppelin and the Power of Rock Music.* Oxford: Oxford University Press, 2001.

Ferris, Timothy. "David Bowie in America." *The Bowie Companion.* Ed. Elizabeth Thomson and David Gutman. New York: Da Capo Press, 1996. 87–94.

Ferry, Bryan. *These Foolish Things.* 1973. CD. Virgin Records, 1999.

———. "Whatever Turned Me On." *New Musical Express,* August 26, 1972: 6.

Fornäs, Johan. "Listen to Your Voice! Authenticity and Reflexivity in Karaoke, Rock, Rap and Techno Music." *Popular Music: Style and Identity.* Ed. Will Straw, Stacey Johnson, Rebecca Sullivan, and Paul Friedlander. Montreal: Center for Research on Canadian Cultural Industries and Institutions, 1995. 99–110.

Frith, Simon. "The Bryan Ferry Story—A Hollywood Production." *Creem,* June 1974: 28–31+.

———. "1967: The Year It All Came Together." *The History of Rock,* 1981. *Rock's Back Pages.* December 9, 2003. http://www.rocksbackpages.com/print.html?ArticleID=2587.

———. *Performing Rites: On the Value of Popular Music.* Cambridge: Harvard University Press, 1996.

———. *Sound Effects: Youth, Leisure, and the Politics of Rock 'n' Roll.* New York: Pantheon, 1981.

———. "Sweet Notes." *Creem,* November 1973: 42–44+.

Frith, Simon, and Angela McRobbie. "Rock and Sexuality." *On Record: Rock, Pop, & the Written Word.* Ed. Simon Frith and Andrew Goodwin. London: Routledge, 1990. 371–89.

Gaar, Gillian G. *She's a Rebel: The History of Women in Rock & Roll.* Seattle: Seal Press, 1992.

Gambaccini, Paul. "Beethoven Rolls Over Again." *Rolling Stone,* May 23, 1974: 14–15.

Geyrhalter, Thomas. "Effeminacy, Camp and Sexual Subversion in Rock: The Cure and Suede." *Popular Music* 15 (1996): 217–25.

Glitter, Gary. "Rock and Roll (Part 2)." *Glitter.* LP. Bell Records, 1972.

Goffman, Erving. *Gender Advertisements.* New York: Harper and Row, 1979.

Goldman, Albert. *Freakshow.* New York: Atheneum, 1971.

Gore, Leslie. "I Wish I Were a Boy." 1964. *Growin' Up Too Fast: The Girl Group Anthology.* Polygram Records, 1996.

Gorman, Paul. *The Look: Adventures in Pop & Rock Fashion.* London: Sanctuary, 2001.

Gottlieb, Joanne, and Gayle Wald. "Smells Like Teen Spirit: Riot Grrrls, Revolution and Women in Independent Rock." *Microphone Fiends: Youth Music and Youth Culture.* Ed. Andrew Ross and Tricia Rose. New York: Routledge, 1994. 250–74.

Gracyk, Theodore. *I Wanna Be Me: Rock Music and the Politics of Identity.* Philadelphia: Temple University Press, 2001.

The Grateful Dead. "Turn On Your Lovelight." *Live/Dead.* LP. Warner Bros., 1969.

Graver, David. "The Actor's Bodies." *Performance: Critical Concepts in Literary and Cultural Studies*. Ed. Philip Auslander. London: Routledge, 2003. 2:157–74.

Gray, Michael. "The Sex Bar." *Melody Maker*, June 8, 1974: 51.

———. "Sexist Songs." *Melody Maker*, June 1, 1974: 18–19.

———. "Women and Rock." *Melody Maker*, May 25, 1974: 36–37.

Grossberg, Lawrence. "The Media Economy of Rock Culture: Cinema, Postmodernity, and Authenticity." *Sound and Vision: The Music Video Reader*. Ed. Simon Frith, Andrew Goodwin, and Lawrence Grossberg. London: Routledge, 1993. 185–209.

Haden-Guest, Anthony. "Suzi Quatro Flexes Her Leather." *Rolling Stone*, January 2, 1975: 48–51.

Halberstam, Judith. "Between Butches." *Butch/Femme: Inside Lesbian Gender*. Ed. Sally R. Munt. London: Cassell, 1998. 57–65.

———. *Female Masculinity*. Durham, N.C.: Duke University Press, 1998.

———. *Skin Shows: Gothic Horror and the Technology of Monsters*. Durham, N.C.: Duke University Press, 1995.

Hall, Russell. "Alice Cooper." *Goldmine*, October 10, 1997: 14–15.

Hall, Stuart. "The Hippies: An American 'Moment.'" *Student Power*. Ed. Julian Nagel. London: Merlin Press, 1969. 170–202.

Harvey, Mike. *The Ziggy Stardust Companion*, June 1996. February 7, 2004. http://www.5years.com.

Haynes, Todd. Foreword. *Glam! Bowie, Bolan and the Glitter Rock Revolution*. By Barney Hoskyns. New York: Pocket Books, 1998. x–xi.

———. *Velvet Goldmine: A Screenplay*. New York: Miramax/Hyperion, 1998.

Hebdige, Dick. *Subculture: On the Meaning of Style*. London: Routledge, 1979.

Hibbert, Tom. "Oh, Suzi Q! How Quatrophenia Conquered the UK." *The History of Rock*, 1983. *Rock's Back Pages*. April 11, 2003. http://www.rocksbackpages.com/print.html?ArticleID=537.

Hodenfield, Chris. "Tyrannosaurus Enters Rock Age." *Rolling Stone*, September 16, 1971: 25.

Holmes, Peter. "Gay Rock." *The Bowie Companion*. Ed. Elizabeth Thomson and David Gutman. New York: Da Capo Press, 1996. 77–78.

Hoskyns, Barney. *Glam! Bowie, Bolan and the Glitter Rock Revolution*. New York: Pocket Books, 1998.

———. *Waiting for the Sun: Strange Days, Weird Scenes and the Sound of Los Angeles*. N.p: Bloomsbury, 1997.

Hull, Robot A. Rev. of *Suzi Quatro*. By Suzi Quatro. *Creem*, May 1974: 64–65.

Innes, Neil. "Randy Raquel." *Taking Off*. LP. Arista Records, 1977.

Irwin, Lou. Interview with Mu. *Earth News Radio*. Date unknown. *Mu*. CD. Sundazed, 1997.

Jett, Joan. *Bad Reputation*. LP. Boardwalk, 1981.

Jett, Joan, and the Blackhearts. *I Love Rock & Roll*. LP. Boardwalk, 1981.

The Jimi Hendrix Experience. "1983." *Electric Lady Land*. LP. Reprise, 1968.

———. "Up from the Skies." *Axis Bold as Love*. LP. Reprise, 1968.

Jones, Mablen. *Getting It On: The Clothing of Rock 'n' Roll*. New York: Abbeville Press, 1987.

Kantner, Paul, and Jefferson Starship. *Blows against the Empire*. LP. RCA, 1970.

Keightley, Keir. "Reconsidering Rock." *The Cambridge Companion to Pop and Rock*. Ed. Simon Frith, Will Straw, and John Street. Cambridge: Cambridge University Press, 2001. 109–42.

Kennedy, Kathleen. "Results of a Misspent Youth: Joan Jett's Performance of Female Masculinity." *Women's History Review* 11.1 (2002): 89–114.

Kent, Nick. "A Whole Hunk-A Human He-Man." *New Musical Express*, May 23, 1974: 28–29.

Kimmel, Michael. *Manhood in America: A Cultural History*. New York: Free Press, 1996.

The Kinks. *20 Golden Greats!* LP. Ronco, 1978.

Kirby, Michael. *Happenings*. New York: E. P. Dutton, 1965.

Kirk, Andrew. "'Machines of Loving Grace: Alternative Technology, Environment, and the Counterculture." *Imagine Nation: The American Counterculture of the 1960s and '70s*. Ed. Peter Braunstein and Michael William Doyle. New York: Routledge, 2002. 353–78.

Kogan, Frank. Rev. of *Glitzkrieg*. By the Spiders. *Village Voice*, December 3–9, 2003. December 5, 2003. http://www.villagevoice.com/print/issues/0349/kogan.php.

Laing, Dave. *One Chord Wonders: Power and Meaning in Punk Rock*. Philadelphia: Open University Press, 1985.

Lennon, John. *Rock 'N' Roll*. LP. Capitol, 1975.

Lhamon, W. T. *Deliberate Speed: The Origins of a Cultural Style in the American 1950s*. Cambridge: Harvard University Press, 2002.

Lipsitz, George. "Who'll Stop the Rain? Youth Culture, Rock 'n' Roll, and Social Crises." *The Sixties: From Memory to History*. Ed. David Farber. Chapel Hill: University of North Carolina Press, 1994. 206–34.

Lydon, Michael. *Flashbacks: Eyewitness Accounts of the Rock Revolution, 1964–1974*. New York: Routledge, 2003.

Mahal, Taj. "Blues Ain't Nothing." *Dancing the Blues*. CD. Private Music, 1993.

———. "Blues with a Feeling." *Like Never Before*. CD. Private Music, 1991.

Marc Bolan: 20th Century Boy. Videotape. Channel 5, 1986.

Marsh, Dave. *The First Rock & Roll Confidential Report*. New York: Pantheon, 1985.

———. "Marc Bolan and T. Rex: Can the Electric Warrior Conquer America?" *Creem*, May 1972: 36–41.

Matthews, Ian. "Da Doo Ron Ron (When He Walked Me Home)." *Tigers Will Survive*. LP. Vertigo, 1971.

McLenehan, Cliff. *Marc Bolan 1947–1977: A Chronology*. London: Helter Skelter, 2002.

McLeod, Ken. "Space Oddities: Aliens, Futurism and Meaning in Popular Music." *Popular Music* 22 (2003): 337–55.

McNeil, Legs, and Gillian McCain. *Please Kill Me: The Uncensored Oral History of Punk*. New York: Grove Press, 1996.

McRuer, Robert. "Gay Gatherings: Reimagining the Counterculture." *Imagine Nation: The American Counterculture of the 1960s and '70s*. Ed. Peter

Braunstein and Michael William Doyle. New York: Routledge, 2002. 215–40.

Melly, George. *Revolt into Style: The Pop Arts.* Garden City, N.Y.: Doubleday, 1971.

Meltzer, Richard. *The Aesthetics of Rock.* New York: Da Capo, 1987.

Middleton, Jason. "Heroin Use, Gender, and Affect in Rock Subcultures." *Echo* 1.1 (1999). February 26, 2004. http://www.humnet.ucla.edu/echo/Volume1-Issue1/middleton/middleton~article.html.

Miles. "Dazed and Infused: The Summer of Love." *Vox,* August 1992. *Rock's Back Pages.* December 9, 2003. http://www.rocksbackpages.com/print .html?ArticleID=745.

Mockus, Martha. "Queer Thoughts on Country Music and k. d. lang." *Queering the Pitch: The New Gay and Lesbian Musicology.* Ed. Philip Brett, Elizabeth Wood, and Gary C. Thomas. New York: Routledge, 1994. 257–71.

Monterey Pop. Dir. D. A. Pennebaker. 1968. *The Complete Monterey Pop Festival.* DVD. Criterion Collection, 2002.

Morthland, John. "Rock Festivals." *The Rolling Stone Illustrated History of Rock & Roll.* Rev. ed. Ed. Jim Miller. New York: Random House, 1980. 336–38.

Mosse, George L. *The Image of Man: The Creation of Modern Masculinity.* New York: Oxford University Press, 1996.

The Move. *Movements: 30th Anniversary Anthology.* CD. Westside, 1997.

———. *Split Ends.* LP. United Artists, 1972.

Mu. "On Our Way to Hana." 1972. *Mu.* CD. Sundazed, 1997.

Mud. "Tiger Feet." *Glam Rock.* Vol. 2. Videotape. Virgin Music Video, 1988.

Murray, Charles Shaar. "David at the Dorchester." *New Musical Express,* July 22, 1972. *NME Originals* 1.15 (2004): 48–50.

Negus, Keith. *Popular Music in Theory.* Hanover, N.H.: Wesleyan University Press, 1996.

The New York Dolls. "Frankenstein." *The New York Dolls.* LP. Mercury, 1973.

Nicholl, Charles. "Bryan Ferry: Dandy of the Bizarre." *Rolling Stone,* April 24, 1975: 48–50.

Novick, Jeremy, and Mick Middles. *Wham Bam Thank You Glam: A Celebration of the 70s.* London: Aurum Press, 1998.

Nuttall, Jeff. *Bomb Culture.* New York: Delacorte Press, 1968.

Oglesbee, Frank W. "Suzi Quatro: A Prototype in the Archsheology of Rock." *Popular Music and Society* 23.2 (1999): 29–39.

Onkey, Lauren. "Voodoo Child: Jimi Hendrix and the Politics of Race in the Sixties." *Imagine Nation: The American Counterculture of the 1960s and '70s.* Ed. Peter Braunstein and Michael William Doyle. New York: Routledge, 2002. 189–214.

Owens, Craig. *Beyond Recognition: Representation, Power, and Culture.* Berkeley and Los Angeles: University of California Press, 1992.

Padel, Ruth. *I'm a Man: Sex, Gods and Rock 'n' Roll.* London: Faber and Faber, 2000.

Palmer, Robert. *Rock & Roll: An Unruly History.* New York: Harmony, 1995.

The Paris Sisters. "Dream Lover." 1964. *Growin' Up Too Fast: The Girl Group Anthology.* CD. Polygram Records, 1996.

Pavis, Patrice. *L'Analyse des spectacles.* Paris: Editions Nathan, 1996.

Paytress, Mark. *Bolan: The Rise and Fall of a 20th Century Superstar.* London: Omnibus Press, 2002.

———. Liner notes. *The Definitive Tyrannosaurus Rex.* CD. Sequel Records, 1993.

Phantom of the Paradise. Dir. Brian DePalma. 1974. Videotape. Twentieth Century Fox Home Entertainment, 2001.

Pinch, Trevor, and Frank Trocco. *Analog Days: The Invention and Impact of the Moog Synthesizer.* Cambridge: Harvard University Press, 2002.

Pink Floyd. *The Piper at the Gates of Dawn.* LP. Capitol, 1967.

"Portsmouth Sinfonia—The World's Worst Orchestra." *Chachacha.co.uk.* 1999. October 14, 2004. http://www.chachacha.co.uk/cgi-bin/mt/mt tb.cgi/107.

Quatro, Suzi. "Can the Can." 1973. *Suzi Quatro: Greatest Hits.* CD. EMI, 1999.

———. "Devil Gate Drive." *Glam Rock.* Vol. 2. Videotape. Virgin Music Video, 1988.

———. E-mail to the author. October 23, 2000.

———. E-mail to the author. November 6, 2000.

———. E-mail to the author. January 24, 2001.

———. "Glad All Over." *Rock Hard.* LP. Dreamland, 1980.

———. *If You Knew Suzi . . . .* LP. RSO Records, 1979.

———. *Suzi Quatro/Quatro.* 1973/1974. CD. BGO Records, 2000.

Quigley, Mike. "Alice Cooper: Vancouver 1969." *Poppin,* September 1969. *Rock's Back Pages.* December 9, 2003. http://www.rocksbackpages.com/ print.html?ArticleID=3169.

Rée, Jonathan. "Funny Voices: Stories, Punctuation, and Personal Identity." *New Literary History* 21 (1990): 1039–58.

Reed, Lou. *Transformer.* LP. RCA, 1972.

Reynolds, Simon, and Joy Press. *The Sex Revolts: Gender, Rebellion, and Rock 'n' Roll.* Cambridge: Harvard University Press, 1995.

Rice, Anne, "David Bowie and the End of Gender." *The Bowie Companion.* Ed. Elizabeth Thomson and David Gutman. New York: Da Capo Press, 1996. 183–86.

Roberts, Vera Mowry. *On Stage: A History of Theatre.* 2nd ed. New York: Harper and Row, 1974.

Rock, Mick. *Blood and Glitter.* London: Vision On, 2001.

Rook, Jean. "Waiting for Bowie." *The Bowie Companion.* Ed. Elizabeth Thomson and David Gutman. New York: Da Capo Press, 1996. 133–35.

Rosenbaum, Michael. "Jimi Hendrix and Live Things." *Crawdaddy,* May 1968: 24–29.

Ross, Ron. "David Bowie: Fleeting Moments in a Glamorous Career." *Phonograph Record,* October 1972. *Rock's Back Pages.* April 16, 2003. http://www.rocksbackpages.com/print/html?ArticleID=3748.

———. "Roxy Music: 'Love Is the Drug' in Bi-centennial Year!" *Phonograph*

Record, March 1976. *Rock's Back Pages.* December 9, 2003. http://www
.rocksbackpages.com/print/html?ArticleID=3813.

Rossinow, Doug. " 'The Revolution is about Our Lives': The New Left's Counterculture." *Imagine Nation: The American Counterculture of the 1960s and '70s.* Ed. Peter Braunstein and Michael William Doyle. New York: Routledge, 2002. 99–124.

Roszak, Theodore. *The Making of a Counter Culture.* Garden City, N.Y.: Doubleday, 1969.

Roxy Music. *For Your Pleasure.* LP. Atco Records, 1973.

———. *Roxy Music.* 1972. CD. Virgin Records, 1999.

Ruby, Jay. "Donovan." *Giants of Rock Music.* Ed. Pauline Rivelli and Robert Levin. 1970. New York: Da Capo, 1981. 61–67.

The Runaways. *The Best of the Runaways.* CD. Mercury, 1987.

Rundgren, Todd. *Faithful.* LP. Bearsville Records, 1976.

Sandford, Christopher. *Bowie: Loving the Alien.* New York: Da Capo, 1998.

Savage, Jon. "Odysseys and Oddities: Jon Savage Compiles the Definitive Space-Rock Tape." *Mojo,* March 1995. *Rock's Back Pages.* May 5, 2004. http://www.rocksbackpages.com/print/html?ArticleID=2783.

Schechner, Richard. *Between Theater and Anthropology.* Philadelphia: University of Pennsylvania Press, 1985.

———. *Performance Studies: An Introduction.* London: Routledge, 2002.

———. "Performers and Spectators Transported and Transformed." *Kenyon Review* n.s. 3.4 (1981): 83–113.

Scheuring, Dick. "Heavy Duty Denim: 'Quality Never Dates.' " *Zoot Suits and Second-Hand Dresses: An Anthology of Fashion and Music.* Ed. Angela McRobbie. Boston: Unwin Hyman, 1988. 225–36.

Sedgwick, Eve Kosofsky. *Between Men: English Literature and Homosocial Desire.* New York: Columbia University Press, 1985.

Senelick, Laurence. *The Changing Room: Sex, Drag and Theatre.* London: Routledge, 2000.

Sha Na Na. *Hot Sox.* LP. Kama Sutra, 1974.

———. *Sha Na Na.* LP. Kama Sutra, 1971.

Sharp, Ken. "Roy Wood: The Wizzard of Rock." *Goldmine,* September 30, 1994. *The Move Online.* September 3, 2004. http://www.themove online.com/archive_01.html.

Shaw, Greg. "Suzi Quatro, Queen of Pop." *Phonograph Record,* August 1974. *Rock's Back Pages.* April 11, 2003. http://www.rocksbackpages.com/ print.html?ArticleID=1964.

She. *She Wants a Piece of You.* CD. Big Beat Records, 1999.

Shuker, Roy. *Key Concepts in Popular Music.* London: Routledge, 1998.

Simmons, Sylvie. Introduction. *Kiss.* New York: St. Martin's Press, 1997.

Sims, Joshua. *Rock/Fashion.* London: Omnibus Press, 1999.

Slik. "Forever and Ever." 1976. *Dynamite: The Best of Glam Rock.* CD. Repertoire Records, 1998.

Sly and the Family Stone. "Everybody is a Star." *The Best of Sly and the Family Stone.* CD. Sony, 1992.

Smith, Patricia Juliana. "You Don't Have to Say You Love Me: The Camp

Masquerades of Dusty Springfield." *The Queer Sixties*. Ed. Patricia Juliana Smith. New York: Routledge, 1999. 105–26.

The Song Remains the Same. Perf. Led Zeppelin. Dir. Joe Massot. Videotape. Warners Home Video, 1991.

Spirit. "Water Woman." *Spirit*. LP. Epic, 1968.

Stable, Simon. "The Crimson King Talking about Bolan, Badfinger and the Force of Magic." *New Musical Express*, June 24, 1972: 14.

Stambler, Irwin. *Encyclopedia of Pop, Rock & Soul*. Rev. ed. New York: St. Martin's, 1989.

Stokes, Geoff. "The Sixties." *Rock of Ages: The Rolling Stone History of Rock & Roll*. New York: Summit, 1986. 249–463.

Street, John. *Rebel Rock: The Politics of Popular Music*. Oxford: Basil Blackwell, 1986.

Sweet. "Blockbuster." *Glam Rock*. Videotape. Virgin Music Video, 1988.

Sweet Toronto. Dir. D. A. Pennebaker. Perf. John Lennon and the Plastic Ono Band. DVD. Pioneer Artists, 2001.

Sweeting, Adam. "The Boy Looked at Bowie." *Uncut*, March 2003. February 7, 2004. http://www.btinternet.com/~s.essom database.

T. Rex. "Cadillac." 1972. *The Slider*. CD. Polygram, 1997.

———. *Electric Warrior*. 1971. CD. A&M Records, 2001.

———. "Jeepster." *Glam Rock*. Videotape. Virgin Music Video, 1988.

———. "London Boys." 1976. *Great Hits, 1972–1977: The A-Sides*. Polygram, 1997.

———. *The Slider*. 1972. CD. Polygram, 1997.

———. *T. Rex*. 1970. CD. A&M Records, 1998.

———. "Thunderwing." 1972. *The Slider*. CD. Polygram, 1997.

———. "Woodland Rock." Ca. 1971. *The BBC Recordings, 1970–1976*. CD. New Millennium Communications, 1997.

Taylor, Ian, and David Wall. "Beyond the Skinheads: Comments on the Emergence and Significance of the Glamrock Cult." *Working Class Youth Culture*. Ed. Geoff Mungham and Geoff Pearson. London: Routledge and Kegan Paul, 1976. 105–23.

Taylor, Timothy D. *Strange Sounds: Music, Technology & Culture*. New York: Routledge, 2001.

Thomas, Michael. "T. Rex is Gonna Fuck You into the Mick Jagger Gap." *Rolling Stone* March 16, 1972: 32–34.

Thompson, Dave. *20th Century Rock and Roll: Glam Rock*. Burlington, Ont.: Collector's Guide Publishing, n.d.

Thomson, Elizabeth, and David Gutman, eds. *The Bowie Companion*. New York: Da Capo Press, 1996.

Toynbee, Jason. "Fingers to the Bone or Spaced Out on Creativity? Labor Process and Ideology in the Production of Pop." *Cultural Work: Understanding the Cultural Industries*. Ed. Andrew Beck. London: Routledge, 2003. 39–55.

Turner, Steve. "Marc Bolan." *Other*, February 1971. *Rock's Back Pages*. April 14, 2003. http://www.rocksbackpages.com/print.html?ArticleID=1817.

———. "Moving History with Sha Na Na." *Beat Instrumental*, November

1972. *Rock's Back Pages*. August 26, 2003. http://www.rocksback
pages.com/article.html?ArticleID=1916.

———. "Roxy Music." *Beat Instrumental*, October 1972. *Rock's Back Pages*.
December 9, 2003. http://www.rocksbackpages.com/article.html?ArticleID
=1845.

Turner, Victor. *From Ritual to Theatre: The Human Seriousness of Play*. New
York: PAJ Publications, 1982.

The Turtles. *The Turtles Present The Battle of the Bands*. LP. White Whale,
1968.

Tyrannosaurus Rex. *A Beard of Stars*. LP. Blue Thumb, 1970.

———. *The Definitive Tyrannosaurus Rex*. CD. Sequel Records, 1993.

Uhelszki, Joan. "Suzi Quatro: Elvis as Virgin Queen." *Creem*, November 1974:
48–51.

Unterberger, Richie. "The Move." *All Music Guide to Rock*. 2nd ed. Ed. M.
Erlwine et al. San Francisco: Miller Freeman, 1997. 638–39.

———. "Suzi Quatro." *All Music Guide to Rock*. 2nd ed. Ed. M. Erlwine et
al. San Francisco: Miller Freeman, 1997. 745.

Utopia. *Deface the Music*. LP. Bearsville Records, 1980.

Van Gennep, Arnold. *The Rites of Passage*. 1908. Trans. Monika B. Vizedom
and Gabrielle Caffee. Chicago: University of Chicago Press, 1960.

Velvet Goldmine. Dir. Todd Haynes. Miramax, 1998.

Vermorel, Fred, and Judy Vermorel. *Starlust: The Secret Life of Fans*. London:
W. H. Allen, 1985.

Visconti, Tony. Liner notes. *Electric Warrior*. By T. Rex. CD. A&M Records,
2001.

Waksman, Steve. *Instruments of Desire: The Electric Guitar and the Shaping
of Musical Experience*. Cambridge: Harvard University Press, 1999.

Walser, Robert. *Running with the Devil: Power, Gender, and Madness in
Heavy Metal Music*. Hanover, N.H.: Wesleyan University Press, 1993.

Watts, Michael. "Oh you pretty thing." *The Bowie Companion*. Ed. Elizabeth
Thomson and David Gutman. New York: Da Capo Press, 1996. 47–51.

Watts, Michael, and Robert Partridge. "Made in Britain." *Melody Maker*, July
6, 1974: 8–10.

Weinstein, Deena. "The History of Rock's Pasts through Rock Covers." *Mapping the Beat: Popular Music and Contemporary Theory*. Ed. Thomas
Swiss, John Sloop, and Andrew Herman. Malden, Mass.: Blackwell, 1998.
137–51.

Wham Bam, Thank You Glam! Audiocassette tape. Sony, 1994.

Whiteley, Sheila. "Little Red Rooster v. the Honky Tonk Woman: Mick Jagger, Sexuality, Style and Image." *Sexing the Groove: Popular Music and
Gender*. Ed. Sheila Whiteley. London: Routledge, 1997. 67–99.

———. *The Space Between the Notes: Rock and the Counter-Culture*. London: Routledge, 1992.

———. *Women and Popular Music: Sexuality, Identity and Subjectivity*. London: Routledge, 2000.

———, ed. *Sexing the Groove: Popular Music and Gender*. London: Routledge, 1997.

Wiener, Jon. *John Lennon in His Time*. New York: Random, 1984.

Wilde, David. "Bowie's Wedding Album." *The Bowie Companion*. Ed. Elizabeth Thomson and David Gutman. New York: Da Capo Press, 1996. 214–16.

Williams, Richard. "Roxy in the Rock Stakes." *Melody Maker*, August 7, 1971. *Rock's Back Pages*. December 9, 2003. http://www.rocksback pages.com/print/html?ArticleID=2046.

Willis, Paul E. *Profane Culture*. London: Routledge and Kegan Paul, 1978.

Wilson, John S. "Phil Ochs Fans are Won Over by Rock." *New York Times*, April 3, 1970: 44.

Winter, Edgar. "Frankenstein." *They Only Come Out at Night*. LP. Epic, 1973.

Wizzard. "Are You Ready to Rock." 1974. *Roy Wood and Wizzard*. Archive Series. CD. Rialto, 1997.

———. "Ball Park Incident." *Glam Rock*. Videotape. Virgin Music Video, 1988.

———. "Ball Park Incident." 1972. *The Best Glam Rock Album in the World . . . Ever!* CD. Virgin, 1998.

———. "I Wish It Could Be Christmas Everyday." *Glam Rock*. Videotape. Virgin Music Video, 1988.

———. *Introducing Eddy and the Falcons*. LP. United Artists, 1974.

———. "Rock and Roll Winter." 1974. *Roy Wood and Wizzard*. Archive Series. CD. Rialto, 1997.

———. "See My Baby Jive." *Glam Rock*. Vol. 2. Videotape. Virgin Music Video, 1988.

———. "See My Baby Jive." 1973. *Dynamite: The Best of Glam Rock*. CD. Repertoire, 1998.

———. *Wizzard Brew*. 1973. CD. Harvest Records, 1999.

Wollman, Elizabeth L. "Much Too Loud and Not Loud Enough: Issues Involving the Reception of Staged Rock Musicals." *Bad Music: The Music We Love to Hate*. Ed. Christopher J. Washburne and Maiken Derno. New York: Routledge, 2004. 311–30.

Wood, Elizabeth. "Sapphonics." *Queering the Pitch: The New Gay and Lesbian Musicology*. Ed. Philip Brett, Elizabeth Wood, and Gary C. Thomas. New York: Routledge, 1994. 27–66.

Wood, Roy. *Boulders*. LP. United Artists, 1973.

———. "Forever." 1973. *Roy Wood: The Definite Album*. CD. BR Music, 1989.

———. *Mustard*. LP. Jet Records, 1975.

Woodstock: 3 Days of Peace and Music—The Director's Cut. Dir. Michael Wadleigh. DVD. Warner Brothers, 1994.

Ziggy Stardust and The Spiders from Mars: The Motion Picture. Dir. D. A. Pennebaker. DVD. Virgin/EMI, 2003.

Index

African-American music, 17, 31n25, 113n8, 168–69, 204, 227n1; blues, 87, 129, 158, 187; rhythm and blues, 44, 50, 57, 205–6n13. *See also specific musicians*

"A Hard Rain's A-Gonna Fall" (song), 159–60

Alice Cooper, 19, 29–38, 42n3, 43, 44, 45–46; "Ballad of Dwight Fry," 35–36, 37, 63; Sha Na Na and, 33–34, 37–38; transvestism of, 30, 31–32, 33, 37, 48. *See also* Furnier, Vincent

"All Shook Up" (song), 217–18, 219

"All the Madmen" (song), 36–37

"All the Young Dudes" (song), 68

Andrew Sisters, the, 191, 215

androgyny, 31, 60–63, 67, 133, 145n34, 232. *See also* gender identities; transvestism

"Androgyny in Rock: A Short Introduction" (*Creem*), 33

Arrows, the, 43, 51, 224

"At the Hop" (song), 20, 26

audience. *See* fans

authenticity, 9–19, 66–67n20, 101n21, 162–63, 174, 182–83; Bolan and, 101–3; female rockers and, 204–5, 212; psychedelic rock and, 14, 17–19, 27, 37, 66; Quatro and, 204–5, 212; rock and, 14, 110n6, 112–13, 190, 227; vocals and, 167,

191, 192. *See also* hippie counterculture; psychedelic rock

"Baby I Don't Care" (song), 169–70, 171

Bach, Johann Sebastian, 65, 175–76

Bad Reputation (Jett), 224–25

Bailey, Beth, 30

Bailey, Steve, 168, 190n23

"The Ballad of Dwight Fry" (song), 35–36, 37, 63

Bangs, Lester, 52, 112–13

bass guitar, 202–3. *See also* guitar; instruments

Baxandall, Lee, 11–12, 15

Bayles, Martha, 48

Bayton, Mavis, 164

Beach Boys, 80, 168, 170–71; Wood and, 186, 188, 190, 191

A Beard of Stars (Tyrannosaurus Rex), 83, 94

Beatles, 104, 127n25, 162–63, 168, 172–73, 219. *See also* Lennon, John; McCartney, Paul

Beckenham Arts Lab, 115

Beckenham Free Festival, 115, 128–29, 130

Benshoff, Harry M., 63

Berry, Chuck, 22, 25, 26, 97, 204

Best Glam Rock Album in the World . . . Ever!, The, (compilation), 223

Bevan, Bev, 176, 188

249